Genre and performance: film and television

Manchester University Press

Genre and performance: film and television

EDITED BY CHRISTINE CORNEA

Manchester University Press
Manchester and New York

distributed in the United States exclusively
by Palgrave Macmillan

Published by Manchester University Press
Oxford Road, Manchester M13 9NR, UK
and Room 400, 175 Fifth Avenue, New York, NY 10010, USA
www.manchesteruniversitypress.co.uk

Distributed in the United States exclusively by
Palgrave Macmillan, 175 Fifth Avenue, New York,
NY 10010, USA

Distributed in Canada exclusively by
UBC Press, University of British Columbia, 2029 West Mall,
Vancouver, BC, Canada V6T 1Z2

British Library Cataloguing-in-Publication Data
A catalogue record for this book is available from the British Library

Library of Congress Cataloging-in-Publication Data applied for

ISBN 978 0 7190 7980 1 *hardback*

First published 2010

Typeset by Servis Filmsetting Ltd, Stockport, Cheshire
Printed in Great Britain
by CPI Antony Rowe, Chippenham, Wiltshire

Contents

List of illustrations vi
List of contributors vii
Acknowledgements xi

Editor's introduction *Christine Cornea* 1

1 Film noir: gesture under pressure *Cynthia Baron* 18
2 Captured ghosts: horror acting in the 1970s British television drama *Richard J. Hand* 38
3 Docudrama performance: realism, recognition and representation *Jonathan Bignell* 59
4 Living stories: performance in the contemporary biopic *Dennis Bingham* 76
5 Borders and boundaries in *Deadwood* *Steven Peacock* 96
6 *The Colbert Report*: performing the news as parody for the postmodern viewer *Gwendolyn Audrey Foster* 113
7 Contemporary comedy performance in British sitcom *Brett Mills* 130
8 2-D performance and the re-aminated actor in science fiction cinema *Christine Cornea* 148
9 The multiple determinants of television acting *Roberta Pearson* 166
10 Bollywood blends: genre and performance in Shahrukh Khan's post-millennial films *Rayna Denison* 184

Index 205

List of illustrations

1.1 Mitchum's appliquéd gesture and expression let audiences see that Jeff is acting the part of the flirt in *Out of the Past* (Jacques Tourneur: 1947, RKO Radio Pictures) 29

1.2 Washington's tightly bound stillness conveys Easy's intense effort to mask his anger in *Devil in a Blue Dress* (Carl Franklin: 1995, Clinica Estetico, Mundy Lane Entertainment, TriStar Pictures) 33

2.1 Ultra-feminine heroine and arrogant anti-hero: Jane Asher and Michael Bryant in Nigel Kneale's *The Stone Tape*, 25 December 1972 (BBC Photograph Library) 43

2.2 The Professor's discovery: Michael Hordern in Jonathan Miller's M. R. James adaptation 'Whistle and I'll Come to You', 7 May 1968 (BBC Photograph Library) 44

2.3 The Professor's nightmare: Michael Hordern in Jonathan Miller's M. R. James adaptation 'Whistle and I'll Come to You', 7 May 1968 (BBC Photograph Library) 46

2.4 Stage actors on the small screen of horror: Iain Cuthbertson and Michael Bryant in Nigel Kneale's *The Stone Tape*, 25 December 1972 (BBC Photograph Library) 53

4.1 Giamatti grimaces: 'a cross between realism and the comics'. *American Splendor* (Shari Spriner Berman and Robert Pulcini: 2003, Good Machine and Home Box Office) 85

4.2 Davis counterbalances with impatient calm. *American Splendor* (Shari Spriner Berman and Robert Pulcini: 2003, Good Machine and Home Box Office) 86

4.3 Male icon re-imagined as female biopic subject. Cate Blanchett as Bob Dylan (and vice versa) in *I'm Not There* (Todd Haynes: 2007, Killer Films and Weinstein Company) 94

5.1 A pivotal moment in *My Darling Clementine* (John Ford: 1946, Twentieth Century Fox) 98
5.2 Merrick's brief gain of the upper hand in *Deadwood* (2004–06, HBO/Red Board and Roscoe Productions) 104
5.3 Swearengen's bedtime story in *Deadwood* (2004–06, HBO/Red Board and Roscoe Productions) 105
5.4 Bullock's rocky situation in *Deadwood* (2004–06, HBO/Red Board and Roscoe Productions) 106
8.1 Sebastian Caine/Kevin Bacon makes the traumatic transition to invisible presence in *Hollow Man* (Paul Verhoeven: 2000, Columbia Pictures Corporation, Global Entertainment Productions GmbH and Company Medien KG) 149
8.2 Indented outline on gurney marks the otherwise invisible presence of Caine/Bacon in *Hollow Man* (Paul Verhoeven: 2000, Columbia Pictures Corporation, Global Entertainment Productions GmbH and Company Medien KG) 149
8.3 Wearing his 'scramble suit', Fred is asked to observe Arctor on the monitors at the Sheriff's Department in *A Scanner Darkly* (Richard Linklater: 2006, Warner Independent Pictures, Thousand Words, Section Eight, Detour Filmproduction, 3 Arts Entertainment) 158
8.4 The digitally rotoscoped Keanu Reeves (Arctor/Fred) and Winona Ryder (Donna) in *A Scanner Darkly* (Richard Linklater: 2006, Warner Independent Pictures, Thousand Words, Section Eight, Detour Filmproduction, 3 Arts Entertainment) 160
10.1 Don/Khan carries the unconscious Vijay/Khan in *Don* (UTV) 195
10.2 Publicity still taken from 'Dhoom Taana', *Om Shanti Om*, (reproduced with kind permission of Eros International Ltd) 198
10.3 Publicity still from Khan's performance in 'Dard-e-Disco', *Om Shanti Om* (with kind permission from Eros International Ltd) 200

List of contributors

Cynthia Baron is Associate Professor in the Department of Theatre and Film and an Affiliated Faculty member of the American Culture Studies Program at Bowling Green State University in Ohio. She is co-author of *Reframing Screen Performance* (University of Michigan Press, 2008) and co-editor of *More Than a Method: Trends and Traditions in Contemporary Film Performance* (Wayne State University Press, 2004). Her publications include work in star studies, political censorship, women's cinema, and food, film and culture. She is currently involved in audience reception research that brings Q methodology into cultural analyses that draw on political economy and cultural studies principles to examine corporate media effects and circumstances surrounding audiences' varied readings of film and media.

Jonathan Bignell is Professor of Television and Film at the University of Reading. He is the Director of the Centre for Television Drama Studies and specialises in the history and theory of television. His books include *Postmodern Media Culture* (Edinburgh University Press, 2000), *Big Brother: Reality TV in the Twenty-first Century* (Palgrave Macmillan, 2005), *An Introduction to Television Studies* (Routledge, 2003), *Beckett on Screen* (Manchester University Press, 2009) and (as co-editor) *Popular Television Drama: Critical Perspectives* (Manchester University Press, 2005) and *A European Television History* (Wiley Blackwell, 2008). He serves on the editorial advisory committees of the *New Review of Film & Television Studies*, *Journal of Science Fiction, Film & Television* and *Critical Studies in Television*. He is a Series Editor for Manchester University Press's 'Television Series' which publishes volumes on the work of individual screenwriters, producers and directors. His own contribution to the Series was *Terry Nation* (written with Andrew O'Day) on the work of the British science fiction screenwriter.

Dennis Bingham teaches Film Studies and English at Indiana University-Purdue University, Indianapolis. He has written on film acting and stardom, on gender in film and on film genres. His new book, *Whose Lives Are They Anyway? The Biopic as Contemporary Film Genre*, is forthcoming from Rutgers University Press.

Christine Cornea is Lecturer with the School of Film and Television at the University of East Anglia, Norwich, UK. She is the author of *Science Fiction Cinema: Between Fantasy and Reality* (co-published by Edinburgh University Press/Rutgers University Press, 2007) and has published various articles/chapters on science fiction in film and television. Most recently, her piece 'Showrunning the Doctor Who Franchise' appeared in *Production Studies: Cultural Studies of Media Industries* (Routledge, 2009) and she edited an 'In Focus' segment in the *Cinema Journal* which looked at 'The Practitioner Interview in Film and Television Studies' (2008). Christine is currently working on a further monograph, entitled 'Post-Apocalypse on the Small Screen'.

Rayna Denison is Lecturer in Film and Television Studies at the University of East Anglia, Norwich UK, and writes and teaches on various aspects of Asian film and television cultures. Rayna is currently writing two books, one on Ang Lee for Palgrave and another called *Film Genres: Anime* for Berg. Rayna has also published in the area of vocal performance in film; for example, her article 'Star-Spangled Ghibli: Star Voices in the American Versions of Hayao Miyazaki's Films' recently appeared in *Animation: An Interdisciplinary Journal.*

Gwendolyn Audrey Foster is Professor in the Department of English, University of Nebraska, Lincoln, and Coordinator of the Film Studies Program. Her most recent books include *A Short History of Film*, co-written with Wheeler Winston Dixon (Rutgers University Press, 2008); *Class-Passing: Social Mobility in Film and Popular Culture* (Southern Illinois University Press, 2005); and *Performing Whiteness: Postmodern Re/Constructions* (State University of New York Press, 2003), cited by the journal *Choice* as 'Essential . . . one of the Outstanding Academic Books of the Year' for 2004.

Richard J. Hand is Professor of Theatre and Media Drama at the University of Glamorgan, Cardiff, UK. He is the author of *Terror on the Air: Horror Radio in America, 1931–52* (McFarland, 2006), *The Theatre of*

Joseph Conrad: Reconstructed Fictions (Palgrave, 2005) and is founding co-editor of the *Journal of Adaptation in Film and Performance* (Intellect, 2007 onwards). He has published journal articles and book chapters on a wide range of performance media, including theatre, radio, film, graphic narratives and digital gaming, with a special interest in horror studies and adaptation studies. As a collaborator, he co-edited *Monstrous Adaptations: Generic and Thematic Mutations in Horror Film* (Manchester University Press, 2007) with Jay McRoy; and with Michael Wilson has written *Grand-Guignol: The French Theatre of Horror* (University of Exeter Press, 2002) and *London's Grand-Guignol and the Theatre of Horror* (University of Exeter Press, 2007).

Brett Mills is Senior Lecturer in Film and Television Studies at the University of East Anglia, UK, and an Associate Tutor for the Open University. He is the author of *Television Sitcom* (BFI, 2005) and *Television Genres: Sitcom* (Edinburgh University Press, forthcoming 2009) and co-author with David Barlow of *Reading Media Theory: Thinkers, Approaches, Contexts* (Pearson, 2009). He is the Associate Editor of Palgrave's 'Adaptations' book series. His research interests include comedy, popular culture, television's relationship to the real world, and issues of entertainment.

Dr. Steven Peacock is Senior Lecturer in Film at the University of Hertfordshire, Hatfield, UK. He is the author of monographs *Colour: Cinema Aesthetics* (Manchester University Press, forthcoming) and 'Scaling Intimacy', in *Close-Up 04* (Wallflower, forthcoming 2009). He is the editor of *Reading 24: TV against the Clock* (I. B. Tauris, 2007) and has written extensively on television aesthetics, with a particular interest in the American serial drama. He is also co-editor, with Jonathan Bignell, of the ongoing book series, *The Television Series* (Manchester University Press).

Roberta Pearson is Professor of Film and Television and Director of the Institute of Film and Television Studies at the University of Nottingham. She is the editor of *Reading Lost: Perspectives on a Hit Television Show* (I. B. Tauris, 2009) and co-editor of *Cult Television* (University of Minnesota Press, 2004).

Acknowledgements

Firstly, I would like to thank my contributors for their individual chapters. In approaching contributors, I was especially struck by their enthusiasm for this book project. I was also very pleased to be working with such a diligent and lively group of fellow academics, who, in my view, produced innovative pieces of outstanding quality.

I owe a debt of gratitude to the School of Film and Television at the University of East Anglia and I am also indebted to the staff at Manchester University Press for their help and advice.

Finally, thanks are owed to my family and friends, for their unswerving support. In particular, I would like to thank my friend, Agi Andreou, for donating his computer after mine finally bit the dust in the middle of writing the introduction for this book. I would also like to thank Phil Cockrell, Aparna Chahal and Rebecca de Young for their patience and understanding – you are the best of friends.

Editor's introduction

Christine Cornea

Before I took up an academic career as a researcher and lecturer, I was an actor. Having said that, back in the 1980s, I remember making the decision to call myself a performer instead of an actor. If, in its most constricted sense, acting is understood as a sub-set of performance caught up in the rendering of a dramatic character, then this did not fully encompass what I felt I was doing at the time. In practical terms, I was not only employed to convey characters in plays, television series and feature films, but also performed in experimental productions, musical shows, satirical comedy shows, television adverts, in-house training videos, corporate shows and documentaries. In short, I was also employed in productions that did not necessarily involve the sort of 'character building' most readily associated with 'acting'. Beyond the semantics of strict definition, my decision at this time was actually guided by the sense that the term 'performer' denoted a more consciously active and dynamic positioning. Although I had little knowledge then of academic debates in the fields of theatre, drama, film or television studies, it seems that the desire to re-brand myself fell into line with contemporary currents. In the 1980s and 1990s, a number of academics and practitioners working in higher education were busy reconceptualising what was meant by acting and arguing for a more expansive approach to performance. Famously, for Richard Schechner 'performance' became a kind of umbrella term, covering not only 'theatre, dance, music and performance art', but also 'a broad spectrum of activities including at the very least the performing arts, rituals, healing, sports, popular entertainments, and performance in everyday life' (Schechner, 2004: 7). Moving into territory associated with anthropological or cultural studies, Schechner saw this expansion as necessary in order to carve out a more relevant, critical and sustainable academic domain.

Within the narrower field of theatre and drama studies certain shifts in perspective were also inevitable as forms such as the theatre of the absurd, performance art and the 'happenings' of the 1960s began to impact upon more mainstream or traditional practices, raising questions about the very nature of dramatic character and the processes of acting. In this regard Philip Auslander usefully tracks his own interests and theoretical perspectives alongside a trajectory from modernist avant garde theatre towards contemporary postmodern performance practices. Concerned with identifying the politically 'resistant' aspects of postmodern performance, Auslander notes a 'progressive redefinition of theatrical mimesis away from "character" toward "performance persona" with consequent redefinitions of the function of the performer's self in relation to performance' (1997: 6). For Auslander, this shift allows for resistant practices in alternative and popular, live and recorded performance,[1] which I would say is largely made possible by foregrounding the activity in and of performance. Back in the day, I could not always have laid claim to being involved in politically 'resistant' performance, but I was resistant to the notion of the compliant actor simply servicing the needs of the script writer or director. So, Auslander's ideas resonate with my own experiences; my desire to re-evaluate and elevate my own activities and to explore different approaches to the presentation of character.

Although I would certainly distinguish my current academic role from past involvement in the entertainment industry, I have paid attention to the ways in which acting and performance are analysed and discussed within my chosen realm of film and television studies. It has been satisfying to see performance studies in general expand and grow, and, in a more limited fashion, to see serious consideration given over to issues surrounding screen performance in film and television studies. Of course the idea of a 'performance persona' is not new to film and television. This has largely been developed to denote the ways in which a star or celebrity performer's identity is constructed by the media and popular press and the consequent interplay and tensions between off-screen persona and on-screen character or role. Following Richard Dyer's lead in *Stars* (1979) and *Heavenly Bodies: Film Stars and Society* (1986), what is now commonly called 'star studies' has examined these modes of star construction and the wider meanings that an individual star persona therefore brings to a film text. While Dyer stresses the extra-textual elements in the building of a star persona, he also defines and examines performance to underpin his discussions of stars and authorship. For Dyer:

> Performance is what the performer does in addition to the actions/functions s/he performs in the plot and the lines s/he is given to say.

> Performance is how the action/function is done, how the lines are said. (1998 [1979]: 134)

But, even as Dyer placed some emphasis in his early work upon the activity of performance and its importance in the creation of meaning, subsequent star studies often led away from analysis or discussion of actual performance and the ways in which meaning is created in narrower performance contexts.

That said, in the late 1980s and 1990s, some valuable work did appear that explicitly engaged with screen performance. For example, Roberta Pearson's adroit examination of performance in D. W. Griffith's Biograph films provided a foundation for future work (see Pearson, 1990, 1992). In charting the shift from the histrionic to the verisimilar performance style in the Biograph films, Pearson also brought to the fore some of the problems in attempting to analyse, in particular, the 'naturalistic' performance styles that came to dominate later film and television drama. For instance, while a semiotic approach to analysis might seem appropriate in analysing performance, it is not really possible to identify the kinds of discrete, 'digital' distinctions that make up the sign system of something like language. Instead Pearson offers a way forward through analysis of the interaction of a combination of elements that make up broader codes in verisimilar performance. Also, James Naremore's detailed account of film acting in *Acting in the Cinema* (1988) provided some useful tools in the analysis and discussion of screen performance. Naremore's expert account of the 'performance frame' in combination with his engagement with underlying methods of acting opened the door to a more nuanced understanding of screen performance. For Naremore, 'the activity of any performer can be described in terms of a mode of address and a degree of ostensiveness' (1988: 34), which he applied in the second half of this book by presenting a series of case studies focused upon key Hollywood films and stars. Using this basic formula, Naremore looked at both representational and presentational modes and naturalistic and non-naturalistic performance styles, as well as the degrees of reflexivity apparent in performance and as signalled by the performer in conjunction with the performance frame. At its most basic, Naremore's 'frame' is literally delineated by the margins of the camera lens and the borders of the finished film. However, on a more conceptual level, it is possible to understand the 'performance frame' as the way in which a meaningful context is constructed for the performances.

Although some earlier star studies could be criticised for a lack of engagement with performance and performance theory, they certainly succeeded in making the performer a central concern. Some lines of inquiry initiated by Dyer, Naremore and Pearson might have taken longer to impact upon film and television studies more generally, but there has been an increasing acknowledgement of the significance of performance over the past few years. For example, Jeremy G. Butler's edited collection, *Star Texts: Image and Performance in Film and Television* (1991) and, more recently, Karen Hollinger's *The Actress: Hollywood Acting and the Female Star* (2006), provide prominent examples in which the central figure of the star is analysed with reference to acting and performance theory. Also, Virginia Wright Wexman's book, *Creating the Couple: Love, Marriage, and Hollywood Performance* (1993) relies heavily upon aspects of performance theory in her examination of stars, alongside a more expansive project concerning the portrayal of courtship, romance and gender. Indeed, the performance of gender on screen has long been a concern in film and television studies. After Laura Mulvey's ground-breaking work and the development of 'gaze theory' (see Mulvey, 1975, 1981), successive studies tended to view the performer as part of the mise-en-scène, as a gendered object to be looked at or as a point of identification for the audience. This approach largely dominated in the 1970s and early 1980s, but further strands of investigation were also underway. Heavily influenced by Michel Foucault's and Judith Butler's work on the construction of gender and identity, academics have been encouraged to explore the possible links between performance and performativity (see Parker and Kosofsky Sedgwick, 1995: 1-18). This kind of inquiry elicits a rather different perception, one that recognises the constraints and ritual dimensions of performance at the same time as the performer can be understood as an active participant; a participant who intervenes in what amount to complex iterative and citational processes. Against this backdrop, those working in fields like star studies have begun to pay more attention to the activity of performance, partly as a route to exploring the star as a more active agent in the process of their own construction.

The advent of star studies certainly challenged the traditional notion of the director as the single or most important creative force in a film. However, a focus upon the film director has not disappeared and continues to co-exist in parallel to star studies. In fact, the director emerges as a kind of central convergence point in two of the most recent edited collections looking at screen performance. Collectively the pieces in these books enrich a field looking at screen performance, bringing together new work that is undoubtedly detailed and illuminating. Nevertheless, it is worth noting that contributions in *Falling for You: Essays on Cinema and Performance* (Stem and Kouvaros, 1999) are more or less split down the middle in terms of a focus upon either director or star, and in *More than a Method: Trends and Traditions in Contemporary Film Performance* (Baron, Carson and Tomasulo, 2004) are predominantly framed with reference to a particular director. While individual pieces stress the importance of performer and performance, chapter titles that reference the likes of Robert Bresson, Michelangelo Antonioni, Robert Altman, John Sayles, Neil Jordon, John Cassavetes, Hal Hartley, John Woo and so forth indicate that the influence of the director is important. Having said that, these collections do shift primary focus away from mainstream Hollywood to look at art house films, films that emanate from other countries, films that are more marginal or that come under the category of independent cinema. These kinds of cinema acquire special significance for researchers looking at performance because they are frequently marked apart from Hollywood in the employ of different or alternative styles or modes of performance. Moreover, performance per se becomes obvious, more tangible in these films and appears readily to invite analysis at this level. So, perhaps reflecting an interest in the 'resistant' practices that performance studies academics like Auslander commonly seek out, these collections work to counterpoint an overwhelming focus upon mainstream Hollywood productions. What is also evident in these recent collections is a shift away from discussions centred upon a particular acting or training practice, which I would say suggests an editorial effort to carve out a more interdisciplinary approach. For example, in their introduction to *Falling for You*, Lesley Stern and George Kouvaros make clear their instructions to contributors to concentrate upon 'particular texts or performers', at the same time as they state an interest in 'how performance is manifested cinematically, how it registers semantically and somantically' (1991: 3). Further, Cynthia Baron, Diane Carson and Frank P. Tomasulo declare that their collection 'challenges the idea that reference to training or working method is the best or only way to categorize performances' (2004: 2). So both of these books aim to encourage the further development of an interdisciplinary account of screen performance; an account that may acknowledge performance and acting traditions, but that also recognises the necessity for shifts in theoretical approach and methodology when dealing with performance as presented on the film and television screen.

For me, coordinating a new edited collection around either individual directors or performers comes too close to re-establishing the romantic idea of the author or auteur as sole creator of meaning in film or television. Therefore, as the title of this book suggests, I asked my contributors to concentrate specifically upon performance in conjunction with the concept of genre. It has always seemed strange to me that this confluence has not been explored more fully in the past, for if anything immediately defines or creates a conceptual frame for the meaning of screen performance it is surely the notion of genre. Returning again to my past life as a performer, genre was definitely a central concern when it came to auditions for film or television roles. For instance, I recall one audition for a lead role in a film in New Zealand which consisted of a series of shocked and fearful expressions made straight into the lens of a camera. A planned scene for the film was described to me in which a young woman sees a ghostly and threatening figure through the windscreen of her car. Without dialogue I was then instructed to arrange my face into a suitable expression and to freeze. My reaction was recorded several times over and if I was not sure beforehand about the exact nature of the film, I certainly cottoned on quickly to the fact that I was dealing with a supernatural horror and was being asked to draw upon the familiar codes and conventions of performance associated with that genre. On another occasion, when auditioning for a central role in a television series, I was acutely aware of the codes and conventions that I needed to tap into if I were to win the role. This was a long-running series set around a medical practice in the late 1940s and, having previously watched episodes on television, I was familiar with the performance style adopted to convey a sense of period. Assuming a tense and slightly high-pitched tone, clipped articulation, and delivering the dialogue at an energetic and fast pace seemed to do the trick: unlike the horror film I was successful in being cast in this television role. My point is that an awareness of screen genres comes into play even at the level of performance method or craft. Ultimately I made a part my own when it came to recording or filming, but I was frequently aware of the generic constraints and frameworks within which I was expected to work.

Aside from the personal experience related above, further study of screen performance together with genre has been called for repeatedly in academic circles. As Richard de Cordova argued in 'Genre and Performance: An Overview', back in 1991, an 'examination of the ways that different genres circumscribe the form and position of performance in film is an important and underdeveloped area' (see Butler, 1991: 117). More recently, in the editorial introduction to *Movie Acting: The Film Reader*, Pamela Robertson Wojcik bemoaned the lack of attention given to performance in film genre studies, stating: 'modes of performance differ sufficiently among melodrama, the Western, comedy, film noir, and the musical to enable genre theorists to characterize acting style as a defining feature of genre' (2004: 5). Therefore, my own edited collection answers those appeals for further work to bring issues in performance together with film genre. At the same time my collection expands the field of study to look at the specificities of television performance and the concept of genre as it has developed in television studies.

Anyone familiar with film or television studies knows that the very term, genre, has multiple and contested meanings. Without rehearsing the debates and arguments that abound within genre studies, I shall briefly outline some of the levels upon which it is possible to conceive of screen genres. Genre theory emerged as an academic area in the 1960s and 1970s, partly as a reaction to the auteurism of the period and partly as a way of addressing popular cinematic forms. Heavily influenced by literary theory and the advent of structuralism, film theorists set about delineating, defining and categorising particular screen genres, thereby enabling critical engagement with the structures of repetition/variation, similarity and difference within and between film productions. Arguably, some of the major genres that have emerged in film studies include the Western, the comedy, the musical, and the animated film, with various other genres like the horror film, science fiction, film noir and so forth making up a more frequently contested list. The classification of most film genres has been intimately linked to narrative, in which particular genres become identifiable through narrative theme and structure. However, simply glancing at the short list above indicates that even major genres have not always been classified in this way. For instance, at their most basic, comedy and horror are defined by their affective modes, the musical by its overt mode of address and the presence of diegetic musical performance, the highly contentious film noir by its visual stylistics, and the animation by its very methods of production in conferring the illusion of movement to literally drawn, modelled or computer-created characters. Add to this list, genres like the teenpic, biopic and documentary film and things become even more complicated. The teenpic is obviously defined by the age of its intended audience, and the biopic and documentary by their particular and declared relationship with the 'real world'. Television studies have also developed catalogues of genres, some specific to the medium and some that refer to familiar cinematic genres. For instance, within the broader category of television drama (including the single play, series and/or serial, and mini-series) the Western, science fiction and horror are all discernable genres, as well as dramatic forms in television that are usually classified according to their occupational setting (i.e. the police series, the hospital series, the courtroom drama series, the traditionally domestic setting of the soap opera, and so forth). Furthermore, important to television are a plethora of non-narrative genres, like the documentary, talk show, quiz and game show, and news and current affairs programme.

As Rick Altman has pointed out, 'film genre's consistent connections to the entire production–distribution–consumption process make it a broader concept than literary genre has typically been.' In film studies the concept of genre, according to Altman, can therefore be understood as a blueprint, a structure, a label, a contract (1999: 14). In part, this explains the variety of aspects alighted upon in classifying film genres. It also goes some way towards explaining the often fierce debates surrounding the 'proper' classification of individual films. What is clear is that an understanding of genre that encompasses its many functions and possible affects calls for a variety of critical approaches. Critics may concern themselves with the ways in which the film industry is able to use genre to maximise efficiency of production, or may look at the ideological function of the textual structures of genre. They may also look at how genre operates as a branding device or how it functions in association with audience expectations. While early genre critics liked to see genres as more or less fixed (if not by their own academic theorising, then by the industry), this has been challenged by discrepancies in genre definition that occur in the way a film is categorised at different times. As both Steve Neale (2000)and Rick Altman (1999) have pointed out in their recent work on film genres, these are not a-historical and a film can be classified in a certain way when it is released and later re-classified to fit into a different generic category. In addition, categorical differences can be found among the various academic factions vying to define and/or interpret a particular film, as well as between how the industry, the popular press and the academic might define a particular film. Similar inconstancies have been shown to exist in defining television genres; as Graeme Turner points out in *The Television Genre Book*, the competing industry term, 'format', can complicate notions of genre in television (see Creeber, 2001: 5). Furthermore, as both film and television genre critics have been forced to take on board a view of the active or participatory audience, engagement with fan discourses and the like has revealed a further level of struggle over the meaning of particular films, television shows and generic categories in general. Clearly, the setting up of a commonly accepted catalogue has enabled analysis, as much as it has encouraged diverse and contrary discourses surrounding particular films or television productions and generic categorisation.

Although continuing debates may signal some of the weaknesses inherent in genre theory, they also signal the degree to which genre remains an important focal point for critics, the industry and audiences alike. In fact, it is possible to say that notions of genre have taken on a renewed importance of late. In an increasingly competitive, multi-media, global era of information and entertainment, genre frequently offers a convenient nexus with which to negotiate and organise meaning across media platforms. In this respect, it is interesting to note that alongside the massive growth in the numbers of available television channels, the importance of genre and genre theory has grown in the field of television studies. Of course, this may suggest that film and television studies academics are busy widening their field of vision, or that interdisciplinary dialogue is becoming more crucial as traffic between the two mediums increases, but the presence of both freeview and pay TV channels literally demarcated by genre (e.g. Sci-Fi Channel, Cartoon Channel, Discovery Channel, numerous news channels, and so on) underlines the powerful influence of generic assumptions in contemporary television. If this were not evidence enough then turning to the menus used for various 'On Demand' services in television reveals a further level of genre classification: my own service lists films under the generic headings of comedy, drama, family, horror + sci-fi, romance, thriller and crime, and independent cinema, with television productions listed under comedy, drama, entertainment, kids, lifestyle, factual, and so forth. Even as individual films and television productions in these accessible archives can find their way onto more than one of these lists, reference to genre has certainly become pivotal in contemporary television's delivery and niche marketing practices.

As genre studies takes stock of ongoing trends in the film and television industry as well as in academia, there has also been an increasing acceptance of the hybrid or multi-generic status of films and programmes. Taking issue with earlier film genre theory, Altman argues that 'Hollywood's stock-in-trade is the romantic combination of genres, not the classical practice of generic purity' (1999: 59). While Altman is referring back to Hollywood cinema of the classical period to support this argument, critics have claimed that a special feature in post-classical cinema is the rising prevalence of generic impurity and hybrid forms apparent in films from the 1960s onwards (see Kramer, 1998). Likewise,

Graeme Turner insists that 'television genres and programming formats are notoriously hybridised and becoming more so' (Creeber, 2001: 6). Aside from the recent erosion of boundaries between the series and serial, this is evident in the sheer number of overtly hybrid television genres like docudramas and so called info-tainment programmes, as well as the unparalleled number of combination police/courtroom series, medical/police series, and so on. A further challenge to genre theory has been presented by those who have noted an escalating use of parody, pastiche and allusion in both film and television that confuses generic certitude, some claim to the point of collapse (see Bordwell, 1989; Stam, 2000). But surely devices like these rely upon the recognition of genre on some level.

Classically, film has been associated with modernity and its aesthetic forms examined with reference to modernist theory. So, on the one hand, the use of devices associated with a fragmented, ironic and playful postmodern aesthetic appears to undermine conceptual frameworks, like genre, through which film has been understood. On the other hand, given its continuous stream of programming, it is easy to see how television can more easily be aligned with a postmodern aesthetic. Television seems to exemplify the blurred boundaries of the postmodern experience, and allusion, intertextuality and fragmentation are perhaps fundamental to the medium. However, it is my contention that the concept of genre rather than losing its usefulness, in either film or television studies, becomes ever more valuable. If under modernity, genre operated to resolve or smooth over contradictions, to provide determinacy and satisfying closure, then the postmodern sense of genre is quite the contrary. In these circumstances, genre often works to demythologise, to indicate a mode of reflexivity, to foreground the constructed and mediated nature of a film or programme. Furthermore, the activity of performance becomes more crucial and noticeable, as generic modes are deliberately juxtaposed or melded and as the performance of generic character types becomes increasingly palpable. For films, this is true of both mainstream and independent productions. For example, a self-reflexive mode has almost become the norm in post-classical Hollywood cinema, which extends to the part ironic/part celebratory performance of stock generic types by many a Hollywood star. Also, independent cinema's frequent make-over of the most recognisable Hollywood genres (the Western and science fiction being two of the most common genres adopted by independents), has produced performances that play to and with familiar generic character types. The arrival of what is commonly called 'quality' television has also increased the relevance of performance as central to the meaning and success of a genre series: if film genres were often criticised for their one-dimensional characters, then recent television drama series seem to have taken those characters and added a depth, complexity and degree of reflexivity that foregrounds the work of the performer. Witness the bravura performance of eccentric and dysfunctional detectives and doctors (e.g. *Monk*, *Silent Witness*, *House*), the complex ensemble performances in series/serial from *The Sopranos* to *The West Wing* to *Sex and the City*, and the compellingly elusive performances in series/serials like *Twin Peaks*, *The X-Files* and *Lost*. Not to mention the ways in which performance has become ever more relevant in looking at factually based entertainment programmes or documentary forms. So, questions around genre and performance are now more vital than ever to both film and television studies. This book is certainly not promising an exhaustive coverage of generic forms and associated styles and modes of performance, or of the issues and arguments that can be brought to light – this would not have been possible in a book of this size. Instead, I hope this collection proves the need for further study in this area. For instance, while working on the collection I was all too aware of what was *not* being covered. I would have liked to have included more chapters and covered more film and television genres, in particular, looking at those genres and associated performances that might be understood as culturally 'feminised' (TV Soap, romance, more on contemporary film musicals and so forth). But I do believe that the following chapters offer a promising taster of what can be achieved in approaching screen performance together with an awareness of genre and I also hope that this book works to inspire interest and further investigations in this area.

While the collection reflects the particular interests of contributors, certain limitations were deliberately built into the original brief. For instance, I specifically limited the primary focus of each chapter to films or television programmes from the 1970s to the present day. This was partly because of the points made above about the rising significance of both genre and performance in later years and also because of my intention to encourage fresh ideas. While US- and UK-produced films and television programmes are more substantially covered in this collection, there is some very interesting work that looks at genre and performance in the context of Bollywood and Canadian television in ways that provide an illuminating comparison. Also, I have arranged some chapters so as to encourage comparison and a kind of dialogue between individual contributions. For instance, readers will notice that science fiction is covered in both film and television, as well as the biopic film and celebrity docudrama. These comparative allegiances were not specifically sought out, but it was my aim to provide a further level of interdisciplinary dialogue in bringing film together with television. In this respect, I hoped to raise questions concerning the specificities of performance and genre within these media forms as well as looking at how approaches overlap or differ within film and television studies.

Having outlined the meanings and relevance of the terms that are brought together to frame this collection and having justified its layout and limitations, what remain are a few brief statements concerning individual chapters. The collection opens with Cynthia Baron's detailed examination of contemporary film noir, which specifically builds upon de Cordova's account of 'dissimulation' as performed within the genre. Classically this genre required that audiences become aware and pay attention to performance as various characters feign reactions and emotions in order to deceive, con or outwit a central detective character. In an updated account of performance in later noir films, Baron brings Laban Movement Analysis into play for this chapter. Baron's analysis here is therefore meticulous and her lucid reading reveals the specific ways in which diegetic performance is revealed and illustrates how various performance strategies work within the confines of this film genre.

Following this chapter is Richard J. Hand's more expansive account of shifts in performance styles associated with the British television horror play. In the 1970s this television genre attracted well respected and established performers, perhaps because it allowed the performer to expand upon and extend the more limited expressive style associated with other television drama. Noting similarities between the earlier Théâtre du Grand-Guignol and television horror, Hand sees the virtuoso performance style evidenced in the 1970s television horror play as linked with earlier melodramatic performance styles and as a necessary component in communicating and exteriorising the extremes of emotion that are central to the genre. However, tracing television horror through to more recent examples, Hand remarks on how styles of performance have become more technically mediated and thereby less 'stagey'. It seems that 'heightened gestures' have been all but replaced within this television genre by what Hand refers to as 'subtle intensity'.

Moving on from those genres that deal in extreme situations and that place deliberate pressure upon character, performer and performance, the next two chapters focus upon the dramatic portrayal of 'real people' in cinema and television. While both the film biopic and the celebrity docudrama dramatise the lives of historical figures or celebrities of one sort or another, the 'realism' that arises in these portrayals is inevitably foregrounded and brought into question. For example, Jonathan Bignell notes that television docudrama seems to invite a knowing audience to draw upon their knowledge of other television genres as well as anterior knowledge of reported events. Likewise, Dennis Bingham identifies the biopic as a genre located between fiction and actuality. For Bingham, while pleasure may be found in the biopic's invitation to intimacy, it also operates as a showcase for performers and performance. Similarly, Bignell sets the docudrama within a television tradition that relies on intimacy and immediacy and the medium's overall aims to 'contain and explain the real' while making some reference to hybrid documentary and dramatic modes as prominent in contemporary cinema. Bingham reads biopic performance alongside a Hollywood tradition of star performances, as well as accounting for the parodic and self-reflexive devices witnessed in more recent engagements with the genre and an increasing integration of documentary style segments and newsfilm. So, while the specificities of each medium are dealt with in these separate chapters, interesting intersections are also acknowledged by both writers.

Likewise, Steven Peacock's examination of the US serial drama, *Deadwood*, pays attention to both film and television forerunners in the Western genre. In a comparative analysis, Peacock sees a depth and complexity achieved in the performance of generic character 'types' in this recent serial and notes the different meanings that therefore accrue in performance. For example, Peacock compares performances in the serial to those witnessed in earlier television and film Westerns, as well as the revisionist Westerns of post-classical Hollywood cinema. Moving on, Peacock notes that although *Deadwood* 'holds true to the form of stock characters', certain performers are particularly restrained, casting themselves in 'performative profile', while other performers push at the boundaries of character 'types' in a way that refuses parody. In this regard, especially fascinating is Peacock's account of the use and performance of language in the serial, as particularly associated with the swearing and swaggering Swearengen (Ian McShane), whose strategic use of expletives can be read as 'at once florid and foul'.

Focusing upon comical 'fake news' programmes produced in both the US and Canada, Gwendolyn Audrey Foster is concerned with a kind of blurring of boundaries between fiction and actuality, seen here as evidential tensions in contemporary factual reporting on television. Concerned with a burgeoning mistrust of traditional news formats, Foster examines the ways in which comedic performance strategies are utilised by the 'left-leaning' presenters of *The Colbert Report* and *The Daily Show*. By mimicking the often overblown presentational style of many a 'straight news' presenter or in adopting an entirely fictitious interviewing persona, Foster argues that both Jon Stewart and Stephen Colbert offer an alternative and ironically authentic perspective on current news events and the state of television reporting in general. In their ostensive production of a heavily loaded and utterly reflexive presentation performance, Stewart and Colbert appear to place themselves and, by extension, their audience, both at one remove and somehow closer to the news of the day. With particular reference to *The Colbert Report*, Foster argues that these programmes encourage a questioning of more conventional news and current affairs programmes, exposing a 'truth' by imploring audiences to 'reject "truthiness"'.

Following Foster is Brett Mills' chapter, which is also concerned with a certain mixing of truth and falsehood in performance and the overt blurring of generic boundaries in recent British comedy series like *The Office* (BBC2, 2000) and *Marion and Geoff* (BBC2, 2000). Having coined the term 'comedy vérité' to describe this hybrid form, Mills comments on the relationship between recent comedy serials and the various factual and documentary forms of television that they appear to emulate. For Mills, by adopting techniques associated with factual television these comedy series work to question 'the ability of documentary to "capture" the truth of the world in the manner the format suggests'. From another perspective, they also operate to critique 'the ways in which comedy is conventionally signalled'. What is interesting in a comparison with the more excessive and postmodern performance strategies of Colbert and Stewart, as detailed by Foster, is a certain movement in the opposite direction evidenced in 'comedy vérité'. Here more 'naturalistic' modes of address, which Mills distinguishes as 'acting', dominate and are only occasionally offset by moments when characters clumsily 'perform' for the camera.

A clear shift in generic focus comes with the following two chapters, which look at issues surrounding performance in science fiction film and television respectively. Concentrating on films like *Heavy Metal* (1981), *Titan A. E.* (2000), *Hollow Man* (2000), *Final Fantasy: The Spirits Within* (2001) and *A Scanner Darkly* (2006), my own chapter sets the emergence of the so called 'synthespian' and 'virtual acting' within a broader history of animation techniques. At the heart of this exploration are the uncertain 'presence' of the performer and the genre's relentless scrutiny of the relationship between the technological and the human. While science fiction film is often reluctant to dispense altogether with 'naturalistic' acting, its insistence on foregrounding technological intervention poses some interesting questions concerning the assumption of an 'actorly self' as the grounding force of human performance and characterisation in the genre. With reference to a variety of film reviews and written and 'promotional documentary' interviews, the chapter assesses the reception of performance for these films and grapples with the evident confusions brought about by the heavily mediated presentation of being human.

Aside from a brief outtake from an interview I carried out with the director Paul Verhoeven, my approach for Chapter 8 differs from the following Chapter 9. Here, Roberta Pearson draws heavily upon original interviews that she carried out with the cast and crew of *Star Trek: The Next Generation* to examine the 'unique challenges for actors' in science fiction television. Setting the series within the wider context of television production and generic modes, Pearson's piece provides a detailed account of the practical determinants of acting and performance in this famous series. Concentrating on the particular constraints of the genre, Pearson offers comment on dealing with constrictive costumes and make-up, interacting with unfamiliar and futuristic machinery, supplying reactions for computer-generated effects, delivery of 'technobabble' and so forth, as well as noting the relative autonomy of individual performers in this series. Indeed, Pearson's description of the hierarchical power play between cast and crew members is fascinating. While observing instances of correspondence between science fiction and other television genres, Pearson concludes by identifying a 'theatrical performance mode' that is encouraged by the 'epic' American science fiction series; a mode that sets the genre apart from realist television drama.

The final chapter, by Rayna Denison, examines the specifically different ways in which genre and performance operate in the context of popular Bollywood films. Concentrating upon the star performances given by Shahrukh Khan, Denison explores how Khan's 'generically aware' performance intersects with his star persona and how his skill and energy as a star performer are signalled by prolifically diverse performance strategies. In contrast to other Bollywood stars and contrary to most western screen stars, Khan's overt generic adaptability marks him as 'unexceptional' at the same time as it distinguishes him as the 'King of Bollywood cinema'. In comparison with other chapters, Denison's work here suggests that looking at the operations and functions of genre and performance beyond the more familiar confines of the UK or US context is highly revealing and it also indicates that there is a lot more useful work to be done in this area.

Note

1 While Auslander is concerned most with live performance, he also engages with, for instance, *The Roseanne Barr Show* (HBO, 1987) in this collection. See 'Brought to You by Fem-Rage: Stand-up Comedy and the Politics of Gender', Chapter 10 in Auslander (1997).

References

Altman, R. (1999) *Film/Genre*, London: bfi publishing.

Auslander, P. (1997) *From Acting to Performance: Essays in Modernism and Postmodernism*, London and New York: Routledge.

Baron, C., D. Carson and F. P. Tomasulo (eds.) (2004) *More than a Method: Trends and Traditions in Contemporary Film Performance*, Detroit: Wayne State University Press.

Bordwell, D. (1989) *Making Meaning: Inference and Rhetoric in the Interpretation of Cinema*, Cambridge, MA: Harvard University Press.

Butler, J. (1990) *Gender Trouble: Feminism and the Subversion of Identity*, London and New York: Routledge.

Butler, J. (ed.) (1991) *Star Texts: Image and Performance in Film and Television*, Detroit: Wayne State University Press.

Creeber, G. (ed.) (2001) *The Television Genre Book*, London: bfi publishing.

De Cordova, R. (1991) 'Genre and Performance: An Overview', in Jeremy Butler, ed., *Star Texts*, Detroit: Wayne State University Press, 115-124.

Dyer, R. (1986) *Heavenly Bodies: Film Star and Society*, London: British Film Institute.

Dyer, R. (1998 [1979]) *Stars*, London: bfi publishing.

Foucault, M. (1980) *The History of Sexuality, Volume 1: An Introduction*, Robert Hurley, trans., London: Vintage.

Hollinger, K. (2006) *The Actress: Hollywood Acting and the Female Star*, London and New York: Routledge.

Kramer, P. (1998) 'Post-Classical Hollywood', in J. Hill and P. Church Gibson, eds., *The Oxford Guide to Film Studies*, Oxford: Oxford University Press, 289-309.

Mulvey, L. (1975) 'Visual Pleasure and Narrative Cinema', *Screen*, 16, No. 3: 6–18.

Mulvey, L. (1981) 'Afterthoughts on "Visual Pleasure and Narrative Cinema" Inspired by *Duel in the Sun*', *Framework*, 15/16/17: 12–15.

Naremore, J. (1988) *Acting in the Cinema*, Berkeley and Los Angeles: University of California Press.

Neale, S. (2000) *Genre and Hollywood*, London and New York: Routledge.

Parker, A. and E. Kosofsky Sedgwick (1995) 'Introduction', in *Performativity and Performance*, London and New York: Routledge, 1-18.

Pearson, R. (1990) 'O'er Step not the Modesty of Nature: A Semiotic Approach to

Acting the Griffith Biographs', in C. Zucker, ed., *Making Visible the Invisible: An Anthology of Essays on Film Acting*, Metuchen: Scarecrow Press.

Pearson, R. (1992) *Eloquent Gestures: The Transformation of Performance Style in the Griffith Biograph Films*, Berkeley and Los Angeles: University of California Press.

Robertson Wojcik, P. (ed.) (2004) *Movie Acting: The Film Reader*, London and New York: Routledge.

Schechner, R. (2004) 'Performance Studies: The Broad Spectrum Approach', in H. Bial, ed., *The Performance Studies Reader* (second edition), London and New York: Routledge, 7-9.

Stam, R. (2000) *Film Theory*, Oxford: Blackwell Publishers.

Stern, L. and G. Kouvaros (eds.) (1999) *Falling for You: Essays on Cinema and Performance*, Sydney: Power Publications.

Wright Wexman, V. (1993) *Creating the Couple: Love, Marriage, and Hollywood Performance*, Princeton: Princeton University Press.

1

Film noir: gesture under pressure

Cynthia Baron

Noting that film 'genres circumscribe the form and position of performance' in discrete ways, in the 1980s Richard de Cordova identified the need for 'a general account of performance and its role within an economy of genres' (1986: 129, 138). Before his untimely passing, de Cordova began that account by outlining examples of acting choices in 'the western, film noir, and the melodrama' that reflected 'genre-specific rules' (1986: 129). Building on his work and on scholarship that has considered noir and masculinity, I would like to make a minor contribution to the ambitious project de Cordova envisioned by using his observation – that noir performances follow 'a model of dissimulation' (1986: 135) – as the starting point for my study.

My goal is to describe certain acting patterns in the classic noirs *Maltese Falcon* (John Huston, 1941), *The Big Sleep* (Howard Hawks, 1946) and *Out of the Past* (Jacques Tourneur, 1947) and the neo-noirs *Chinatown* (Roman Polanski, 1974), *Devil in a Blue Dress* (Carl Franklin, 1995) and *Brick* (Rian Johnson, 2005). Recognising that there are unmistakable contrasts between classic and neo-noir, I will look at acting choices that tend to be constants, rather than exceptions, in the evolving phenomenon of film noir. I hope to show that noir narratives require portrayals of tough guys to include a dizzying combination of (a) caricatured and exaggerated performance moments, (b) occasions of understated gestures and expressions, and (c) instances when performance details prompt audiences to see a distinction between the public face that noir tough guys show to other characters and their subjective experience that is visible only to audiences. The point is to clarify just how *gestures under pressure* work with other aspects of film noir narratives to communicate the complex inner life of vulnerable tough guys.[1]

Performance details that convey characters' efforts to conceal or disguise their thoughts, feelings and identities are not confined to noir, for as James Naremore points out, 'the breakdown of repressive constraints on behavior – the "failure" of performance – is a telling moment in any sort of theater' or film (1988: 76). However, some of noir's most memorable scenes are about characters' failed 'performances' for one another. For instance, acting choices that make a character's concealment plainly visible to other characters and the audience seem essential to portrayals of femme fatales. De Cordova notes that Mary Astor's performance as Brigitte O'Shaughnessy in *The Maltese Falcon* typifies how noir leads viewers to ask: 'Is the character lying or not lying, performing or not performing?' (1986: 135). Noting how Astor/O'Shaughnessy 'behaves like a sheltered innocent, casting demure glances down at the floor, wringing her hands and touching her brow in an appeal for sympathy', only to be told by Spade/Bogart that her performance is 'good . . . very, very good', Naremore explains that Spade and the audience are prompted to see through the 'performance' because Astor slightly overplays the scene, 'registering what Lawrence Shaffer has called "appliquéd" expressions' (1988: 76).

Along with the many occasions when femme fatales' 'performances' fail to mask their intentions, and so instead telegraph their attempt at concealment, there are times when 'playacting' by detective-heroes goes unnoticed by characters but reveals to audiences the emotion and psychological pressure underneath the tough guy's 'performance'. A range of details can convey 'expressive incoherence', if only because actors' physical characteristics differ (Naremore, 1988: 76). As Barry Grant notes, the 'hard-boiled detective Philip Marlowe is different as played by Dick Powell (*Murder, My Sweet*, 1944), Humphrey Bogart (*The Big Sleep*, 1946) or Elliott Gould (*The Long Goodbye*, 1973)' (2007: 18).

There are also a variety of acting choices that can suggest a noir tough guy is concealing or disguising something, for, as with any aspect of film, audiences encounter gestures and expressions in relation to other cinematic elements and, as in theatre, performance details acquire dramatic significance through their relationship to other formal elements. Still, when gestures and expressions are distinguished from characters, actors and star images, it becomes apparent that combinations of and variations in the spatial, temporal and energy qualities of filmic movements, gestures, and facial and vocal expressions prompt audiences to see when and why noir tough guys are masking their 'true' thoughts and feelings. Terms from Laban Movement Analysis can facilitate description of how performances details, or what Stephen Heath (1981: 213) calls *intensities*, convey the subjective experiences noir tough guys try to hide.

Caveats and context

Writing about noir performances makes one feel a bit like a noir character, 'embarrassed by a visibility' and at risk of making a misstep on someone else's turf (Copjec, 1993: ix). For instance, given the range of opinions on how noir 'should be classified within the scope of cinema history and criticism', any observation about patterns of performance within 'the genre' could be challenged (Erickson, 1996: 308). However, by now many scholars have tired of the 'dryly academic' debates about how noir should be seen – as 'a genre, a tone, a mood, a style, or a moment in film history' (Dimendberg, 2004: 11). Synthesising diverging perspectives, Mark Bould echoes and acknowledges the view that noir is 'an intersubjective discursive phenomenon' but he also points out that genres in general 'arise – or more accurately, are identified, named and developed – through complex feedback mechanisms involving producers, distributors, exhibitors, consumers, interpreters and other discursive agents' (2005: 15). Moving beyond the debates, Naremore proposes that noir occupies 'a liminal space somewhere between Europe and America, between high modernism and "blood melodrama," and between low-budget crime movies and art cinema' (2008: 220).[2]

Focusing on noir performances might also be suspect because the films have been thoroughly identified with their visual style.[3] As Alain Silver (1996: 7) explains, 'the evocation of a "noir look" goes all the way back' to *Panorama du film noir américain, 1941–1953*, the seminal work by Raymond Borde and Étienne Chaumeton published in 1955. Thus, there are now recognised 'visual conventions of film noir', which include 'chiaroscuro lighting, contrasts of dark and light in the image, imbalanced compositions that suggest powerlessness and geometric compositions that imply entrapment and doom' (Grant, 2007: 24). There are also cultural studies of noir and urban space that examine the 'quintessential emptiness' of its cityscapes (Murphet, 1998: 26).[4]

While studies of iconography and visual culture look more at urban space and less at the movements, gestures and expressions within those spaces, they are not antithetical to studies of screen performance. Their inquiries into the way noir depicts 'mechanisms of surveillance', for example, can be taken up in the analysis of gestures and expressions that convey instances when a noir hero feels 'encumbered by his own overexposed being' (Dimendberg, 2004: 211; Copjec, 1993: ix). Studies of noir's urban spaces can show how compositional details suggest that characters are under surveillance; but taking a different tack, analyses of performances can examine a 'change in the activation and involvement of the [actor's] body and in the quantity and quality of energy' that colour the gestures and expressions to see if and how they reveal a character's experience of being watched (Moore and Yamamoto, 1988: 184). In work that reckons with variations in the specific qualities of filmic movements, the shift from a light, free-flowing gait to a controlled and weighted one takes on as much importance as a change in the setting, with alteration in the expressive qualities of the gait revealing that the character feels exposed and vulnerable.

Inquiries into noir performance are rare but they do exist. Raymond Durgnat's (1951) work on emotional melodramas touches on questions related to performance, as does Thomas Elsaesser's (1972) analysis of melodramatic narration, for both scholars identify the role that small, seemingly insignificant performance details can play in representations that preclude emphatic physical expression, as when the Western hero arrives on the scene, guns blazing (Baron, 1993: 46-59). Mitchell Cohen has discussed noir's need for 'a new, largely beneath-the-surface acting style that combined force and vulnerability' (1974: 27). Writing about individual actors offers insights into how their physical embodiments of characters shape viewers' understanding of noir heroes. For example, Andrew Spicer describes Bogart as an actor who 'exemplified the new minimalist, pared-down acting technique in which his stiff face . . . is only allowed an occasional smile' (2002: 94). He notes that it is 'the eyes, knowing and sad, that express the sentiment that gave depth to his tough guys', and that Bogart's 'rasping voice, with the famous lisp, could convey scornful cynicism and bemused irony' as well as 'confused feelings churning inside' (2002: 94).

Writing about *Out of the Past*, Spicer observes that 'Mitchum's modulated baritone narration is capable of greater inflection than the dead-pan drawl of Bogart or [Dick] Powell, and [that] it contributes powerfully to the [film's overarching] mood of blighted hope' (2002: 56). Spicer, however, also notes: 'Like Bogart, Mitchum was a minimalist – with somnolent movements and hooded, lazy eyes – [and] a performance style that lent meaning to the smallest gesture' (2002: 96). Explaining that Mitchum's portrayal of Jeff Bailey 'has become one of the most celebrated noir performances', Spicer finds that it is Mitchum's 'measured yet evocative narration, intoned in the gruff voice summoned as if by an act of great will' that conveys the character's emotional vulnerability (2002: 96).

Bogart also serves as a point of comparison for Jack Nicholson's performance in *Chinatown*. Naremore finds that with Nicholson's portrayal of Gittes, the noir hero 'emerges as a slightly more believable version of a fantasy Bogart sometimes embodied – the tough man whose exterior disguises compassion and an outraged sense of justice' (2008: 206). Roger Ebert calls attention to the actor's ability to convey his character's inner life, noting that Nicholson so completely 'inhabits the character of J. J. Gittes . . . that there are scenes in the movie where . . . we know what he's thinking' (1974: 2). James Berardinelli, noting that the performance suggests sensitivity behind a tough guy mask, finds that *Chinatown* 'shows off the multiple facets of [Nicholson's] talent – tenderness, quiet intensity, bulldog tenacity, and bravery in the face of danger' (2001: 2). Denzel Washington's performance in *Devil in a Blue Dress* has also been linked to classic noir, with Washington described as possessing 'all the presence and laid-back gravity of a Robert Mitchum' (Pawelczak, 1996: 62). Richard Schickel's review of the film identifies key features of Washington's performance. He writes: 'Reserved but agile, wary but thrusting when he needs to be, [Washington] gracefully reanimates a lost American archetype, the lonely lower-class male' (1995). Ed Guerro also locates salient details of Washington's performance by noting that Washington 'plays Rawlins with social vulnerability and caution mixed with a persistent toughness that gradually builds into a cunning, assertive rage against injustice as the narrative evolves' (1996: 38). Joseph Gordon-Levitt's performance in *Brick* has been linked to Bogart, in that Gordon-Levitt also embodies a character who is 'tough and cynical, but . . . funny, too' (Grady, 2005: 1). Describing Gordon-Levitt as 'a hard-boiled romantic in bloom', Meghan O'Rourke explains that the signature gesture he creates for the 'gawky high-school sleuth', 'a hands-in-the-pocket, hunched stride', conveys the idea that Brendan is continually 'hiding in plain sight' (2007: 1, 2). Highlighting a feature of Gordon-Levitt's performance that links it to other portrayals of noir heroes, O'Rourke argues that the 'quietude' of his performance is engaging '*because* we can sense the effort it takes' (2007: 2). In other words, audiences see that measured, carefully modulated physical expressions are *gestures under pressure* and thus signs of subjective experience.

Vocabulary for analysing performances

Some observations about noir performances highlight the specific acting choices that convey tough guys' interiority, as when O'Rourke notes that Gordon-Levitt signals the pain Brendan feels 'on the inside . . . through averted glances and a flicking wit' (2007: 2). As O'Rourke might argue, by themselves the actor's averted glances do not express the character's emotional pain, but seen in relation to his intrusive, flicking vocal expressions, the glances highlight the disparity between the cocky attitude Brendan 'performs' for other characters and the fear and uncertainty visible only to the audience.

Even when not so specific, observations about noir performances provide a valuable resource for inquiries into the *performance montage* that depicts noir heroes. For example, Spicer's comment that Bogart has the 'ability to project opposing attitudes' invites us to identify the acting choices that establish the different attitudes (2002: 94). The remark that Gittes is 'another of Nicholson's volatile but vulnerable screen characters [whose] façade begins to crack once he comes to care for others' can prompt us to locate the specific features in Nicholson's performance that cause audiences to see Gittes as volatile, vulnerable, a character who has a façade, and a character whose façade cracks (Albright, 1980: 335). Similarly, O'Rourke's insight that Gordon-Levitt's 'minimalist' performance reveals his ability to project 'emotion by containing it' (2007: 1) can lead us to search for the order and combination of performance details that generate the impression Brendan tries to contain his feelings.

Framing the inquiry more broadly, one could ask, for example, how does the order and selection of salient physical expressions create the impression that audiences learn more about the central character's hopes, fears and moral code? How do contrasts between 'performances' for other characters and gestures and expressions visible only to the audience influence our view of noir tough guys? Answers to these questions can be found by examining the selection and combination of observable physical details that represent the noir hero. These details come into sharper focus when they are distinguished from the character, the actor and the inter-textual star image. While distinctions between those elements seem obvious, discussions of screen performance often conflate them, thus obscuring the connotations carried by the fragments of gestures and expressions that belong to filmic discourse in the same way that framing, lighting, sound and design details do (see Baron and Carnicke, 2008: 62–85).

Heath (1981: 176–193) has outlined categories that clarify distinctions relevant to analysis of film performance. These include: (1) *agent* – fills a narrative function, often organised into pairs of oppositions; (2) *character* – can be an agent, belong to subplots, contribute to mood and theme; (3) *person* – an actor or nonprofessional who represents agents or characters; (4) *image* – star image that influences the way characters in commercial films are encountered; (5) *figure* – an instance in which star image, narrative and performance intersect meaningfully for cinephiles; (6) *idea* – when people represent social types or convey points in an intellectual argument; (7) *moments, intensities* – gestures and expressions present in film representations, evocative in themselves.

These categories reflect the cultural reality through which audiences approach screen performances and in terms of material outside films themselves. They also illuminate the fact that performance details are a source of meaning – distinct from (a) agents and characters within a fictional narrative, (b) actors who pay bills, go to auditions and exist outside of films, and (c) star images, figures and ideas that are established by marketing and social developments outside of films. What distinguishes intensities is that they function as meaningful, connotatively charged discursive elements 'outside a simple constant unity of the body as a whole [or] as the property of some *one*' (Heath, 1981: 183). Because performance details, working in concert with other filmic details, convey impressions about characters, it can be productive to analyse noir performances by focusing on gestures and expressions in the films themselves, temporarily setting aside the extra-textual associations that colour responses to the screen appearances of Bogart, Mitchum, Nicholson, Washington, or Gordon-Levitt.

One way to identify the meanings created by intensities is to draw on Laban Movement Analysis, which takes it name from its originator, Rudolf Laban, who first became known for establishing an alternative vision of dance by seeing 'body rhythm rather than musical meter as the impetus for movement' (Partsch-Bergsohn, 1994: 15). In 1921, Laban's appointment as ballet director of the National Theatre in Mannheim, Germany, secured his reputation as a key figure in Modern Dance, and between World War I and II 'there was hardly a major European city [that] did not have its Laban School' (Hodgson, 2001: 3). However, in 1936, at the height of his career, Laban was put under house arrest. He fled Nazi Germany and in the 1940s began working in the U.K. with Littlewood's and McColl's Theatre Workshop. Here, actors relied on Stanislavskian techniques 'to create the inner truth of the characters' and Laban principles 'to structure the expressive [qualities] of performance', with actors' choices about physical and vocal expressions arising from experiments with the different spatial, temporal, weight and flow qualities that shaped 'the rhythmic patterns' of the performances in the company's productions (Barker, 2000: 115, 119). Since that time, physical approaches to performance have served to balance various forms of Method acting. Laban's insights are especially compatible with Stanislavsky's method of physical actions, which approaches the emotional life of the character through the physical dimension of the role; they also dovetail with Grotowski's interest in creating an authentic connection between impulse and physical action. Used in a variety of applications, the Laban system is recognised by the Association of Theatre Movement Educators as a theoretical and practical taxonomy.

For audiences interested in analysing performances, Laban principles can provide a way to locate the impelling inner action that colours gestures and expressions, because Laban terms prompt us to attend to 'actual movement, rather than its completed result' (Lamb and Watson, 1979: 7). That focus facilitates analysis of acting choices, for the meaning of actors' gestures and expressions is not disclosed by a single frame but instead by the players' movements through space, the speed of their movements, and the degree of resistance and control in their movements, gestures and expressions. Laban vocabulary illuminates observable aspects of physical expression, so that the nuanced connotations conveyed by gestures, facial expressions, and vocal intonations become more legible.

Laban Movement Analysis seeks to identify: (a) *the spatial aspects of movement*: is a movement direct or flexible/indirect; what is the direction, place, and shape of physical and vocal expression; (b) *the temporal aspects of movement*: is a movement sudden or sustained; what is the speed and rhythm of gestures and expressions; (c) *the weight or strength of movement*: is a movement strong/weighted or light; what is the degree of resistance to gravity in movements and expressions; (d) *the energy flow of movement*: is a movement bound or free flowing; what is the degree of control suggested by filmic movements, gestures, facial expressions and vocalisations?

The weight or strength of actors' movements, their spatial aspects and their temporal qualities can also be described in terms of eight 'efforts' identified by Laban. Four of these efforts are strong: *pressing* movements are strong, direct and sustained, while *thrusting* movements are strong, direct and sudden; *wringing* movements are strong, indirect and sustained, whereas *slashing* movements are strong, indirect and sudden. In contrast to efforts defined by the strong or weighted quality of the movement, other efforts are distinguished by their lightness: *gliding* movements are light, direct and sustained, while *dabbing* movements are light, direct and sudden; *floating* movements are light, indirect and sustained, while *flicking* movements are light, indirect and sudden.

By highlighting the spatial, temporal, weight and energy dimensions of physical and vocal expression, Laban concepts might lead us to ask, for example, in portraying a scrappy, working-class character calling on a well-heeled city operator, does an actor move through space in a *direct or indirect manner*? For instance, in *The Big Sleep* when Marlowe has his initial meeting with General Sternwood, are Bogart's gestures and vocal expressions direct, indirect; or do they perhaps start off indirect, and so show Marlowe getting his bearing, and then become more direct, and so suggest that the shamus, rather naively, feels he is capable of handling the situation? Similarly, when a noir tough guy finds himself in a dangerous situation, is there a *sudden or sustained quality* to the way the actor moves? For instance, in *Out of the Past* whenever Jeff is at Whit Sterling's Lake Tahoe estate, could we say that Mitchum's movements, gestures and vocal expressions tend to be bound, weighted and sustained?

When a noir hero is trying to stir up a little dust to get the investigation started, does the actor use *weighted or much lighter movements*? When Jack Gittes is making sure people connected to Hollis Mulwray know that he is investigating Hollis's concern about water diversion, is it possible to say that there is a light, ebullient quality in the way Nicholson raises his hat in grand farewell to Gittes's plodding nemesis Claude Mulvihill and the untrustworthy deputy engineer Russ Yelburton? In the wake of recognition scenes that somehow implicate the noir tough guy in events he is supposed to be sorting out, do the actor's gestures tend to be marked by a *bound quality or do they seem to be free flowing*? In the case of *Brick*, might we say that there is a distinctly bound quality to Gordon-Levitt's movements after Brendan learns that Emily was pregnant (perhaps with his child) when she was murdered?

Gestures, expressions and noir narrative demands

While the specific selection and combination of movements, gestures, vocal inflections and facial expressions differ from film to film, productions like *The Big Sleep*, *Out of the Past*, *Chinatown*, *Devil in a Blue Dress* and *Brick* reveal an integral relationship between narrative demands and performance details, with the scenarios requiring various forms of expressive incoherence that lead audiences to see when the heroes are disguising or masking their 'true' thoughts, feelings and intentions. In these and other noir films, carefully crafted arrangements of observable, connotatively rich performance details, anchored by narrative circumstance and amplified by lighting, framing, editing, sound and design elements, contribute a great deal to the sense that audience members know what the central tough guys are thinking and feeling, especially when the characters in the fiction do not.

The effects of performance, meaning the orchestrated ensemble of movements, gestures and expressions present in films' visual and aural representation, are, as one might expect, consistent with the effects of the narratives' signature features. Just as character voice-overs and flashbacks linked to characters' narration 'foreground the subjectivity and "interiority" of *noir*'s principal characters', gestures and expressions that convey expressive incoherence establish the noir tough guy's 'psychological complexity' (Neale, 2000: 168; Naremore, 1988: 80). In these instances, an actor might make 'two different faces, both clearly visible to the audience, one coded as "suppressed," the other coded as "ostensive"' (Naremore, 1988: 80). Or it might involve contrasting physical expressions. As Meghan O'Rourke notes in describing *Brick*'s opening flash-forward when Brendan discovers Emily's body, Gordon-Levitt 'lets perceptions flicker in his eyes, tightening a few muscles [and at the same time] keeps so still that he shakes almost imperceptibly' (2007: 1).

Of course, isolated performance details do not by themselves convey moments of expressive incoherence. Much like the notes in musical compositions, which 'can only be appreciated as the piece sequentially progresses through time to its ending', it is the crafted selection and combination of differing poses, gaits, movements, gestures, facial expressions, vocal intonations and vocal inflections that let audiences, but not the other characters, see how smart, socially compromised tough guy characters think and feel as they encounter the physical and emotional dangers presented by noir scenarios (Moore and Yamamoto, 1988: 121). In noir, the tough guy's way of moving, gesturing, and speaking in unguarded moments serves as a point of reference. For instance, in *Out of the Past*, Mitchum's gait has a light, swinging quality when we first see Jeff walking along the shoreline towards Ann, the small town girl he wants to marry. However, when Jeff is with threatened and threatening femme fatale Kathie Moffat, Mitchum's movements and gestures shift between extreme, almost slack looseness and sustained, tightly bound rigidity.

Noir tough guys are consistently 'framed, imprisoned for crimes they did not commit or caught up unwittingly in conspiracies and plots' (Bould, 2005: 51). The emotional and psychological toll these experiences have on them is frequently conveyed by the observable contrast in the performance details found in opening and closing scenes. Initially, noir heroes are often distinguished by the light, relaxed qualities of their physical expression. By the end of the saga, however, there is often a weighted quality that conveys the subjective experience of the wiser, sadder, but still vulnerable tough guy.

In *The Big Sleep* when Marlowe first arrives at the Sternwood mansion, there is a light, free-flowing quality to Bogart's exchange with Carmen/ Martha Vickers; when she 'accidentally' trips and falls into his arms, Bogart catches her in a gentle, flexible embrace that is light and quick, and thus as graceful as a ballroom dance move. In *Devil in a Blue Dress* when we are first introduced to Easy Rawlins as he calmly enjoys a cigarette and a whisky while scanning the newspaper for job openings, there is a smooth, even, direct quality to Washington's inflections in the voice-over that works in tandem with the quick but light and relaxed way he takes a drag off his cigarette and the light, effortless pose that balances the focused way he scans the newspaper.

These types of performance details establish the noir hero's 'natural' attitude, which soon must be masked, for the investigation's initial stage requires the hero to enter the world surrounding the crime. To gain entry, the tough guy makes himself vulnerable, with acting choices suggesting that the hero naively begins his investigation as a lark. Exemplified by the Marlowe/Bogart book collector impersonation in *The Big Sleep*, noir films often feature scenes in which performance details convey the sleuth's flare for the dramatic. For the hero gets the investigation going by creating a persona who intrudes into situations and leads other characters to take notice of the fabricated, caricatured character; all the while, the actors' overt overplaying and use of 'appliquéd' physical and vocal expression allow audiences to be in on the act.

The detective-hero's 'playacting' is entertaining and gives audiences a sense of having intimate knowledge about the character. For instance, Mitchum's light, flexible, free-flowing, quick but relaxed, almost skipping gait in the early scene by the lake with Ann establishes our sense of Jeff's private, 'natural', unguarded way of being. Of course, those qualities disappear when Jeff gets the assignment from Whit Sterling/Kirk Douglas; there, Mitchum's gestures and expressions are weighted, bound, so sustained and yet so direct that he seems to press his words out. Later, when Jeff first meets Kathie/Jane Greer in Acapulco, it is significant that the qualities in Mitchum's physical expression do not echo those in the scene at the lake; instead Jeff 'acts' the part of the silly flirt to get her attention. The scenes that depict Jeff's initial encounters with Kathie verge on 'self-parody' in part because Mitchum 'overplays' the flirtation and thus makes the contrast between authentic and artificial behaviour visible (Naremore, 2008: 201).

1.1 Mitchum's appliquéd gesture and expression let audiences see that Jeff is acting the part of the flirt in *Out of the Past*

Watching *Chinatown*, audiences get to enjoy the 'performance' Gittes turns in at the water engineers' office, for Nicholson 'overplays' the part of the obnoxious private eye, as he plops himself in a chair, taps his cigarettes, hums loudly, looks at pictures in the office, pesters the secretary with questions. Here, Nicholson's performance is marked by an odd, irregular rhythm and a light, indirect feeling that gives each gesture a flicking quality that is so annoying that the officious secretary caves in to Gittes's request to see Yelburton. In *Devil in a Blue Dress*, audiences are privy to a play-within-a-play in the sequence that shows soft-spoken, clean-cut Easy Rawlins become a loud-mouthed, pool-playing, heavy-drinking lowlife to get Frank Green to contact him so that he can find the mystery woman Daphne Monet.

'Performances' such as these not only place audiences in a privileged position of knowledge, they also illuminate the temperament of the noir hero. For example, while the details in Nicholson's portrayal make Gittes's 'performance' for the secretary a change in degree – from cocky, self-assured guy who is making a living to intolerable jerk who is looking for his comeuppance – the 'performance' Easy turns in for the characters in the club, pool hall and liquor store reveals a sharp contrast between Easy's 'natural' attitude and the persona he temporarily assumes. That is, Washington's portrayal prompts us to see that Easy 'naturally' moves through the world in a grounded, direct manner, while the lowlife he pretends to be is so flexible he is off-balance; and whereas Easy 'naturally' moves and speaks in an even, measured, sustained way, as a lazy, drunken lowlife his 'performance' is marked by rapid, irregular vocal expressions that make him seem testy, hot-tempered and not very bright.

The narrative/performance pattern of the sleuth making himself visible by 'pretending' to be an insufferable character carries over into *Brick*. Here, in the scene in which the disaffected loner gets the investigation started, the qualities in Gordon-Levitt's performance shift from their baseline – of weighted, contracted, wringing gestures and expressions – to 'uncharacteristic' sudden, irregularly paced, flicking vocal expressions and then strong, sudden slashing movements and gestures. Creating a visible contrast with the tense and subdued qualities that characterise Brendan's standard way of being in the world, to shake things up Gordon-Levitt 'overplays' the part of the smart-mouthed punk when Brendan picks a fight in the high school parking lot to get the attention of the lazy jock's drug contacts. Once again, performance choices give audiences special access to the tough guy's intentions, for the free-flowing, expanding qualities of Gordon-Levitt's movements, gestures and vocal expressions signal that Brendan is 'putting on a show'.

In sequences late in noir scenarios, often following melodramatic recognition scenes, performance details illuminate the tough guy's burgeoning understanding of his own implication in the larger crime that has been revealed by his investigation. In *The Big Sleep*, when Marlowe/Bogart calls and then waits for Eddie Mars at Geiger's house, there is no trace of the oddball book collector, and in place of the quick, light, flexible qualities in Bogart's gestures and expressions in the opening scene, there are sustained, weighted and direct qualities to convey Marlowe's fear as he finally knows what he is up against. In *Out of the Past*, as Jeff has a drink at Sterling's estate before he and Kathie drive into the police road block he has arranged, the silly flirt is long gone, and in contrast to the light, flexible qualities visible when he walks up from the lake towards Ann, Mitchum's direct, sustained and very weighted gestures and expressions convey his resolve to bring Kathie and himself to justice.

In *Chinatown*, once Gittes learns that the mystery girl is Evelyn's sister and daughter, Nicholson's demeanour becomes uncharacteristically quiet, resigned, the cockiness replaced by earnestness. The other characters, of course, do not register the change; Lou Escobar treats Gittes as an annoying buffoon until after Evelyn is killed and even he grasps the disastrous consequences of his attempt to intervene in the affairs of Noah Cross. In *Devil in a Blue Dress*, when Easy finally gets the answers he needs – what Terrell has on Daphne and who killed his erstwhile lover Coretta – in the few moments before the thugs arrive, the strong, direct, sudden qualities in Washington's body and voice melt into a quiet, weighted energy that suggests Easy has learned more than he wanted to. In the final moments of *Brick*, after Laura finally ties up all the loose ends of the story, any trace of the smart-mouthed kid has gone, and in place of the restless energy that infuses Gordon-Levitt's gestures and expressions throughout the film, there is now a lightly weighted stillness that suggests the wind has been taken out of his sails.

The contrast between performance choices in the opening scenes and the scenes that reveal the true stakes of the detective's investigation allows audiences to trace and assess the noir hero's existential journey from casual investigator to entrapped participant. Between those two dramatic moments, performances give depth to the main characters by revealing their private responses to tight situations. In those instances, tiny performance details can function like 'Shakespearean asides' that telegraph the thoughts and feelings the tough guys cannot let other characters see (Naremore, 1988: 75).

In *Out of the Past*, when Whit and Joe suddenly appear at Jeff's hotel room in Acapulco, Mitchum establishes a contrast between the slow, measured gestures Bailey 'performs' for the other characters and the darting glances he uses to make audiences see Bailey's fear, anger and strategising. For audiences, even the bound, sustained quality of Mitchum's movements conveys Jeff's fear, for in the moments prior to Whit's and Joe's arrival there had been a light, direct quality to his whistle and an open, outstretched, free-flowing quality to his movement as he packed his suitcase. These qualities disappear the moment Mitchum opens the door; and for the remainder of the scene, that smooth, lyrical pace is replaced by an irregular rhythm that conveys Jeff's scramble to regain balance. For example, Mitchum slowly squeezes out the words, 'I like surprises' then suddenly whips through the explanation: 'when I was a kid we were so busted if we got anything at all it was a big surprise'. Still off-balance, Mitchum conveys Jeff's alarm at seeing the telltale earrings; he quickly raises his eyebrows and then glides over to get the earrings.

Then, 'overplaying' the role of the sleuth, hands shoved in his pockets and his voice low, Mitchum's strong, direct and sudden thrust of a comment, 'I know how far you trust people', shows Jeff hunkering down, trying to square off and put Whit on the defensive. From there, he shifts 'performance' tactics again, this time 'overplaying' the breezy confidence of the guy who is just looking out for Whit's best interests. But even Whit sees through the ruse, and the scene is choreographed so that audiences get to see Jeff/Mitchum catch his breath 'off-stage' by going into the bathroom to get a towel to wipe his by now very likely sweating hands.

Following this reprieve, Mitchum 'overplays' Jeff's indifference, tossing the towel on the bed with a jerk and directing more than casual attention to closing his cufflinks. Then, just after Jeff/Mitchum has made another strong, direct verbal thrust at Whit, Mitchum communicates the desperation Jeff feels at hearing what he thinks is Kathie knocking at the door; he holds his body completely still in counterpoint to the quick moments of his eyes. Conveying the relief Jeff experiences when it is a porter with his shoes, Mitchum again 'overplays' the clever detective as he pokes out, 'like I said before, I thought the others squeaked'.

In the scenes in the hotel lobby and bar, performance details continue to convey Jeff's fear and anger at being cornered and his attempts to survive the situation. Mitchum combines strong, slow, pressing line deliveries with sudden shifts in his eyes and a quick exhale of breath to blow out a match. Still 'overplaying' his indifference, Jeff/Mitchum scribbles his signature on the bar tab, then tosses the pencil down on the table with a flick. To show Jeff still struggling to conceal his feelings, when the characters leave the hotel, Mitchum pushes the door open with a strong, direct gesture in combination with a quick glance down that lets audiences see Jeff's confidence is an act. Finally, as Jeff watches Whit and Joe leave in a cab, Mitchum takes a full breath – the bound, weighted quality that had pervaded his physical expression now followed by the light, free-flowing sigh confirms the earlier tension and gives audiences a privileged view of Jeff's relief after surviving this dangerous situation.

There is a comparable but more dangerous episode in *Devil in a Blue Dress*. Again, the noir hero finds himself surprised, cornered and threatened by the powerful man who has hired him. Returning home in the early morning, Easy sees Albright's car parked outside his house. Using quick, light, direct movements as he puts his car in park, rolls up the window and closes the car door, Washington conveys Easy's confidence that he can handle the situation. Then, shifting to more sustained, more weighted movements, Washington reveals Easy's growing concern as he approaches the house and hears several voices. But, as Washington's performance reveals, when Easy enters the house, he goes on the offensive, essentially flicking Albright's men away as he objects to them being in his house. However, Albright throws Easy off-balance, calling him 'nigger'

1.2 Washington's tightly bound stillness conveys Easy's intense effort to mask his anger in *Devil in a Blue Dress*

and soon increasing the danger by threatening him with a knife; Easy is forced to back down.

But in the next units of action, after Albright tells Easy to write down Daphne's address, 'if [he] can write', Washington's strong, tightly bound movements convey the rage Easy feels at being insulted and threatened in his own home. Washington prompts audiences to see that Easy is barely able to play the part of the 'submissive black man'. His line delivery is quiet but strong and very direct when Albright tells him to get him some whisky and Easy replies, 'get it your own damn self'. Holding himself tall and upright, Washington trembles with anger, his eyes glisten with emotion, but he 'conceals' that feeling from the others by averting his eyes and lowering his voice to a whisper. Once again, our impressions about the hero's thoughts and feelings are confirmed by the scene's final performance details: as Easy/Washington watches the thugs leave he relaxes his body in a moment of relief; next, collecting his physical energy to convey Easy's newfound resolve, Washington slams his fist on the table and then strides forward, his head up, shoulders open.

As these scenes suggest, portrayals of tough guys who are required by external circumstances to mask their vulnerability feature crafted but naturalistic modulations in performance details. Often it is simply a slight variation in the spatial, temporal and energy qualities of the physical expression that communicates what the hero is thinking and feeling. Especially when considered as musical notes, that is, over time and in relation to one another, it is possible to see how the connotations carried in physical expressions make noir characters' inner experience visible.

Conclusion

While I have discussed only a few moments in a handful of films, it should be possible to see that patterns in noir narratives lead to patterns in noir performances, that observable performance details help convey characters' experiences, and that acting in noir films illuminates the remarkable paradox that gestures and expressions can make visible the fact that characters are hiding or disguising something. A close look at acting choices in noir can contribute to 'a general account of performance' (De Cordova, 1986: 129) because the films feature so many occasions when performance details communicate the contrast between characters' private experience and their public behaviour.

Analysing noir can also illuminate the role that performance plays 'within an economy of genres' (De Cordova, 1986: 138) by locating the genre-specific rule that audiences alone must see what the hero is thinking and feeling. Interestingly, this rule leads to bravura performances. By portraying characters who 'pretend' to be oddballs, flirts, buffoons, lowlifes and punk kids, actors have a chance to show their acting 'virtuosity by sending out dual signs' that are plausible enough to be convincing to other characters but allow audiences to appreciate the artifice (Naremore 1988: 76). By embodying characters who develop a discernible lack of expressivity that goes unnoticed by other characters but shows audiences how the answers to the mystery have affected the noir tough guy, actors are able to 'convey the sense of *change* so important to classic narrative' (Naremore, 1988: 73).

By paralleling the narrative strategies of character voice-over and flashback, performance choices in noir help create 'a place for affect' in scenarios distinguished by 'action and suspense' (Vernet, 1993: 1; Neale, 2000: 169). By working in concert with narrative strategies, physical expressions with differing spatial, temporal and energy qualities provide a window into and 'sustained focus on the thoughts and feelings' of characters who are physically and emotionally vulnerable (Neale, 2000: 168). A look at performance thus confirms that viewers' privileged access to the inner experiences of noir's clever, earnest and vulnerable tough guys is one of the genre's abiding pleasures. It also suggests that illuminating tough guys' subjective experiences is one of the things that distinguishes 'the form and position of performance' (De Cordova, 1986: 129) in film noir.

Notes

1 The essay builds on work by Bingham, Cohan, Covey, Crowther and Krutnik, and genre/performance analysis in Baron and Camicke's *Reframing Screen Performance* (Chapter 2). Contrasts between classic and neo-noir have been the subject of critical analyses since the late 1970s (see, for example, Borde and Chaumeton, 2002: 155–160). Thanks to Sarah Q. Doyle for suggesting *Brick* as a case study.

2 The view that '*film noir* does not belong to the history of cinema [but rather] to the history of film criticism' has been an integral part of noir scholarship (Vernet, 1993: 26). In his overview of the debates, Steven Neale concludes that noir 'now has a generic status it originally did not possess' (2000: 3; see also 151–177).

3 In addition to visual design (lighting, composition), scholarship has also, of course, addressed narrative design (convoluted plots, flashbacks, voice-over), recurring themes (outcasts, femme fatales that signify a threat to patriarchy, and so on) and sound design.

4 Julian Murphet looks at how noir's 'run-down, dark, mean and empty streets resound with the fear and hatred of a race/class faction that has lost its hold over them' in the wake of cities being abandoned by 'the upper tiers of the white working class and the white middle class' (1998: 29, 28). Paula Rabinowitz, also noting how the American city 'quite literally darked' over the course of the twentieth century, considers the postwar years and the 'female takeover of urban space' given 'the absence of men who have deserted . . . urban spaces for war' (2002: 28, 30). Tracing 'the changing spatial practices' of film noir, Dimendberg shows that by the end of the 1940s 'the pulsating nocturnal metropolis of neon signs and dark alleys' was no longer the 'dominant spatial mode' as the films came to 'represent social life in an increasingly decentralized America knitted together by highways, radio, and television' (2004: 211, 210, 211).

References

Albright, C., Jr. (1980) '*Chinatown*', in Frank Northern Magill, ed., *Magill's Survey of the Cinema*, Englewood Cliffs: Salem Press, 332–335.

Barker, C. (2000) 'Joan Littlewood', in Alison Hodge, ed., *Twentieth Century Actor Training*, New York: Routledge, 113–128.

Baron, C. (1993) '"Tales of Sound and Fury" Reconsidered', *Spectator*, 13, No. 2 (Spring): 46–59.

Baron, C. and S. M. Carnicke (2008) *Reframing Screen Performance*, Ann Arbor: University of Michigan Press.

Berardinelli, J. (2001) '*Chinatown*' www.reelviews.net/movies/c/chinatown.html.

Bingham, D. (1994) *Acting Male: Masculinities in the Films of James Stewart, Jack Nicholson, and Clint Eastwood*, New Brunswick: Rutgers University Press.

Borde, R. and E. Chaumeton (2002) *A Panorama of American Film Noir: 1941–1953*, trans. Paul Hammond, San Francisco: City Lights Books.

Bould, M. (2005) *Film Noir: From Berlin to Sin City*, London: Wallflower Press.

Chow, L. (2006) '2006 World Poll – Part 1', *Senses of Cinema*, www.sensesofcinema.com/contents/07/42/2006-world-poll-1.html.

Cohan, S. (1997) *Masked Men: Masculinity and the Movies in the Fifties*, Bloomington: Indiana University Press.

Cohen, M. (1974) 'The Actor: Villains and Victims', *Film Comment*, 10, No. 6: 27–9.

Copjec, J. (1993) 'Introduction', in Joan Copjec, ed., *Shades of Noir*, New York: Verso, ix–xii.

Covey, W. (2003) 'The Genre Don't Know Where It Came From: African-American Neo-Noir Since the 1960s', *Journal of Film and Video*, 55, Nos 2–3 (Summer/Fall): 59-72.

Crowther, B. (1988) *Film Noir: Reflections in a Dark Mirror*, London: Virgin.

De Cordova, R. (1986) 'Genre and Performance: An Overview', in Barry Keith Grant, ed., *Film Genre Reader*, Austin: University of Texas Press, 129–139.

Dimendberg, E. (2004) *Film Noir and the Spaces of Modernity*, Cambridge, MA: Harvard University Press.

Durgrat, R. (1951) 'Ways of Melodrama', *Sight and Sound*, 21, No. 1: 34–40.

Ebert, R. (1974) '*Chinatown*', http://rogerebert.suntimes.com/apps/pbcs.dl1/article?AID=/19740601/REVIEWS/4081700.

Elsaesser, T. (1972) 'Talks and Sound and Fury: Observations on the Family Melodrama', *Monogram*, No. 4: 2–15.

Erickson, T. (1996) 'Kill Me Again: Movement Becomes Genre', in Alain Silver and James Ursini, eds., *Film Genre Reader*, New York: Limelight, 307–329.

Grady, P. (2005) '*Brick*', Reel.com, www.reel.com/movie.asp?MID=141818&buy=closed&Tab=reviews&CID=13.

Grant, B. K. (2007) *Film Genre: From Iconography to Ideology*, London: Wallflower.

Guerro, E. (1996) '*Devil in a Blue Dress*', *Cineaste*, 22, No. 1: 38.

Heath, S. (1981) *Questions of Cinema*, Bloomington: Indiana University Press.

Hodgson, J. (2001) *Mastering Movement: The Life and Work of Rudolf Laban*, New York: Routledge.

Krutnik, F. (1991) *In a Lonely Street: Film Noir, Genre, Masculinity*, New York: Routledge.

Lamb, W. and E. Watson (1979) *Body Code: The Meaning of Movement*, London: Routledge.

Moore, C. and K. Yamamoto (1988) *Beyond Words: Movement Observation and Analysis*, New York: Gordon and Breach.

Murphet, J. (1998) 'Film Noir and the Racial Unconscious', *Screen*, 39, No. 1 (Spring): 22–35.

Naremore, J. (1988) *Acting in the Cinema*, Berkeley: University of California Press.

Naremore, J. (2008) *More Than Night: Film Noir in its Contexts*, updated edn, Berkeley: University of California Press.

Neale, S. (2000) *Genre and Hollywood*, New York: Routledge.

O'Rourke, M. (2007) 'Joseph Gordon-Levitt', *Slate Magazine* (6 April), www.slate.com/id/2163588.

Partsch-Bergsohn, I. (1994) *Modern Dance in Germany and the United States*, Chur, Switzerland: Harwood.

Pawelczak, A. (1996) '*Devil in a Blue Dress*', *Films in Review* (2 January): 62.

Rabinowitz, P. (2002) *Black & White & Noir: America's Pulp Modernism*, New York: Columbia University Press.

Schickel, R. (1995) 'Down These Mean, Palm-Lined Streets', www.time.com/time/magazine/article/000,9171,983523,000.html.

Silver, A. (1996) 'Introduction', in Alain Silver and James Ursini, eds., *Film Noir Reader*, New York: Limelight, 3–15.

Spicer, A. (2002) *Film Noir*, New York: Longman.

Vernet, M. (1993) '*Film Noir* on the Edge of Doom', in Joan Copjec, ed., *Shades of Noir*, New York: Verso, 1-31.

2

Captured ghosts: horror acting in the 1970s British television drama

Richard J. Hand

British television drama in the 1970s had a special interest in the genre of horror. Examples of horror television included works with a supernatural theme, such as the BBC's *A Ghost Story for Christmas* series (1971–78), most familiarly featuring adaptations of the short stories of M. R. James, but also works by Nigel Kneale for both the BBC (*The Stone Tape* [1972]) and ITV (*Beasts* [1976]). Of equal significance was horror drama in a somewhat different mould, namely the generally 'real life', more Grand-Guignol terrors of Brian Clemens's *Thriller* (1973–76). Writing in a period of booming DVD culture, the television academic is afforded an exciting opportunity to reappraise examples of 1970s horror television, key examples of which have been released in digitally re-mastered form and substantial collected editions (the *Thriller* DVD box-set totals 2150 minutes) with a variety of extra features. The ongoing release of 1970s television horror reflects three factors: the DVD industry continues to flourish and material is being released to meet this demand; there is a nostalgia industry surrounding 1970s culture; and performance horror enjoys a perennial popularity. With regard to the case studies in this chapter, there is a special place for the writer: Nigel Kneale and Brian Clemens were already veterans of television writing prior to the 1970s while M. R. James' ghost stories created near-perfect paradigms for television adaptation. However, there are other key factors in the case studies we will be analysing: the role of the performer and the practice of 'horror acting' in 1970s British television drama.

In his analysis of television acting, John Caughie signals the problem with approaches to this form of performance. As he states, 'the actor acting is a messily humanist component of the specific signifying practices of film and television, a kind of impressionistic marshland' (2000: 219) and any analysis of an example of acting 'poses the problem of endless description: at what point do you stop?' (2000: 218). Nevertheless, the place and function of the actor as conduit and interactive agent remain centrally important to any television drama, an argument that becomes even more significant when looking at genre-specific works of the 1970s. As a performance genre, horror frequently charts a character's journey from the mundanely realistic into the exceptionally heightened in order to capture, *in extremis*, the supernatural or the brutal. Compared with contemporary television drama, the 1970s now seems technically rudimentary: visual effects are highly simplistic compared with modern CGI technology; the camerawork seems conservative with a typically motionless camera employing long- and mid-shots and few close-ups; and the editing employs a functional rather than artistic purpose. The consequence of these limitations means a foregrounding of performers and their craft. 1970s television horror drama permits and demands the centrality of the performer. Furthermore, as the editing is comparatively minimal and the extreme close-up is rarely used, the spectator is privileged to the corporeal presence and essence of the performer. In other words, the actors in 1970s television drama are frequently like the best kind of stage performers: they act with the whole body and respond acutely to the spatial and temporal contexts within which they are placed. In addition, Caughie's celebration of actors' ability to 'en-act and em-body feelings *as if* they were real, in a way which makes them real for them and *for us*' (2000: 220) takes on a profound resonance when looking at horror. The genre of horror is exceptionally demanding on both the performer and viewer as, typically, it attempts to make the irrational or implausible 'real' and believable, at least for the duration of the drama.

Location shooting is extremely important for many examples of 1970s horror television, especially in the 'period drama' settings of the BBC's *A Ghost Story for Christmas* series with its acute attention to historical context in its use of British architecture and landscape, while the BBC's *Omnibus* adaptation of J. Sheridan Le Fanu's 'Schalcken the Painter' (23 December 1979) employs an exquisite mise-en-scène based meticulously on Dutch interior paintings. In these works, the performer is obliged to engage with the setting which frames their essence and actions. A particularly apposite example of the use of location is to be found in Lawrence Gordon Clark's M. R. James dramatisation 'A Warning to the Curious' (24 December 1972). The adaptation makes careful use of its Norfolk setting, frequently using long-shots to capture dark-clad, solitary figures framed against landscapes and hazy skies. In the work, Paxton (Peter Vaughan) digs up an ancient crown and suffers the consequences of his 'curiosity'.

In the climax to the adaptation, Paxton is chased by the vengeful Ager Ghost (John Kearney): predominantly in long-shot, one is obliged to gauge mood and meaning by the framing of distant, active characters in an austere landscape that shifts from a beach to woodland. Paxton's terror can only be inferred by his running, pursued by the preternaturally determined – and equally rapid – Ager Ghost. When the ghost catches up, Paxton turns and beholds his nemesis. Peter Vaughan, in the role of Paxton, is sweating, wide-eyed with his mouth slightly open, but is otherwise somewhat understated, almost neutral, at this moment of despair and death, certainly when compared with examples of similar nadirs of terror, as we will see in due course.

As much as location shooting is used to great effect in television horror, the use of the studio is equally important, above all in ITV's *Thriller* and *Beasts*. These series use short filmed location sections to structure the predominant use of the studio, most crucially in the opening sequences which 'set the scene' before homing in to the studio. Although on the surface not as evocative as the sustained location sequences employed in numerous BBC horror adaptations, the long studio sequences do not diminish the generically determined atmosphere as they serve to create a claustrophobic, unnerving locale of their own. The studio filming of *Thriller* dictates the settings: time and again, scenes and even whole stories are set in appropriately oppressive or claustrophobic locations. We could even argue that what are now popularly known as 'goofs', such as the cityscape that wobbles outside the penthouse window in 'The Next Victim' (17 April 1976), heighten the claustrophobia: a failed illusion of reality becomes a disconcerting *unreality*. The choice of location and the constraints it places on the drama signals how theatrical *Thriller* is and this is also a quality reflected in the performance practice of the actors. In a recent interview, Clemens reveals that each episode of *Thriller* had a ten-day rehearsal period (a fortnight with weekends off) and a four-day shoot followed by a three-day edit (Clemens, 2003): it is interesting that, proportionately, the process is dominated by the rehearsal of the actors with the time allocated to post-production editing extraordinarily short by today's standards.

Peter Sasdy's production of Nigel Kneale's *The Stone Tape* (25 December 1972) was broadcast as a companion piece to the BBC's *A Ghost Story for Christmas* (which, on Christmas Eve 1972, had been the aforementioned 'A Warning to the Curious'). An ingenious story on the cusp of science fiction and horror, partly reminiscent of H. P. Lovecraft and allusive to Kneale's own *Quatermass* oeuvre, *The Stone Tape* concerns a scientific investigation of a seemingly haunted chamber that a group of scientists believe is not an example of a 'supernatural' phenomenon; rather, they think that the ancient stone walls of the building have in some way 'recorded' a past event. Essentially an extrapolation of the Shakespearean 'There are more things in heaven and earth . . . Than are dreamt of in your philosophy' (*Hamlet* I.v.166–167), *The Stone Tape* presents a group of rational scientists who find themselves abysmally out of their depth. In the 2001 DVD commentary to *The Stone Tape*, Kim Newman is in discussion with Nigel Kneale. During a short sequence involving a minor character, Alan (Michael Graham Cox), Newman says to Kneale: 'I understand this is your least favourite performance in the film – the, er, the "yokel" who's terrified.' Kneale quickly responds with 'No, he's fine' and explains that any discontent with the sequence is because it is, essentially, dramatically redundant as it reiterates previously established plot points. Newman, however, is determined to return to the acting and states:

> I know some people find the acting in this excessive at times but, in fact, for British television in 1972 this is what you had to do because we were looking at tiny monitors, in effect, and in black and white for the most part [. . .] So the tendency to exaggeration and melodrama was predominant and this is excusable in this as we're dealing with something which is on the brink of hysteria. Indeed, only the security guard is underplaying.

The tribute paid to Neil Wilson as the 'security guard' here is supported by Kneale, who points out that Wilson played a policeman in the first series of *The Quatermass Experiment* on British television in 1953. Although Newman emphasises that the context of near-hysteria makes the performances 'excusable', he seems to imply that some of the actors are guilty of excessive 'exaggeration and melodrama'.[1] He has inferred that there were technological constraints (an awareness that the majority of viewers would have been watching monochrome, small-screen television sets), but let us analyse the actors' performances in this example of horror, especially that of Michael Graham Cox as Alan, in close detail.

The episode with Alan is less than four minutes in duration. The reluctant 'yokel' (to remind ourselves of Newman's description) arrives in the haunted chamber where he had played as a child and is evidently nervous as he looks around in agitation. When he senses a supernatural presence Graham Cox gasps and with his right hand clutches where his heart is and clutches his stomach with his left hand. When he hears the scream of the ghost, he demonstrates terror through an almost abstract physical positioning: he thrusts his hands up over his ears with his wrists facing outwards and his forearms at right angles to his head while his facial expression takes on the extreme grimace of a Greek mask of tragedy. After this momentary tableau, he screams and runs, tripping over and scrambling to the door, knocking down equipment in the process. With a bleeding hand and brow he lumbers down the corridor, clinging to the wall before attempting to hide in a corner. When Jill (Jane Asher) and Brock (Michael Bryant) appear, Alan lurches into a room, screaming again as he dives onto the floor. Jill gently placates him with 'it's alright, it's over' while Brock calls 'Get some water, whisky, anything!' before manhandling the hysterical Alan, grabbing him roughly by the collar. By the implication of Newman's commentary, the scene is 'overplayed': certainly there is a 'melodrama' to the scene, in the genuine sense of the theatrical tradition of the term, specifically in this case the clearly defined archetypal characters portrayed by actors with a focused development of their individual roles. Graham Cox plays an unambiguous, emasculated *victim*; Asher plays the sympathetic, ultra-feminine *heroine* whose ultimate demise is inevitable; and Bryant portrays the central character as a consistently arrogant, macho *anti-hero* whose tragic decline is as coherent as it is inexorable.

In the case of *The Stone Tape*, well-realised characterisation becomes heightened into melodramatic, differentiated roles which can even, in the case of Graham Cox, stretch out into an extremely abstract physical realisation of terror and despair. After all, Newman's 'alibi' of small-screen television sets notwithstanding, not only does the cast of *The Stone Tape* consist of high-calibre actors but Peter Sasdy had directed *Taste the Blood of Dracula* (1970), *Hands of the Ripper* (1971) and *Countess Dracula* (1971) for Hammer. In other words, even if some viewers' tastes have changed over time, *The Stone Tape* is imbued with aspects of generic integrity which reflect its place in the legacy of popular horror performance.

One of the BBC's most distinguished adaptations of M. R. James is a work that is a forerunner to *A Ghost Story for Christmas*: Jonathan Miller's production of 'Whistle and I'll Come to You' (7 May 1968) for the BBC's *Omnibus*. Although this adaptation of James's 'Oh, Whistle, and I'll Come to You, My Lad' is a work of television drama from the 1960s, it casts a long shadow of influence over subsequent television horror drama and performance. The adaptation is wholly focused on the remarkable central performance of Michael Hordern in the role of Professor Parkins.

James's story concerns the professor's visit to Norfolk, where he discovers a whistle which when blown summons a spirit that slowly but relentlessly comes to him. Once again, it is an example of a tale which

2.1 Ultra-feminine heroine and arrogant anti-hero: Jane Asher and Michael Bryant in Nigel Kneale's *The Stone Tape*, 25 December 1972

explores the *Hamlet* 'more things in heaven and earth' contention that underpins many tales of the supernatural. Indeed, in 'Whistle and I'll Come to You', Miller gives Hordern a repeated line (not in James's original tale) to emphasise Parkins's hubris: 'There are more things in philosophy than are dreamt of in heaven and earth.' In the short story,

2.2 The Professor's discovery: Michael Hordern in Jonathan Miller's M. R. James adaptation 'Whistle and I'll Come to You', 7 May 1968

Parkins is described as 'young, neat, and precise in speech' (James, 1984: 75) although Hordern is much older (in his late 50s by this time); James goes on to describe Parkins as being 'something of an old woman – rather hen-like, perhaps, in his little ways . . . but at the same time dauntless and sincere in his convictions' (1984: 77), which is captured effectively in the adaptation. Although James describes Parkins as 'totally destitute [of a] sense of humour' (1984: 77), Hordern's Parkins is often chortling to himself or sarcastic to others and yet this humour, such as it is, is mordant and irritating.

The dialogue throughout 'Whistle and I'll Come to You' is minimal, with the narrative focused intensely on the performance of Hordern, who uses a repertoire of scrupulously realised mannerisms and actions in the creation of a highly detailed persona. He captures the pomposity of the character by variously using a flourish in his gestures, rubbing his hands, sighing, shaking his head, sniggering in self-satisfaction, humming indistinct tunes, fidgeting and swaggering. When he speaks he sometimes draws out his words pretentiously and repeats himself with affectation. In a strategy that reveals the (over)rational confidence of Parkins, he seems to regard the world and its objects with superciliousness and treats other people as inferior and inconvenient. In one of the breakfast scenes, two pieces of grapefruit hang together from his spoon and Parkins tuts at them as if they are being disobedient. Hordern was, of course, a highly accomplished comic actor and despite being within the horror genre his portrayal can be described as a comic characterisation. At one point he stretches with his hands placed on the small of his back in a position distinctly allusive to Jacques Tati's trademark physical stance in a feature film also about an isolated eccentric on vacation: *Les Vacances de Monsieur Hulot* (Jacques Tati, 1953).

After he blows the whistle, Hordern gradually begins to utilise a new repertoire of techniques on the journey towards the terror of the final moments: sitting up in bed he frowns in consternation which develops into a more evident disquiet when he lies down. In the nightmare sequences, an unusually intense (even dismembering) close-up is used which fills the screen with Hordern's eyes and nose to reveal him snapping in and out of uneasy (un)consciousness. In the final moments of the adaptation, when Parkins sees the ghost, his puffed-up persona is humbled into an awkward, cowed figure, his hair is dishevelled and he makes indistinct utterances of terror. In a final audacious but brilliantly effective physical action to conclude the carefully mapped descent of Parkins, Hordern sucks his thumb like a terrified infant. Saved by the Colonel (Ambrose Coghill), Parkins then makes an utterance that repeats and gradually clarifies into 'Oh, no' – which is emitted some 13 times before the emphatic 'No!' concludes the adaptation. Hordern's virtuoso performance is different from what James suggests in the original story, where Parkins utters 'cry upon cry at the utmost pitch of his voice' after which he sinks forward 'in a faint' (James, 1984: 90). James's description is more akin to conventions of melodrama and although Miller's dramatisation avoids this, other adaptations do not.

Tony Scull's M. R. James adaptation 'Mr Humphreys and his Inheritance' (21 June 1976) was produced for ITV schools broadcasting. This short adaptation was produced to demonstrate the role of music in film soundtracks. Despite being ostensibly a pedagogical exercise, the adaptation is interesting with regard to horror performance, particularly in the dramatic climax. The protagonist, Mr Humphreys (Geoffrey Russell), inherits a house and its garden maze from his deceased uncle. The maze is overgrown, eerie and disorienting, but Mr Humphreys, unflappably rationalistic like nearly every Jamesian protagonist, is determined to reclaim and clean up the labyrinth. Part of his endeavour is to draw a plan of the maze. Late at night in his study, Humphreys works on his map: as one would expect, the drawing is neat and precise until Humphreys notices an inkblot. He leans

2.3 The Professor's nightmare: Michael Hordern in Jonathan Miller's M. R. James adaptation 'Whistle and I'll Come to You', 7 May 1968

closer and realises the smudge is, in fact, a hole which descends through the paper, the desk and deeper. As he peers into the peephole, he sees the decaying face of his uncle leering back at him. Geoffrey Russell, who has played Humphreys with calm severity up to this point, emits a scream as he falls convulsively backwards to the floor bringing his chair down onto him as, in a melodramatic signature, he places the back of his hand over his eyes; from here he screams again and then gasps. It is interesting to compare this sequence with the corresponding moment in the original short story where James writes: 'with a convulsion of despair Humphreys threw himself back, struck his head against a hanging lamp, and fell' (James, 1984: 204). The filmed version may change the furnishing from a lamp to a chair, but Russell's physical sequence captures the 'convulsion of despair' and the backward fall while the melodramatic covering of the eyes is an effective acknowledgement of a Victorian/Edwardian melodramatic milieu.

The *ITV Playhouse* production of 'Casting the Runes' (24 April 1979) is another example of independent television competing with the BBC at the adaptation of M. R. James. Instead of creating the usual Gothic-featured Victorian/Edwardian locale and context habitually favoured by the BBC's James adaptations, the writer Clive Exton and director Lawrence Gordon Clark (ironically, a key figure in the establishment of the BBC's *A Ghost Story for Christmas*) prefer to set James's story of black magic in a contemporary 1970s. The world of James is transferred to a world of suns setting by electric pylons, airports, television studios and – in a remarkable precursor to Nakata Hideo's *Ringu* (1998) and *Ringu 2* (1999) – films that change after editing to present the spectator with a doom-laden warning. It is an adaptation that uses real-world surroundings very successfully: the snowy locations – both rural and urban – are a pathetic fallacy to reflect the impending curse. Although the ostensible ten-year gap between the four-minute 'prelude' before the credits begin and the equally snowy world of the focal narrative reveals that the film was shot in the same time frame, it provides an effective dramatic unity. The most radical aspect to the adaptation is in terms of gender: the updating of the tale results in the hero of the short story, Edward Dunning, being replaced by a woman, Prudence Dunning (Jan Francis). Although the name 'Prudence Dunning' would not be out of place in a work of Victorian/Edwardian fiction, in this adaptation the protagonist is a successful, unmarried career woman working in the television media who can utter words unthinkable in M. R. James, such as 'Write and tell him to *piss off!*' But this is not to imply that the 1970s 'Casting the Runes' rejects a melodramatic formula of clear-cut hero(ine) and villain. For the sake of this exploration, the performances of three central characters are of particular interest: Christopher Good as the hapless first victim, Jan Francis as the heroine and Iain Cuthbertson as the villain.

In his portrayal of John Harrington, Christopher Good is on screen for scarcely three minutes and is dead before the opening credits: a narrative which takes him from walking his dog to having 'almost every bone in his body broken'. With little editing, the focus is on Harrington's death in a wide, snowy field – a highly physical interpretation by Good as he throws himself down and writhes in agony. In terms of horror performance, Jan Francis's most interesting sequence is the 'bedtime' episode. Prudence climbs into bed with a book and almost immediately struggles and gasps (she emphatically does not scream) and leaps out of bed as we see the legs of a gigantic spider wriggle from beneath her quilt. Prudence moves through two rooms, closing the doors behind her, before entering into a highly melodramatic sequence: she faces the door with a fixed, wide-eyed stare with her lips moving silently before raising her hand up and covering her mouth with her palm as she walks backwards across the room. Iain Cuthbertson as Mr Karswell plays the villain with melodramatic relish, most apparently when he sees through Prudence's disguise and allows his sneering smile to become sardonic laughter which crescendos until his dismembered head is shown roaring with laughter. However, this is in remarkable contrast to his final scene in which he realises his fate is sealed. When Prudence tricks him into taking back the cursed runes in the airport, his performance is completely understated, utilising nothing more than a furrowed brow and two gulps. 'Casting the Runes' offers the audience a mixed mode of horror performance ranging from high physical embodiment and melodramatic set pieces through to subtle understatement.

The examples of horror we have looked at so far in this analysis of 1970s British television drama have all been explorations of the supernatural. But there is another branch in the genre of horror which explores the ostensibly 'real'. The title of Brian Clemens's *Thriller* defines a generic specificity, but there is a case to argue that *Thriller* is very much in the tradition of Grand-Guignol 'horror theatre'. The Théâtre du Grand-Guignol flourished from 1897 to 1962 in Paris (with significant experiments in London in the 1920s) and its focused dramas presented real, if implausible, terror: in other words, it showcased examples of horror perpetrated by the ultimate monster, the *bête humaine*. The 40-plus episodes of *Thriller* present a diverse range of stories but with a number of unifying stylistic features. Like the plays of the Grand-Guignol repertoire, they are all self-contained dramas with small casts that exploit the careful manipulation of suspense strategies, structured by moments of extreme violence and/or psychological terror. The studio filming of *Thriller* dictates the locale: time and again, scenes and even whole stories are set in remote cottages, rooms in oppressive mansions, train compartments, flats and apartments, basements, cellars and laboratories. Similarly, the Grand-Guignol attempted an optimisation of the limiting conditions with which it found itself working. As Hand and Wilson explain, the Grand-Guignol set plays in 'bedrooms in brothels, the ramparts of besieged consulates, lighthouses, rooms in museums, sitting rooms, boats, opium dens, doctors' surgeries, operating theatres [. . .], cells in prisons and asylums, execution courtyards, carnival caravans, and barber shops. The claustrophobic potential of all these locations is exploited to the full' (Hand and Wilson, 2002: 32).

Clemens's dialogue is honed and sometimes the plays develop through actions rather than words. This is partly because the protagonists, victims and villains are often isolated figures although they are sometimes granted a brief monologue, talking to themselves in an evolution of the melodramatic aside. Clemens's dialogue can be violent or ominous but is often mordantly witty with a keen sense of irony. Each episode of *Thriller* exploits the three commercial breaks demanded by ITV through the use of cliff-hangers or 'shock' revelations. *Thriller* typically concludes with an abrupt ending that functions like a quick curtain in melodrama or chooses to leave the spectator with a shocking finale as used in the Grand-Guignol form. The endings of *Thriller* generally resist moralising or cod-psychologising: the denouement is purely dramatic, the conclusion – the 'point' of each experiential play – is left for the viewers to construct for themselves.

The world of *Thriller* is also usually Anglo-American inasmuch as its dramas are set in Britain but with the presence of American characters. This transatlantic exchange of personnel – and values – is partly because ABC television had an important role in commissioning the series. Each episode of *Thriller* is approximately 72 minutes, an unlikely duration, even for the commercial television of the period in Britain. The reason for this was entirely dictated by the US market. In the US broadcast of the plays, American commercial breaks (and an additional opening and closing credit frame added by ABC) would make the *Thriller* slot exactly 90 minutes long. The US market also dictated casting, which explains the presence of North American actors (such as Gary Collins, Linda Thorson, George Chakiris, and so on.) and/or American characters in focal roles (e.g. the English Susan Hampshire plays an American tourist in 'Kill Two Birds' [8 May 1976]). US television invested in the creation and continuation of *Thriller* (allegedly, ABC dictated the termination of the series in 1976) largely because Brian Clemens was perceived as a bankable figure. Clemens was, of course, the creative force behind *The Avengers* (1961–69) which, as Toby Miller reveals, is still the only 'UK show that aired during prime-time sweeps on the US networks' (Miller, 2001: 20).[2]

Thriller is a series that made exceptional use of music. In writing about television music, Karen Lury explains:

> [Music on television is used] to 'thicken' the audio-visual experience. Music colours, provides mood and atmosphere and imparts a 'meaningfulness' (if not always a concrete meaning) to events and images seen on screen. (Lury, 2005: 71)

In the case of *Thriller*, Laurie Johnson's theme tune and incidental music are a quintessential example of how music, as in nineteenth-century melodrama, can play a major role in the establishment of mood and atmosphere around economically deployed dialogue, turning the most innocuous scene into one of foreboding and lending enormous dramatic impact to climactic sequences. In this regard, the soundtrack to *Thriller* draws on the achievement of the composer and conductor Bernard Herrmann and his work on *The Twilight Zone* television series from 1959–63 and on *Psycho* (Alfred Hitchcock, 1960). In fact, the work of Alfred Hitchcock is useful to consider when looking at Clemens's work as a whole. In his analysis of *The Avengers*, James Chapman argues that Clemens draws on the Hitchcock antecedents of *The Man Who Knew Too Much* (1934), *The 39 Steps* (1935) and others in the various 'spy rings and enemy agents' (Chapman, 2002: 54) that occur in the television series. By the time of *Thriller*, there are only a few examples of espionage dramas (mainly reflecting the Cold War context), and yet Hitchcock remains a key paradigm for Clemens, but by now it is the Hitchcock of *Psycho* and *Frenzy* (1972). For example, allusions are made to *Psycho* thematically in 'The Colour of Blood' (12 May 1973) in which a blonde female estate agent's attempt to steal a fortune leads, coincidently, to her murder. Also, stylistically, 'Dial a Deadly Number' (1 May 1976) uses a repeated murder sequence on a staircase that is directly modelled on the murder of Arbogast (Martin Balsam) in *Psycho*.

There are key thematic characteristics to the *Thriller* repertoire. The world of *Thriller* is very much a white, bourgeois world with a lack of ethnic presence, and the working class, when present, is often menacing.

In this respect, *Thriller* is a very 'aspirational' series typically presenting its popular audience with visions of upper-middle-class affluence and luxury including, in 'One Deadly Owner' (16 February 1974), a scene which foregrounds the demonstration of a Rolls Royce's automatic window. Nevertheless, although *Thriller* may titillate its viewers' desire for material comfort, the bourgeois world it displays is inevitably the setting for death, psychosis and destruction. *Thriller* seems utterly nihilistic compared with the quintessential 1960s flamboyance, glamour and happy endings of *The Avengers*, which resonated, as Toby Miller states, with 'progressive political practice' (Miller, 2001: 20). *Thriller* presents the spectator with many disquieting endings and the nightmare of aspiration.[3]

The class issue aspect to *Thriller* is also a prevalent theme in some other contemporaneous television horror drama, such as 'The Exorcism' (5 November 1972) in the BBC series *Dead of Night* in which a middle-class couple hold a dinner party in their cottage, haunted by a victim of starvation, and 'During Barty's Party' (*Beasts*, 23 October 1976) in which a similarly affluent couple find themselves under siege by a highly symbolic – yet unseen – plague of rats. In writing about female Gothic adaptations on television, Helen Wheatley describes 'the threatening, cage-like, labyrinthine and, ultimately, un-homely domestic spaces' (Wheatley, 2005: 156) that are characteristic of her chosen genre. We can see that *Thriller* and some other examples of 1970s horror plays create a similar mood and function to their suspenseful drama, but target a socioeconomic place rather than a domestic space.

Watching *Thriller* in the early twenty-first century one is struck by its 1970s morality, not least in what could be construed as a thoroughgoing misogyny. Admittedly, the violence in *Thriller* is modest compared with the sexual violence in feature films on general release shortly before the television series premiered, such as *Straw Dogs* (Sam Peckinpah, 1971), *A Clockwork Orange* (Stanley Kubrick, 1971) and Hitchcock's *Frenzy*. Nevertheless, *Thriller*'s victims are nearly always female and the episodes present sequences and lines which can be shocking to the contemporary viewer. In 'A Midsummer Nightmare', for example, Jody (Joanna Pettet) is punched in the face by Ingram (Norman Rodway), who she fights off by smashing a bottle over his head, after which she carefully tends to the wounds she inflicted on him! When she sees the policeman Detective Sergeant Briggs (Brian Blessed) he comments, 'It suits you - the bruise. I like all my women with a little imperfection.' In 'The Next Victim' (17 April 1976) there is a short 'comic' sequence in which the serial killer is frightened off by the presence of the would-be victim's male lover. This becomes, for the modern viewer, not so much comic as a violent misogynist narrative in its own right – we hear the woman's erotic laughter, the lover's off-screen accusation and a slap as he presumably hits her face. But perhaps the most problematic sequence in *Thriller* is at the finale of 'File It Under Fear' (2 June 1973). The plot concerns a serial rapist and murderer, played in an astonishing example of casting against type by the comic actor John Le Mesurier, most popularly known at the time for his role in the BBC sitcom *Dad's Army* (1968–77).[4] The central female character, the somewhat 'mousy' (and hence stereotypical) librarian Liz Morris (Maureen Lipman), is rescued by the police in the nick of time and the play concludes with the following line: '[He] had to come back for me - tried to kill me - because I'm a woman. A very desirable woman, see?' The fact that Lipman – playing a victim of sexual assault – utters the line with *pride* is deeply disturbing. However, just because the morality may be problematic to the modern viewer, it does not mean that the quality of the acting is diminished. Indeed, the conviction with which many of these performances are delivered may add to the genre's potential to disturb.

Jonathan Bignell and Stephen Lacey remind us that 'television drama has always been marketed to audiences in relation to performance' (Bignell and Lacey, 2005: 219) and 1970s horror television is no exception: as respected as the writers were, it is the performance of their scripts that garnered the audience. *A Ghost Story for Christmas* always made use of performers who would have been regarded as 'quality' actors. Michael Bryant – star of *The Stone Tape* and the M. R. James adaptation 'Treasure of Abbot Thomas' (23 December 1974) – was a highly respected stage actor as well as an established television actor who also had a horror pedigree, having appeared in genre-specific feature films such as *Torture Garden* (Freddie Francis, 1967). Ian Bannen, who makes two appearances in *Thriller*, and the aforementioned Iain Cuthbertson, were not only familiar screen actors but leading stage actors of their generation. T. P. McKenna, appearing in episodes of *Thriller* and *Beasts*, was a well-known television actor but also had an important role in *Straw Dogs* and was a significant figure in Irish theatre. Even more prestigious is the presence of Patrick Magee in two episodes of *Thriller* and one episode of *Beasts*. Magee had horror genre experience with a role in *And Now the Screaming Starts!* (Roy Ward Baker, 1973) and had appeared in *A Clockwork Orange*, but was also a major figure in theatre.

In the *Thriller* episode 'A Killer in Every Corner' (1 February 1975) Magee plays a psychologist whose habitual action is to record his voice into a tape-recorder, an explicit allusion to Magee's own performance

2.4 Stage actors on the small screen of horror: Iain Cuthbertson and Michael Bryant in Nigle Kneale's *The Stone Tape*, 25 December 1972

in the world premiere of Samuel Beckett's *Krapp's Last Tape* (1958), a role which Magee re-created for television for the BBC's *Thirty-Minute Theatre* (29 November 1972). If Magee alludes to his role of Krapp, the Shakespeare-themed *Thriller* episode 'A Midsummer Nightmare' (15 May 1976) affords the stage and screen actor Freddie Jones the opportunity to explore lyrical extracts from Shakespeare as well as Clemens's clipped dialogue. *Thriller* also features popular British stars or character actors such as Diana Dors, Ian Hendry and Charles Gray and even two former child film actors: Hayley Mills and Pamela Franklin. Interestingly, Mills's earliest appearances were in works with a significant 'suspense' element such as *Tiger Bay* (J. Lee Thompson, 1959) and *Whistle Down the Wind* (Bryan Forbes, 1961) and she had also acquired a horror pedigree with the lead role in *Twisted Nerve* (Roy Boulting, 1968). Franklin was also experienced in the horror genre with central roles in the horror feature films *The Innocents* (Jack Clayton, 1961) and *And Soon the Darkness* (Robert Fuest, 1970). Even more associated with the horror genre were the *Thriller* actors Ingrid Pitt and Ralph Bates, who appeared in numerous early 1970s horror movies including Hammer productions. In addition to these well-known actors from cinema or theatre, the 'backbone' of *Thriller* was provided by an enormous number of television actors including stalwarts who had become very familiar to the contemporary viewer such as David Daker, Ronald Lacey, Robert Powell, Tony Selby and Patrick Troughton, as well as featuring the comparatively early career appearances of actors such as Bob Hoskins, Stephen Rea, Helen Mirren and Don Henderson.

We will now draw to a close by looking at two specific examples of horror acting in *Thriller* and *Beasts*. The *Thriller* play 'Possession' (21 April 1973) stars John Carson in the central role of Ray Burns. Carson was an experienced screen actor, having featured in Hammer's *The Plague of the Zombies* (John Gilling, 1966) and *Taste the Blood of Dracula* (Peter Sasdy, 1970). In 'Possession' he plays a man who has moved into a house in which a murder took place, after which history seems to repeat itself and murders start again with the Burns couple set up as the ultimate victims whose time is running out. In a sequence near the end of the play (approximately three minutes and fifteen seconds in duration), we see Burns distractedly coming downstairs in his dressing gown and slippers, apparently 'being watched'. His expression seems neutral: will he be the victim or heroically catch the voyeur? He takes a kitchen knife and is interrupted by wife Penny Burns (Joanna Dunham). She accuses him of being the murderer himself and having buried a corpse in the cellar: he admits it. He embarks on a split body persona: his right arm rigidly holds the knife while his left arm is agitated. He utters in despair 'It's not me. It's the thing that's possessing me!' His hands are both slightly raised, his mouth slightly open, accompanied by gentle shakes of the head. Carson turns a full 180 degrees, stopping with his back to the camera, placing his hand over his eyes and uttering 'No! I won't have it!' through choking tears. This is countered by his wife's 'You didn't become the murderer. *You always were*.' Carson becomes rigid, the erratic left arm starts the serial killer trademark click of the fingers. The grimace of despair becomes almost neutral with fixed eyes. He raises the knife. The sudden entrance of the police follows and they force him to his knees; he leaps from a squatting position and tries to escape the police, who manhandle him near the top of basement stairs where he falls to his death. The short sequence takes him from potential victim and/or hero to being revealed as the villain to his death. There is a debt to the heightened performances of Hammer, and Carson's transformation from hero to villain is so stylised and painstakingly engineered it even acknowledges John Barrymore in *Dr Jekyll and Mr Hyde* (John S. Robertson, 1920), a melodramatic paradigm of metamorphosis which itself alludes to the heightened performances of Richard Mansfield in the role in the 1880s (see Hand, 2007: 13-16). One is also reminded of the heightened posturing and facial expressions of Henry Irving in *The Bells*, as revealed in the photographs collected in David Meyer's *Henry Irving and The Bells* (1980). Likewise, the skills of the horror actor in Grand-Guignol theatre were to negotiate a journey that leads 'from bourgeois security to mortal danger, from the rational to the insane, from – in effect – naturalism to melodrama' (Hand and Wilson, 2000: 269).

The implication of this is that the 'exaggeration' that Kim Newman finds problematic in *The Stone Tape* is, in fact, part of the long tradition of horror performance. After all, Carson's horror performance in 'Possession' was obviously deemed appropriate as Clemens also cast him in Hammer's *Captain Kronos – Vampire Hunter* (Brian Clemens, 1974). As well as drawing on long traditions of horror performance, some 1970s horror performance can be seen as being avant-garde in scope. In the case of Jane Wymark in the *Beasts* episode 'Baby' (5 November 1976), one is even reminded of Antonin Artaud's belief in the power of the scream as a primal force. Artaud claimed, in the 1930s, that 'no one knows how to scream anymore, particularly actors in a trance no longer know how to cry out, since they do nothing but talk, having forgotten they have a body on stage, they have also lost the use of their throats' (Artaud, 1995 [1935]: 273–274).

In 'Baby', we are presented with a couple who have moved into a cottage. The wife, Jo Gilkes (Jane Wymark), is pregnant and after a dried-up creature is found in an urn in a wall there is an atmosphere of encroaching peril. The audience realises that the 'baby' of the title is not the forthcoming Gilkes offspring but the relic in the urn. At the end of the play, Jo encounters the 'mother'. In the two minutes and forty-five second sequence up to the closing credits, Jo wakes up in the middle of the night and ventures downstairs in her nightgown. When she sees the monstrous creature nursing the reanimated relic, she screams and collapses, presumably losing her own baby. Wymark's triple-screamed 'No' and her subsequent collapse to wail, cry and whimper on the floor are a virtuosic seventeen seconds of performance. The focus is on Wymark's face and her body and the scream she emits is raw, desperate and angry. Perhaps this is another melodramatic exaggeration but it is also an intensely physical moment, Artaudian in register.

In 2005, the BBC offered a return to the *A Ghost Story for Christmas* tradition with a brand-new M. R. James adaptation, 'A View from a Hill'

(23 December 2005). The following year the BBC presented the James adaptation 'Number 13' (22 December 2006) and, for Halloween, broadcast a longer play, *The Haunted Airman* (31 October 2006), an adaptation of Dennis Wheatley's novel *The Haunting of Toby Jugg*. Like the BBC's horror adaptations of the 1970s these are highly atmospheric, concisely scripted dramas with an impressive and evocative use of location filming and period design (from costume to props). However, there are major differences on the technical front, primarily with regard to a more sophisticated approach to special effects, camerawork and editing. Although more attuned to the sensibilities of the contemporary viewer, there is a consequent effect whereby there is less focus on the performance practice of the actor: in other words, they may be less 'stagey' than their antecedents but they are also less *theatrical*.

The horror genre typically uses shifts in inner psychology (the revelation of a victim's terror or the demented psychology of the killer) and this needs to be exteriorised: in the 1970s, this requirement fell upon the actor, depending more on how they performed rather than how their performance was mediated technically. This is not to cast any doubt on the skill of the contemporary actors: the protagonists of the James adaptations, Mark Letheren in 'A View from a Hill' and Greg Wise in 'Number 13' (ably supported by Tom Burke), offer well-realised performances while Julian Sands is an effectively malevolent presence in *The Haunted Airman*. However, the sophisticated filming and editing means that for the actor in some respects 'less' has become 'more'. The heightened gestures of the melodramatic tradition have disappeared and a subtle intensity has replaced it, whereas 1970s horror television often had both. Perhaps the new ethos creates something more 'real' for the contemporary viewer of these supernatural tales, perhaps it is less risible for many, but it is certainly less dynamic. Moreover, it is also somewhat ironic to extinguish the melodramatic element to performance horror, a genre which at its heart thrives on melodramatic narrative.

In conclusion, let us return to *The Stone Tape* commentary. At the end of the film, Kim Newman asks Nigel Kneale if he would consider sanctioning a remake of the film to which Kneale responds: 'If it could be as good as this, yes. Just to see it again, and have it done probably with a little more cash expended which is always good. But as to the acting, not a thing I'd change [. . .] I'm very pleased at how well they did it and that's largely due to some very good acting' (Kneale, 2001). Despite the perceived lack of polish, the rudimentary editing and wobbly sets, 1970s horror television drama presents the viewer with superbly crafted original scripts and adaptations mediated through its all-important 'captured ghosts': consummate actors of the very highest standard.

Notes

1 Newman is using 'melodrama' as an insult here to mean that the acting is over the top and unbelievable. In a more serious sense, the tradition of nineteenth-century melodrama, which has a major role in the establishment of subsequent popular performance culture, involves archetypal characters and a heightened gestural mode of performance that go against the concepts of realism and naturalism.

2 Although *Thriller* is an expressly single-drama series, one can still perhaps detect Clemens striving to find a new *Avengers* formula. In the 40-plus episodes of *Thriller* only one character reappears in the form of the detective Matthew Earp (Dinsdale Landen) in 'An Echo of Theresa' (5 May 1973) and 'The Next Scream You Hear' (6 July 1974), suggesting hopes for a possible series. Towards the end of the *Thriller* run, 'A Midsummer Nightmare' (15 May 1976) presents a divorced but still loving couple of Jodie and Johnny Baxter who seem to suggest a possible detective double act in the style of the US series *Hart to Hart* (1979–84).

3 In the case of the luxury car in the aforementioned 'One Deadly Owner', a very rare foray into the supernatural for *Thriller*, the Rolls Royce turns out to be homicidally possessed in a precursor to Stephen King's *Christine* (1983).

4 A similar example occurs in 'A Killer in Every Corner' (1 February 1975) in which the veteran comedian Max Wall also plays a serial rapist and murderer.

References

Artaud, A. (1995 [1935]) 'An Effective Athleticism', in Richard Drain, ed., *Twentieth-Century Theatre: A Sourcebook*, London: Routledge, 272–74.

Bignell, J. and S. Lacey (2005) 'Editors' Afterword: Directions and Redirections', in J. Bignell and S. Lacey, eds., *Popular Television Drama: Critical Perspectives*, Manchester: Manchester University Press, 215–221.

Caughie, J. (2000) *Television Drama: Realism, Modernism, and British Culture*, Oxford: Oxford University Press.

Chapman, J. (2002) *Saints and Avengers: British Adventure Series of the 1960s*, London: I. B. Tauris.

Clemens, B. (2003) '*Thriller* with Brian Clemens', London: Granada Ventures (DVD).

Hand, R. J. (2007) 'Paradigms of Metamorphosis and Transmutation: Thomas Edison's *Frankenstein* and John Barrymore's *Jekyll and Hyde*', in R. J. Hand and

J. McRoy, eds., *Monstrous Adaptations: Generic and Thematic Transmutations in Horror Film*, Manchester: Manchester University Press, 9-19.

Hand, R. J. and M. Wilson (2000) 'The Grand-Guignol: Aspects of Theory and Practice', *Theatre Research International*, 25, No. 3: 266–275.

Hand, R. J. and M. Wilson (2002) *Grand-Guignol: The French Theatre of Horror*, Exeter: University of Exeter Press.

James, M. R. (1984) *The Penguin Complete Ghost Stories of M. R. James*, Harmondsworth: Penguin.

Kneale, N. (2001) *The Stone Tape*, London: BFI (DVD).

Lury, K. (2005) *Interpreting Television*, London: Hodder Arnold.

Meyer, D. (1980) *Henry Irving and The Bells*, Manchester: Manchester University Press.

Miller, T. (2001) '*The Man from UNCLE* and *The Avengers*', in G. Creeber, ed., *The Television Genre Book*, London: BFI, 20–21.

Wheatley, H. (2005) 'Haunted Houses, Hidden Rooms: Women, Domesticity and the Female Gothic Adaptation on Television', in J. Bignell and S. Lacey, eds., *Popular Television Drama: Critical Perspectives*, Manchester: Manchester University Press, 149–165.

3

Docudrama performance: realism, recognition and representation

Jonathan Bignell

The hybrid television form of docudrama, blending documentary and drama conventions and modes of address, poses interesting methodological problems for an analysis of performance. Its topics, mise-en-scène and performers invite a judgement in relation to the real events and situations, settings and personae represented, and also in relation to the ways the viewer has perceived them in other media representations such as news, current affairs interviews and documentary features. In other words, docudrama's performance of the real asks the viewer to evaluate it in relation to anterior knowledge. But because of their adoption of conventions from drama, docudramas also draw on performance modes from fictional television forms and invite audiences to invest their emotions and deploy their knowledge of codes used in fictional naturalism or melodrama. These hybrid frameworks for viewing militate against docudrama being able to cultivate the authenticity or sobriety associated historically with documentary, and this has been a key reason for criticisms of the form. However, on the other hand, the multiplicity of available interpretive frameworks and routes of access for the audience can also enrich and broaden the pleasures and social purchase of docudrama. In this chapter, I range over examples of docudramas of the post-1990 period, mainly made wholly or partly in the UK, to discuss some of the distinctions between kinds of docudrama performance, the implications of their links with related television forms and how docudrama performance exploits the capacities of television as a medium.

Docudrama performance and documentary practices

The aim of television docudrama is, as Derek Paget (1998: 61) has described, to 're-tell events from national or international histories' and/or 'to re-present the careers of significant national or international figures' in order to review or celebrate these people and events. The key figures and important moments depicted are often familiar to the audience and close in time to the transmission of the programme. Devices like opening statements and captions make clear the factual basis of docudramas, while disclaimers state that some events have been changed or telescoped, and some characters may be amalgamations or inventions. The desire to produce unmediated access to the real, a desire that derives from docudrama's factual base, works alongside this but is potentially contradicted by the necessity to contain and present that factual material by means of dramatic codes of performance and narrative structure. Docudrama sets up a claim for validation based on anterior real events which are then performed using the narrative forms and modes of performance familiar in screen fiction. It is a hybrid form that 'uses the sequence of events from a real historical occurrence or situation and the identities of the protagonists to underpin a film script intended to provoke debate [. . .] The resultant film usually follows a cinematic narrative structure and employs the standard naturalist/realist performance techniques of screen drama' (Paget, 1998: 82). The television medium is especially appropriate for these two divergent components of docudrama because television has always offered both of them to its audiences, though usually in institutionally separated factual and fictional genres.

British docudrama's sobriety is based on a professional production culture with roots in journalistic documentary. Broadly speaking, this tradition is different from the one that underpins US docudrama, which is characterised by its popular address through entertainment and drama forms. However, in both British and US docudrama the characteristic interest of television in the present, addressing current concerns and working over ways of understanding it in and for the culture, has been preserved. Fictional and factual modes are mixed on the assumption that the television audience can recognise their modality, based on the audience's familiarity with television's codes and conventions. These conventions already include elements of hybridity between factual and fictional performance because of the practical necessities of documentary programme making. In the formative period of the socially conscious television documentary, emerging from the British Documentary Cinema movement and migrating to television as it achieved the status of a mass medium in the 1950s, it was accepted that situations that had previously occurred could be reconstructed by the filmmaker (as in the classic wartime documentary *Fires Were Started*, directed by Humphrey

Jennings, 1943). The filmmaker had witnessed the original event's occurrence or had other credible testimony about its truth. Based on this prior witness, it was routine for filmmakers to fully or partially script documentary films, to reconstruct settings in a studio and to coach participants in repeating actions for the camera.

So it is misleading to present documentary as a kind of programme making that represents an authentic reality in an unmediated way, perhaps contrasting it with the staged situations of docudrama. The making of documentary already includes the likelihood if not the necessity of manipulating the real in order to shoot it. Shooting documentary often requires a programme maker to prompt a documentary subject in some way, for example by asking that an action be undertaken so that it can be clearly seen by the camera. When something goes wrong, a documentary maker might reasonably ask the subject to perform an action again so that it can be recorded. After shooting, the procedures of editing very often involve a level of manipulation. Sequences shot at different times can be linked together to give the impression of continuous action, and cutting between sequences shot at different times gives the impression that they happened at the same moment. By acknowledging these practical necessities of production and developing them into a coherent narrative form, docudrama recognises a kind of performance that documentary already necessitated but frequently repudiated. Docudrama makes the necessity of performance into its primary and acknowledged focus of interest, within an overarching intention to inform its audience and to make events accessible.

These docudrama intentions exploit the hybrid functions of television broadcasting as a socially embedded technology, a relationship between the technology, its forms and its audiences which is rendered most accurately by the untranslatable French term *dispositif* (something like 'apparatus' in English). The television medium inhabits a tension between its functions as a window and a mirror (Gripsrud, 1998) for its audience. Television can function as a window on the world, most obviously in news, current affairs and documentary programming. These factual genres have a special claim to present the public world outside, giving access to that world for their audiences. But like a mirror, television's representations of the domestic, of the family, and of ordinary life and the culture of the present have also been crucial to its role. Television shows how people perform their lived realities, offering the possibility of recognising and comparing one life with another. Overlapping this dual function as window and mirror, television also exhibits tensions between characteristics of immediacy and intimacy. In news or the live broadcasting of sport, for example, television claims to bring immediately occurring events to its viewer, and the medium's heritage of liveness is crucial to this. The possibility of live broadcasting was also significant to dramatic performance in the decades before the routine use of videotape or production on film in the 1960s, and still remains as a rare and special event for some drama performances. Intimacy, on the other hand, has more to do with relationships of identification, with an exchange not only of information but also of feeling between viewers and programmes. Television is an intimate medium in the sense that it is broadcast into the private space of the home, and much of its output promises to reveal the detail of individual action through image and sound, with a special emphasis on the ability of the close-up to provide analytical observation of human behaviour. While this capacity is a resource for all television forms, it has been exploited particularly in drama, where ways of expressing psychology and emotion are facilitated by the use of the close-up and the patterning of dramatic forms to emphasise moments of performance that reveal character. These possibilities of television as window and mirror, as immediate and intimate, have been crucial for the development of docudrama in varying ways according to the purposes and subjects of the programmes. As a subset of documentary, docudrama would be expected to emphasise immediacy, the function of the screen as a window and representations of the public world outside of domestic space. However, offering the attractions of drama too, many docudramas are interested in intimacy, character, psychology and the establishment of a mirroring, comparative relationship between the viewer and the people featured in the programme. In these ways, docudrama is a conjunction of the interdependent but apparently opposed cultural functions of the television medium.

One of the variants of the docudrama mode is where a past historical event is analysed in documentary mode, including witness testimony by the actual people involved, with added fictionalised performance and visual effects. Testimony and witness have become crucial to television docudrama because the use of interviews with real or fictional subjects, alongside dramatised reconstruction sequences, emphasises moments of crisis or transformation. The aim of this hybrid form is to allow the audience to reflect on the forces impacting on individuals and how individuals respond to those forces. Its aim is also to enable the documentary subject himself or herself to have a space in which to speak about personal transformation, whether that subject is a real person or an actor standing in for the person. In *Hiroshima* (2005), for example, components from different television forms were combined to tell the story of the atomic bomb raid on the eponymous Japanese city in 1945, from the perspectives of both the US military personnel undertaking it and also of the Japanese people who were its victims. Archive footage, some of it quite familiar from historical documentary series, was placed alongside acted reconstruction. The testimonies of witnesses, such as the survivor Akiko Takakura, expressed their impressions of the blast verbally while CGI sequences portrayed them visually in the manner of a disaster movie (like *Deep Impact*, 1998 or *The Day After Tomorrow*, 2004). In some parts of the programme, performance was used in the same way, such as when verbal testimony from Paul Tibbetts, the pilot of the Enola Gay bomber, was juxtaposed with performance by the actor Ian Shaw playing Tibbetts's younger self. These different kinds of components were brought together by a contextualising voice-over spoken by the actor John Hurt. This linkage of forms questions the priority of any one over the others, since each has different claims to authority. The viewer is able to shift between ways of accessing the meanings of performance, looking both at the performer and also through him or her to a catalogue of other kinds of representation, including audio-visual records from news film, documentary interviews and fictional forms whose conventions derive from (in this case) war films and disaster movies.

The witness statements out of which docudrama is often created, and which are sometimes included in the completed programme, are reports of past events that produce the events in acted reconstructions, and each legitimates the other. The two components are ways of bearing witness to something that happened in reality, but which is inaccessible because there was no camera there at the time to witness it in the intimate and accessible way that a docudrama can do. Instead, the interview and the fictionalised reconstruction witness the event subsequently for the camera, reconstructing it in retrospect. This form of performed witnessing has two contrasting meanings. In the first, the witness is an observer who testifies to the presence and reality of what he or she has experienced. Both the television viewer and the real person on screen can occupy this role since each has access to a version of a real event, reconstructed for the viewer and recalled in memory by the witness. This form of bearing witness is clearly dramatic, whether in the sense that it is scripted and performed, or offered by a real person re-living an emotionally charged experience. The witness statement derives from a documentary tradition, the heritage of the Mass Observation project which collected the comments and personal accounts of a large number of people who kept diaries of their everyday lives and commented on the social and political events of the time. Founded in 1937 and continuing until the 1950s, the Mass Observation organisation recruited both observers and volunteer writers to document everyday life in written records that grew into an invaluable anthropological resource. In television, the BBC's *Video Diaries* and *Video Nation* (1990–) series continued this, focusing on everyday work and leisure, and individuals' attitudes and worries. In relation to the social functions of television, this process of programme creation from witness statement, diary material or recollection presupposes a community of interest in which the witness and the audience both take part. While different narrative structures and balances of factual and fictional components are used in individual programmes, they all assume the criterion of relevance to the audience and adopt a mode of address calculated to produce viewer engagement with the material.

The video diary format has become a component of both conventional documentary and also of created Reality TV formats, as in *Big Brother*'s (1999–) diary room (Bignell, 2005: 12). Participants speak to camera about themselves, knowing that this private speech will become public when the programme is broadcast. Bearing witness is a form of performance in which the presence and speech of the real person testify to the actuality of what he or she experienced. Thus the witness creates the reality of what he or she experienced, rather than observing something that occurs in the same present time. The reality of the past event is re-created at a later time in a reconstruction that can only take place once the person concerned has recounted it, since its detail is unknown until the story is told. However, inasmuch as the witness's narrative may be incomplete or inaccurate, bearing witness after the event or embodying the event in a reconstruction raise further questions of truth and knowledge. Bringing the real person into public visibility to bear witness may be a means of accessing a special truth, but it is also a performance that is necessarily affected by the real person's expectations of how television will represent him or her, and is understood by the viewer in relation to the other factual and fictional components of the docudrama and their relationship with other television forms. The criteria that viewers bring with them to the evaluation of docudrama therefore centre on questions of authenticity, but the kinds of authenticity at stake may derive from the match between the fictionalised performance and the factual base, or between the expressive performance techniques used by real on-screen witnesses or actors and the factual base that legitimates them. In each case, evaluations of docudrama programmes rest on how ideas of modality are brought to bear.

Performance and modes of address to the viewer

The modalities of television are varied because of the medium's breadth of genres, from documentary to naturalist drama to melodrama, for example. The dominant form of naturalism in television fiction is a product of the epoch of modern industrial society, deriving from theatrical antecedents, and also affects performance and performance of self in both docudrama and documentary (Paget, 2002, 2007). The ideology of television naturalism proposes that an individual's character determines their choices and actions, and human nature is seen as a pattern of character-differences. These differences, expressed through performance, permit the viewer to engage with a wide range of characters. The comparisons between performed characters and the viewer, and the judgements consequent on this that are made by viewers about identifiable human figures, are reliant on a common code determining the limits of 'normality'. This normality is the terrain on which the viewer's relationships with characters can occur. Television's psychological naturalism represents a world of consistent individual subjects and addresses its viewers as similarly rational and psychologically consistent. The text of a performance is designed to establish communication and offer involving identification (based on television's capacities as a mirror, discussed above), and television programmes are constructed as wholes which promise intelligibility and significance. The naturalist assumption of the match between the docudrama text and a pre-existing reality underlies this process, by posing the programme as equivalent to a real perception of recognisable social space and the people who function within it. This notion of equivalence rests therefore on the forms of subjectivity that are consensually shared by the viewer and the docudrama's represented characters, in the context of a textual world created in the docudrama. Since that textual world is already proposed by the docudrama's factual base as one that is authentic and plausible, the terrain of identification and shared norms of subjectivity are pre-established to a greater extent than in fictions that cannot make the same claims.

One recent BBC docudrama series makes use of the genre's basis in fact together with its naturalist performance conventions to explore scenarios that are neither in the past nor the present but in an imagined future, thus presenting their performances as a conditional-tense hypothesis.

This example therefore illuminates unusually clearly how docudrama performance works, since the series cultivates authenticity primarily by means of its textual conventions rather than by relying on the acceptance of facts which the viewer may already know. The BBC's five-part *If . . .* series (2004) addressed short- and medium-term social and economic issues that could have been the subject of current affairs programmes and documentaries, but which were realised as docudramas. *If . . . The Lights Go Out* posited a power crisis in 2010 in order to address Britain's dependence on imported energy. *If . . . Things Don't Get Better* imagined social unrest in 2012 because of the escalating gap between the poor and the wealthy. *If . . . The Generations Fall Out* dramatised violent unrest in 2024 as a way of exploring the probable generation gap between middle-class pensioners and the young adults whose taxation will have to support them. *If . . . It Was a Woman's World* presented a feminist society of 2020 in which men had become second-class citizens, and *If . . . We Don't Stop Eating* imagined government policies designed to stigmatise and punish the overweight. Each docudrama began with voice-over to give pertinent factual information about how the future scenario was based on present trends, often exemplified by statistics, then introduced a series of fictional characters representing people affected in different ways by the consequences of the imagined future. The premise of these programmes was that 'it could be you', and their makers cast little-known actors to actualise the ordinary detail of how the future scenario could be experienced, so that relationships of identification and mirroring could be made available to the viewer. Voice-over as a documentary technique and logical extrapolation from factual data claimed one kind of authenticity, while naturalistic performance expressing recognisable action, emotion and incidents claimed another.

One-off docudramas with similar hypothetical scenarios worked in similar ways. *Gas Attack* (2001) portrayed the process and effects of a nerve gas release in a British city, based on an actual incident in Tokyo. *Smallpox: Silent Weapon* (2001, repeated 2002) dramatised the impact of a potential pandemic that had been proposed in many media outlets as the next likely terrorist threat following 9/11. *Dirty War* (2004) explained and documented the likely effect of a small radioactive detonation in London. *The Day Britain Stopped* (2003) was set at Christmas, where multiple pressures on emergency services and political coordination were posed by a plane crash in London, gridlock on the city's orbital motorway the M25, and a terrorist attack on the city's financial district. Each of these programmes combined scripted performance with intercut news footage and other visual material signifying actuality, such as CCTV video. Because they were conditional-tense docudramas they cast actors without established personas deriving from previous programmes, inviting viewers to recognise the performers as equivalent to themselves. They adopted the conventions of television crime and disaster reconstructions, and in some cases also included simulated news interviews and witness statements. In each case, an understated performance style aimed to signify the ordinariness of the characters and their similarities with the imagined audience, by adopting the modified forms of psychological naturalism inherited from theatrical and cinematic modes of acting.

Historically, television fiction has realised the original aims of Naturalist theatre. That nineteenth- and twentieth-century form was characterised by dramas set in domestic and private space, and showed a small group of characters living out their private experience in distinction to a larger public world. But individualisation and privatisation were placed in relation to the pressures and tensions of an unseen public sphere of economic and political restriction. The acting style developing from this is important because of its links with gestural and bodily expression (in distinction to linguistic expression and heightened verbal delivery) and its relationship to ideologies of subjectivity that were discussed above. Psychological naturalism proposes that the actor's performance should be based on the realisation of the character's psychological truth (Baron, Carson and Tomasulo, 2004; Butler, 1991). In the terminology of this acting style, the character has 'tasks' to perform, is motivated by 'wants' and a consistent 'logic' in the 'given circumstances' of the drama. In docudrama based on real past events, these given circumstances are to some degree ready-made, since the historical records, interviews and background research associated with the docudrama's factual base will provide them. The same is much less likely for fictional drama where the script is not closely connected with actual events, so that actors' and directors' research takes different forms such as a programme of improvisation or reference to the actor's own emotional memories. The actor trained in psychological naturalism will look for a 'through-line' which takes the actor through his or her part, and a 'spine' or set of key moments by which the rest of the part is supported. In docudramas reconstructing actual events, or events based (like the BBC's *If . . .* series) on extrapolations of factual evidence, such key moments are determined not only by the dramatic arc of the programme as in fiction, but also by the ways that the docudrama selects moments from a known past or an already hypothesised future. Coherent psychology, contemporary forms of speech and gesture, and an emphasis on the revelation of the internal (wants and needs) through the external (action, movement and gesture) suit docudrama's purposes and restrictions well. The emphasis on motivation and psychology in this performance style tends to reduce the importance of the script, however, and this raises some problems for docudramas based on verbatim records. For docudramas based on verbatim language, or those where the experiences of people in non-western or pre-modern societies are being represented, the inherited predispositions of psychological naturalism make the style much less successful.

Melodramatic docudrama performances

Performance styles are very different in two examples of another kind of docudrama, where in one-off television films already known public personalities are represented by actors. The mode of *Thatcher: The Final Days* (1991) and *Diana: Her True Story* (1993) has much in common with melodrama, which in television is marked by its focus on women characters, on the emotional and the psychological, and on moments of dramatic intensity (Bignell, 2000). *Thatcher* was a dramatised reconstruction based on documentary records and interviews. *Diana: Her True Story* was based on Andrew Morton's bestselling book of the same title, which drew on interviews with Diana and her friends and dramatised her life from her childhood up to her separation from Prince Charles. The dramas were promoted as factual documents of the women's personal struggles, revealing their private lives and their private reactions to public events. Their documentary base was signalled by opening statements about the accuracy of their content and by the appearance of journalists and television cameras within the dramas, where the news media frequently intruded into and commented on the actions of the central figures. There were many documentary programmes about Diana both before and after the *Diana* docudrama, including *Diana: The Making of a Princess* (1989), *Diana: Progress of a Princess* (1991), *Diana: Portrait of a Princess* (1994), and many tribute programmes after her death, such as *Diana: A Celebration* (1997). Similarly, Margaret Thatcher was the subject of documentaries including *The Thatcher Factor* (1989), *Thatcher: The Downing Street Years* (1993) and *Thatcher: The Path to Power – and Beyond* (1995). Granada Television's fact-based dramas, like *Thatcher: The Final Days*, derive their authority and production process from Granada's current affairs programming. The central figures in this tradition conceive docudrama to be based in immaculately researched journalistic investigation (Paget, 1998: 165–168), including a requirement for exactitude of chronology and a sequential narrative structure. Date captions are very common at the beginnings of scenes, and captions also identify the names and job titles of politicians and civil servants. *Diana: Her True Story* is more closely related to US television docudramas about sensational news events (like *Amy Fisher: My Story* [1992] or *Casualties of Love* [1993], each based on the same crime of passion). While *Thatcher* showed no events which could not be confirmed by two or more sources, *Diana* relied heavily on Diana's own point of view and used few written sources. In different ways, these docudramas were legitimated by testimony and their factual base was easy for the audience to recognise because of the iconic presence of the two women in public life and in television factual programming.

The performance style in both *Diana* and *Thatcher* derived from the melodramatic mode, as opposed to more naturalistic, understated performance modes. The cues offered to the viewer for interpreting performance drew on popular gossip and personality reportage about the personal lives and characters of Margaret Thatcher and Princess Diana, supplying the means to interpret dramatic turning-points and crises through a repertoire of stock character-types and codes of gesture and expression. Morton's on-screen introduction to *Diana* alludes to this narrative mode by describing the drama as 'a vivid human interest story about a dream marriage that turned into hell for Diana: it's a story of a fractured fairy-tale'. Action representing the public appearances of Diana and the royal family was counterposed and given significance through its relationship to Diana's private life and her psychological and emotional turmoil. Her increasing stature as an independent player in campaigns and charitable work in the public eye was seen by the media as in part an attack on her husband, Prince Charles, who was having an affair with Camilla Parker-Bowles. Princess Diana became bulimic and occasionally suicidal, and in the docudrama a sequence of scenes aboard the Royal Yacht show Diana (Serena Scott Thomas) first discovering cufflinks on Prince Charles's shirt featuring the intertwined Cs of Charles and Camilla. 'You pig!' she screams, and walks out of the room. There is a cut to Diana voraciously eating cake in the Yacht's kitchen, accompanied by foreboding music in a minor key. The next shot is of Diana leaving a toilet, whose flush is heard in the background. So the sequence attributes Diana's physical problems to emotional disturbances provoked by her husband. The programme marks the emotional dynamics of the sequence by musical cues, as would be expected in melodrama whose historical evolution (and whose name itself) indicates the importance of music as a system to direct audience response. As in melodrama, conflict between characters produces emotional drama in *Diana*, and characters also experience conflicts within themselves which are expressed by rapidly alternating and conflicting emotions, made concrete through physical, bodily behaviour.

Melodrama emerged in the early nineteenth century as a form that could dramatise the ideological changes and contradictions thrown up by capitalism. Rather than focusing on a surface level of realism, melodrama expressed these tensions by 'pressuring the surface of reality' (Brooks, 1985: 15). There was a transition from a spiritual order governed by the institutions of the Church and the Monarchy into a secular order that replaced these legitimating values by an ethical code that infused the everyday with meaning and significance. This ethical dimension of the everyday, Brooks argues, is repressed by realist narrative, but by contrast the mode of melodrama heightens moral conflict and pushes narrative and style towards excess, thus provoking the revelation of an otherwise buried realm of moral and social values. Violent emotions and physical action emerge, which physically catalyse this moral struggle and lead to the liberation and moral triumph of the protagonist. Film and television melodramas have developed these schemas to focus primarily on relationships within the family, and between familial groups and a broader society (Bignell, 2005: 97–100), and a few television docudramas have used the mode to represent female public figures like Thatcher and Diana.

Since media icons like politicians, film stars and members of the Royal Family are recognised by their characteristic media images, their representations are already composed of a restricted repertoire of facial expressions, tones of voice and gestures, like the repertoire of characteristics which define melodrama characters. Reference to the images that the audience already knows, together with the actors' mimicking of familiar bodily movements, facial expressions and tones of voice, both aid perceptions of authenticity and trigger the audience's response to the central figures in terms of television melodrama. In a dramatisation of an interview with a *Times* journalist in *Thatcher: The Final Days*, for example, Thatcher's familiar patterns of speech and gesture and her political dogmatism are brought together in her reaction to Michael Hestletine's candidacy for Conservative Party leadership. Thatcher (Sylvia Syms) leans forward in close-up, speaking loudly and emphatically, saying 'we cannot go that way, we *cannot go that way*', then breaks into a confident smile. Diana's characteristic glance from under the fringe of her hair, and her relative awkwardness in her youth versus a more confident bearing later in life, are used in *Diana* both to recall media images of her on television and in the press and to chart her emotional development. *Thatcher* shows Mrs Thatcher in a simulated broadcast of a parliamentary debate where she famously said 'no, no, no' to European integration, where the camera angle and shot type exactly match the conventions of the real television footage of the parliamentary debate. Re-enacted moments in *Diana* include the positioning of the camera to duplicate the famous press photograph showing her legs through a see-through skirt, and the Royal Wedding itself where close-ups on the actors portraying Diana and her father are carefully integrated with parts of the real broadcast coverage of the event. In both *Thatcher* and *Diana*, lead actors were selected in part because of their physical resemblance to the real people they play, making these matches with real footage more easy to achieve.

In the 1980s prime-time television melodrama *Dynasty* (1981–89), the central woman character Alexis Colby used her (and men's) sexuality in her struggle for power. Alexis was aggressive and sexually manipulative, but all because of her untimely separation from her beloved children. In other words, her masculine behaviour was the result of a thwarted and distorted femininity. Similarly, Margaret Thatcher was represented as a masculinised woman, reputed to be domineering and ruthless, to the extent that satirists sometimes portrayed her in men's clothing or with a male body. In *Thatcher*, Margaret Thatcher maintained control of the male-dominated and patriarchal Conservative Party and the Government. At a Cabinet meeting near the beginning of the drama, Thatcher complains that the drafting of bills is behindhand, asking sharply 'would someone care to tell me why?' A series of brief medium shots follows, showing the assembled Ministers looking down at their notes sheepishly or fiddling with their papers to avoid her gaze. While the scene is based on factual evidence, its dramatic significance comes from the performance's melodramatic characterisation of Thatcher as a domineering boss.

The expression of emotion is both a marker of femininity and of working-class culture (Lusted, 1998). While masculine values (like those of politics, journalism and the British royal circle) entail the suppression of emotion in favour of efficiency, achievement and stoicism, feminine values encourage the display of emotion as a way of responding to problematic situations. Similarly, elite class sectors value rational talk and writing as means of expression, versus emotional release. These distinctions have been important to work in television studies on the relationship between gender and the different genres of television, where news and current affairs are regarded as masculine, and melodrama as feminine. On the basis of these gender, class and genre distinctions, the role of emotional display in *Thatcher* and *Diana* takes on increased significance. Diana's frequent tearful outbursts separate her from the stoical elite group who surround her, some of whom are also women, and parallel her with the ordinary viewer. Thatcher's eventual capitulation to tears at the final meeting with her Cabinet is also a marker of her defeat by masculine forces and the values of the political culture which she had sought to control. She is seen in medium shot across the Cabinet table, making a final statement before withdrawing from the leadership contest, remarking, when her voice breaks, 'I've never done that before.' Christine Geraghty argues of US prime-time soaps that they are set in a world controlled predominantly by men but offer pleasures to the woman viewer by showing that male power can be challenged 'on the one hand by moral questioning and on the other by women's refusal to be controlled' (1991: 74). In contrast to this, *Thatcher* and *Diana* show women failing to hold onto their power within masculine elites. The dramatic climaxes of *Thatcher* and *Diana* attain their climactic status at the cost of the ejection of the women from the masculine public world. The mode of melodrama imposes restrictions on characters, limiting their ability to act and creating a sense of claustrophobia and the domination of particular spaces by social and ethical forces that intrude into them and infuse them. *Thatcher* and *Diana* offer the pleasure of recognising familiar figures, events and issues in the public realms of politics and elite institutions, and also the pleasures of identification and fantasy focused through their private experience. The history of television features on the two women shows an interest in both their public roles and their private lives and personalities, but in *Thatcher: The Final Days* the political environment is depicted in the familial and domestic terms of television melodramas like *Dallas* or *Dynasty*. Discourses of femininity were important to the public images of both Diana and Margaret Thatcher, and performances in the two docudramas also link public and private in their linkage of documentary reconstruction with melodrama.

Docudrama as a vanguard form

The imperatives of television documentary, emerging during the era of scarcity (Ellis, 2000) in British broadcasting when there were few terrestrial channels, matched the ethos of public service to draw together the nation's cultures, classes and regions by showing viewers how other people lived.

Documenting audio-visually ran alongside analysis, often by professional experts, to prompt intervention into material circumstances. Documentary aimed to contribute to the public sphere of rational debate and democratic participation by enabling the exchange of information and the possibility of transcending separations of place, class, education and ideology. But changes in television and in the broader culture have meant that the ambition of documentary to connect with these large-scale ideological strategies has become significantly less important. Individual documentaries are surrounded by many more competing programmes and channels, splitting their audience, and audiences have been understood not as clients but as markets. Assumed relevance to the audience's interests has reduced the number and prominence of factual programmes about other nations and unfamiliar cultures, alongside a surge in factual programmes about ordinary people including the various forms of Reality TV.

Television docudrama has grown in prominence and frequency as part of this shift. It is one of many contemporary audio-visual forms characterised by generic hybridity comprising documentary and dramatic modes (Corner, 2002). In cinema, examples include *Saving Private Ryan* (1998) and *The Queen* (2006) and the bio-pics *The Aviator* (2005), *Capote* and *Walk the Line* (2006). The events of 9/11 were the source for *United 93* and *World Trade Centre* in 2006. In television, the high-budget mini-series *Band of Brothers* (2001) was based on fact and testimony about the Second World War, and docudramas on aspects of this historical conflict included *D Day* (2004), *Hiroshima* (2005), *Conspiracy* (2002) and *Dunkirk* (2004). Four television docudramas addressed the 9/11 events: *The Hamburg Cell* (2004), and in 2006 *9/11: The Twin Towers*, *The Path to 9/11* and *9/11: The Flight That Fought Back*. These docudramas share a concern to investigate recent events of historical significance in a hybrid form, as did *The Government Inspector* (2005) about the controversy over Iraq's absent weapons of mass destruction and *The Road to Guantanamo* (2006) about the 'war on terror'. Reality TV programmes like *Crimewatch UK* (1984–) and history programmes like the Channel 4 series *English Civil War* (2005) also adopted docudramatic performance techniques in order to attract popular audiences. Entertainment and drama producers experimented with hybrids such as the 'mock-documentary' *The Office* (2001) in order to revive established fiction genres (Roscoe and Hight, 2001). Television always aims to contain and explain the real, especially through the form of narrative, in order to address cultural understandings of the real. Docudrama performance is a crucial aspect of generic verisimilitude because it signals to the audience which genre codes should be adduced to evaluate these narratives about the real. Docudrama is a rapidly evolving part of contemporary television culture, and its transgressions of the boundaries between factual and fictional modes foreground performance as an aspect of docudrama's hybridity. The kinds of performance evident in recent docudrama illuminate the tensions between the different claims to authenticity that this hybrid mode can make. More broadly, the hybridity of docudrama that is being explored in ever more innovative and creative ways expresses a widespread interest in calling on the traditions and future potential of the television medium, as an intimate and immediate window and mirror.

Acknowledgement

This chapter is one of the results of the research project 'Acting with Facts: Performing the Real in British Theatre and Television Docudrama since 1990', funded by the Arts & Humanities Research Council. The research is led by Derek Paget at the University of Reading, working with Jonathan Bignell, Lib Taylor and the project's postdoctoral fellow, Heather Sutherland.

References

Baron, C., D. Carson and F. Tomasulo (eds.) (2004) *More than a Method: Trends and Traditions in Contemporary Film Performance*, Detroit: Wayne State University Press.

Bignell, J. (2000) 'Docudrama as Melodrama: Representing Princess Diana and Margaret Thatcher', in B. Carson and M. Llewellyn-Jones, eds., *Frames and Fictions on Television: The Politics of Identity within Drama*, Exeter: Intellect, 17–26.

Bignell, J. (2005) *Big Brother: Reality TV in the Twenty-first Century*, Basingstoke: Palgrave Macmillan.

Brooks, P. (1985) *The Melodramatic Imagination: Balzac, Henry James, and the Mode of Excess*, New York: Columbia University Press.

Butler, J. (ed.) (1991) *Star Texts: Image and Performance in Film and Television*, Detroit: Wayne State University Press.

Corner, J. (2002) 'Performing the Real: Documentary Diversions', *Television and New Media*, 3, No. 3: 255–269.

Ellis, J. (2000) *Seeing Things: Television in the Age of Uncertainty*, London: I. B. Tauris.

Geraghty, C. (1991) *Women and Soap Opera: A Study of Prime Time Soaps*, Cambridge: Polity Press.

Gripsrud, J. (1998) 'Television, Broadcasting, Flow: Key Metaphors in TV Theory', in C. Geraghty and D. Lusted, eds., *The Television Studies Book*, London: Arnold, 17–32.

Lusted, D. (1998) 'The Popular Culture Debate and Light Entertainment on Television', in C. Geraghty and D. Lusted, eds., *The Television Studies Book*, London: Arnold, 175–190.

Paget, D. (1998) *No Other Way to Tell It: Dramadoc/Docudrama on Television*, Manchester: Manchester University Press.

Paget, D. (2002) 'Acting a Part: Performing Docudrama', *Media International Australia*, 104: 30–41.

Paget, D. (2007) '"Acting with Facts": Actors Performing the Real in British Theatre and Television since 1990. A Preliminary Report on a New Research Project', *Studies in Documentary Film*, 1, No. 2: 165–176.

Roscoe, J. and C. Hight (2001) *Faking It: Mock-documentary and the Subversion of Factuality*, Manchester: Manchester University Press.

4

Living stories: performance in the contemporary biopic

Dennis Bingham

There is no film genre to which performance is as crucial as it is to the biopic. The genre's appeal lies in seeing an actual person who did something interesting in life, known mostly in public, transformed into a character. Private behaviours and actions and public events as they might have been in the person's time are formed together and interpreted dramatically. At the heart of the biopic is the urge to dramatise actuality. The function of the biopic subject is to deliver the spectator a story. The genre's charge, which dates back to its salad days in the Hollywood studio era, is to enter the biographical subject into the pantheon of cultural mythology and to show why he or she belongs there.

Like any genre that dates back nearly to the beginning of narrative cinema, the biopic has gone through developmental stages, emerging from each of its historical cycles with certain modes that continue to be available to filmmakers working in the form. These are:

- the classical, celebratory form (melodrama);
- warts-and-all (melodrama/realism);
- critical investigation and atomisation of the subject (or the *Citizen Kane* [1941] mode);
- parody (in terms of choice of biographical subject; what screenwriters Scott Alexander and Larry Karaszewski call the 'anti-biopic – a movie about somebody who doesn't deserve one' [Alexander and Karaszewski, 1999: vii], mocking the very notions of heroes and fame in a culture based on consumerism and celebrity rather than high-culture values);
- minority appropriation (as in queer or feminist, African American or Third World, whereby James Whale or Janet Frame, Malcolm X or Patrice Lumumba owns the conventional mythologising form that once would have been used to marginalise or stigmatise them);

- since 2000, the neo-classical biopic, which integrates elements of all or most of the above.

The biopic dwells in a liminal space between fiction and actuality, if not history. No more documentary than *King Lear*, the biopic nonetheless makes drama out of fact. Thus the actual is put into the form of drama, and for the purposes of drama. Roland Barthes, in a much cited quote, called biography 'the fiction that dare not speak its name' (quoted in Rosenstone, 2007: 13). Robert Rosenstone points out that in a visual medium history 'must be fictional in order to be true' (Rosenstone, 1995: 70). By fiction, Rosenstone refers to the Latin meaning, 'formed', but without ruling out 'fiction' in 'the more modern sense of "an imaginative creation"' (Rosenstone, 2007: 13).

More than fiction, drama, with its remaking of life into enactments, calls for invention. The actor, whose stock in trade is embodiment, behaviour and expression, is the focal point of this invention, the element that literally gets the most attention. The biopic involves research more obviously than does any other genre. Examples of such research are legion, for instance Robert De Niro's learning to box for *Raging Bull* (1980) with the man he was playing, Jake La Motta, as his sparring partner. However, a performance made up only of researched physical traits, skills and habits, looks and characteristics at certain historical points would be mechanical and empty; there has to be embodiment there, a body, as Jean-Louis Comolli (1978) explained, even if the body of the actor supersedes the body of the historical subject, for instance when Greta Garbo plays Sweden's *Queen Christina* (1933). Todd Haynes explained that he prepared for each of the actors playing six 'Bob Dylans' in *I'm Not There* (2007) 'little CD mixes' and 'portfolio books just full of all the images of all the Dylans': 'Actors love having that stuff; it's really helpful', he said. 'And then at a certain point – I noticed this with all of them . . . in the final fine-tunings of hair and wig and costume they would just be like "okay, I just gotta do it." It almost made them too nervous, too freaked out to be thinking about it [the research models] anymore. They just had to start doing it' (IFC News, 2007).

The biopic has always been a showcase for performers; Adolph Zukor cast the stage diva Sarah Bernhardt in *Les Amours de la reine Élisabeth* (*Queen Elizabeth*) in 1912 in order to prove the movies as a 'respectable' medium and to draw middle-class audiences. This coup alone set many precedents still at work today in the genre: that the biopic is a prestige genre, with films made in hopes of winning awards and earning respect.

Because it offers interesting, challenging roles, the biopic is a magnet for well-known actors whose presence will attract financing and also perhaps allow the producers to interest these actors later in other, more commercial genres. More than a showy genre for performance, however, the biopic is a proving ground. From 1980 to 2007, 67 performances of actual personages in biopics have been nominated for Academy Awards for Best Actor and Best Actress (out of 130 nominations for biopics in the 80 years of the Awards). Seventeen of those won (out of 34 for biopics since 1928). Of those 67 and 17, moreover, 24 and 10 respectively, have come between 2000 and 2007.

Clearly, re-creating (or is it creating?) an actual person has become the crucible for acting in the postmodern period, or at least this is how it is viewed by official culture as crystallised in the Academy Awards in the US and the BAFTAs in the UK, both of which awarded Best Actress in 2007 to Marion Cotillard for her embodied, transformative Edith Piaf in *La Môme* (*La Vie en Rose*). It mattered little that foreign-language performances had been honoured with Oscars only twice before (in 80 years!) and that Cotillard's was the first French-language performance to be Oscared. If Hamlet is by legend the ultimate test for a classically trained stage actor, then for an African American male film actor, 'Hamlet' may well be Ray Charles; for a French actress, 'Hamlet' might be Piaf; for a British actress, 'Hamlet' could be Elizabeth I (or II), and for an all-around male character actor 'Hamlet' is perhaps Truman Capote or Ed Wood or Paul Rusesabagina. For an actress 'Hamlet' might even be . . . Bob Dylan? In film history the biopic is practically a barometer of the refinement of film acting as a technical skill. Attention to walk, stance and posture is perhaps no different from an actor's usual construction of character, except that here there is a real-life model for the actor in preparing but also for the audience in assessing the performance. Enacting an actual person calls for a complex degree of precision. The actor must suggest the person with an exactitude that can vary from just a few essential signifiers like hair and dress to a full impersonation of appearance, gesture, posture and voice. All performances call for this orchestration of traits. With the biopic or historical film, however, there is a human model, past or present, against which the actor's success can be measured. At the same time, the pleasure of the biopic performance comes in the private moments, in the performance of emotional depths that no actual person can display publicly, or perhaps privately.

It seems no accident that the biopic performance would reach a point of perfection in the postmodern period when the simulacrum, the synthesis, becomes the standard. The biopic has shifted from a producer's genre during the studio era, as George F. Custen elaborately described it in *Bio/Pics* (1992), to a form that tends to attract auteur directors, both in studio Hollywood and especially in independent art film and internationally. Therefore, the actor must create a character that comes from an overall concept agreed upon by the filmmaker and actor. For his performance in *JFK* (1991), 'I wasn't playing the real Clay Shaw, whoever he might have been', Tommy Lee Jones said of the New Orleans personality who was unsuccessfully prosecuted by district attorney Jim Garrison for the death of John F. Kennedy; 'I was playing Jim Garrison's and Oliver Stone's Clay Shaw' (*Inside the Actor's Studio*, 1997).

There have essentially been, as they have come down to the contemporary period, three categories of biopic performance: embodied impersonation, stylised suggestion and the star performance. Examples of embodied impersonation have been plentiful in the past three decades and account mostly for the number of Oscars in the genre. Such performances include Robert De Niro in *Raging Bull* (1980), Denzel Washington in *Malcolm X* (1992), Jamie Foxx in *Ray* (2004) and Phillip Seymour Hoffman in *Capote* (2005), as well as Toby Jones in *Infamous* (2006) and Charlize Theron in *Monster* (2003). The embodied performance was probably most firmly established in the 1980s by Meryl Streep, who took the realist approach, informed by the Method, to its farthest extremes in her biopics *Silkwood* (1983), *Out of Africa* (1985) and *A Cry in the Dark* (1988). Her performances, capped by Daniel Day Lewis's Oscar-winning turn in *My Left Foot* (1989), established the fully embodied portrayal as the standard.

Look at the difference between two Warren Beatty biopic performances, ten years apart, *Reds* (1981) and *Bugsy* (1991), to see the impact even on star performances. *Reds* shows the power of the star performance. Producer-director-cowriter-star Beatty is the prime mover behind his sweeping magnum opus on the lives of John Reed and Louise Bryant and the left-wing movements of early twentieth-century America. His performance seems at first to draw on little more than the actor's familiar combination of boyish charm and producer's inner will. After the first half-hour, however, a real character starts to grow out of Beatty's (or is it Reed's?) seemingly nonstop motion and energy. The character's passion – as well as Beatty's for his dream project – inform a nontransformative performance; indeed transformation at this time was still left mostly to the supporting characters, such as Maureen Stapleton's Emma Goldman. Accordingly, Stapleton won an Oscar (for Best Supporting Actress); the two leads, Beatty and Diane Keaton, did not.

As Ben 'Bugsy' Siegel, Beatty submits his acting range to its biggest workout to date. Siegel was a handsome man, a snappy dresser and a violent sociopath. Drawn to the glamour of Hollywood, where he moved, and a womaniser like the actor playing him, Siegel requires Beatty to swing crazily but methodically from charm to reasonableness to sadism to irresponsibility. Scripted by James Toback (*Fingers* [1978], *Black and White* [2000]), a writer known for his fascination with the extremes of brutality and civilisation, and directed with impersonal professionalism by Barry Levinson, *Bugsy* allows Beatty to play to his on-screen and off-screen personas but also to stretch to the extremes of human behaviour. A film with the semantics of a classic-era gangster film but the syntax of a biopic, *Bugsy* doesn't quite work. Siegel built the first of the great Las Vegas casino hotels, the Flamingo, when the town was a desert outpost. The film is not sure whether to play Siegel, for all of his monstrosity, as a romantic visionary, much less whether to play this for irony or for commentary on the corruption out of which America creates its entertainment. The greatest irony may simply concern timing. Although Beatty had not been so unrestrained on screen before, the 54-year-old actor almost visibly holds back the clock in order to play a man who was 41 when he died. The heartthrob Siegel would have been better casting for a Beatty 15 years younger; however, nothing the actor had done in the late 1970s showed that he had the technique and depth as an actor that he shows in *Bugsy*, spurred by the new transformative standard for biopic acting.

Two performances nominated for Best Actor in the same year – Washington in *Malcolm X* and Robert Downey Jr. in *Chaplin* (1992) – show again how the 'classical' model for a biopic performance has now changed. The attention given to both the star personas of Washington and Downey exceeded the critical appraisal of their specific performances in each of these movies. Roger Ebert remarked that 'Downey was ready to be Charlie Chaplin in any movie anybody made' (Siskel and Ebert, 1993).

Stylised performances that rely more on suggestion and less on a full impersonation include, as we shall see, Paul Giamatti and Hope Davis in *American Splendor* (2003), as well as Anthony Hopkins in *Nixon* (1995), Johnny Depp in *Ed Wood* (1994) and Hilary Swank in *Boys Don't Cry* (1999). Elizabeth Banks, cast as Laura Bush in *W*, Oliver Stone's 2008 biopic of the 43rd president of the United States, said at the start of production, 'I don't want to do an impression. I just want to honor her voice, her stillness, and her hairstyle' (Svetkey, 2008: 29). Star performances in the biopic are far less prevalent than in earlier periods because the biopic has now become the province of the character actor.

Star performances do not completely go away, however. Steven Soderbergh agreed to direct *Erin Brockovich* (2000) with Julia Roberts already 'attached' because he knew the little-known Brockovich would be a perfect role for Roberts's particular kind of energy and magnetism – her star presence. While the famed cleavage became nearly a running gag in the film, and while Roberts worked on other kinds of biopic-performance embodiments that spectators would not even notice, such as learning to be right-handed like the real-life model, Soderbergh fed Roberts information about Brockovich, as Mike Leigh did in preparing actors for his Gilbert and Sullivan movie, *Topsy Turvy* (1999), while keeping actress and subject from even meeting until shooting was half-completed ('Spotlight on Location', 2000). This way Roberts would be as free to invent her own Erin Brockovich. However, Roberts's performance in *Erin Brockovich* managed to recall past star tours-de-force such as Susan Hayward in *I Want to Live!* (1958) and Barbra Streisand in *Funny Girl* (1968), partly because her subject was almost entirely unknown before the film was made; thus the audience would not be comparing Roberts's portrayal to a real-life model. The coup worked better than could have been imagined. 'For once,' reported *The Times of London*, 'Hollywood appears to have downplayed a character on the screen . . . From the moment that the real Erin Brockovich appeared at the Los Angeles premiere . . . it became clear that while the on-screen character was lifelike, the off-screen one was larger than life' (29 March 2000).

The most fruitful theorisation about acting in historical films remains the article 'A Body Too Much' by Jean-Louis Comolli (1978), whereby the actor playing an actual person becomes the only version of the person that we have as we watch the film. The two bodies – the body of the actor and the body of the actual person as the spectator knows him or her – compete for the spectator's belief: thus, there is 'a body too much'. To Comolli, the actor enacts as much as she can the stance and demeanour of the subject while in performance emphasising her own separateness from her, creating a character from a 'body' (and spirit) who already exists or has existed. Comolli's concept is a product of 1970s and 1980s film studies, when differences between dramatisations and representations of actuality, like any gap between a film's diegesis and its construction, would be considered ruptures through which would show the ideological assumptions at the root of the fiction and its production. As biopics were made up to the time of Comolli's writing, the body of the actor was walled off, psychically, from the body of the actual person, at least for the time the spectator is watching the film.

More and more the biopic in the 1990s came to integrate images from documentary; the film that established this was *Malcolm X*, which ended with the character Denzel Washington played having been murdered and the actual Malcolm resurrected as it were, in photographs and newsfilm, while in voice-over Ossie Davis in present-day read the eulogy that he delivered at Malcolm X's funeral. Spike Lee's move was influenced by the combination of documentary and dramatic sequences in Oliver Stone's films, especially *JFK*, and Warren Beatty's use of on-screen 'witnesses' in *Reds*. Films no longer seemed afraid of threatening their own historical diegesis and the believability of their actors by bringing in shots of the actual person at the end; in fact, it has become almost de rigueur to do this. It is a new way to emphasise the lasting importance of the particular subject, the transcendence of the physical body by accomplishments that render the subject immortal. This was and is always the point that biopics want audiences to take with them out of the cinema. To display both bodies, however, is contradictory; it admits the fictionality and the artifice of the film. In effect this device dares a spectator to compare the authenticity of its performers to the actuality. It also furthers the theme, pervasive from *Citizen Kane*, of questioning the knowability of any human subject.

American Splendor and bodies too much

The scene opens in a legitimate stage house in Pasadena. The camera trains on a couple in the audience as they watch themselves being re-enacted in a play. On stage, a husky man with bad posture and wearing an old flannel shirt stands in a shabby apartment decorated with cheap furniture and a crooked lamp shade. He tells his date, a woman with straight black hair and large horn-rimmed glasses, dressed in overalls and an orange tee-shirt, about the joys of underground comics. 'I didn't come all the way from Delaware to talk about comics,' she says as if she's Bacall seducing Bogart. She kisses him and moves on top of him. The couple in the audience look at each other, a bit embarrassed. The pair in the play have now moved past the prop cat posed at a milk dish to a stage toilet. The woman is bent over it, emotively losing her lunch, while the man solicitously stands by, a cup of chamomile tea at the ready. A troubadour at the side of the stage strums a guitar and sings plaintively, 'Where is my American Splendor? In a world so cloudy and gray?' This is love.

We know because we have seen it before, and so have the couple watching. We have seen them live the same scene not on a stage set, but in a naturalistically dirty apartment, where the woman vomits in cinematic realism, behind a closed door, and tries to clear the air with an aerosol spray, even though it turns out to be WD-40 lubricant. *That* couple is commented on by a third rendition of the pair. These are 'the real deal', as the male protagonist/actual subject Harvey Pekar says. Pekar and his wife Joyce Brabner appear as themselves in *American Splendor*, but in a studio surrounded by a plain white background that looks like a comic book frame. The actual is artificial and the artificial – the performances, the gritty, low-rent locations – are in a realistic style, after a fashion, the fashion being comic books. Moreover, this particular situation – how Harvey and Joyce met and got married two days later – has been played out in a comic book, on the stage and on film. One wonders about the reality behind it, since the situation seems such a comedic setup. Joyce's moans of pleasure while Harvey kisses her are actually the sounds of her becoming sick. Her capper of a line – Harvey, why don't we skip the whole courtship thing and just get married?' – is a wonderfully comic inversion of expectations. The certainty of these two comic book-loving, idiosyncratic misfits, however, that they belonged together and didn't need a lot of 'phoney bullshit', in one of Pekar's favourite phrases, in order to prove it, feels truthful.

Harvey Pekar, a career file clerk in a Veterans' Administration hospital in Cleveland, Ohio, became a kind of pop hero when he began dramatising his hyper-ordinary, lonely life as a 'loser' in a series of underground comics illustrated over the years by hosts of artists. The film works on some of the primary tropes of the biopic. Harvey looks for transcendence in his existence. 'When you croak,' Pekar tells one of his sidekicks (a common type of the film genre), who happens to be R. Crumb, the pioneer underground cartoonist, 'you're gonna leave somethin' behind.' This scene is preamble to Harvey's defining moment. Opening a file drawer marked 'Deceased', Harvey looks into a file describing a Clevelander who died at the early age of 54. 'Occupation: Clerk.' This deadening harbinger of his own futility is Harvey's epiphany; he takes action, doing something no one else had done – writing a comic book about his daily travails and disappointments, using stick figures at first. He shows it to Crumb, who says, 'this is great stuff. I dig it. Can I take 'em home and illustrate 'em?' The scene is one of those biopic moments in which the destiny of the biographical subject is depicted in offhand simplicity, when the importance of the moment is seen in history's hindsight as belied by characters who have no idea how significant their actions are. In the scene's biblical stroke, Harvey, who begins the film's dramatic portions by mysteriously losing his voice, has it restored to him. The triviality of being present at the creation of a comic book is played with the same seriousness as, say, the drafting of William Wilberforce's bill outlawing the slave trade in *Amazing Grace* (2006). Harvey's finding of his voice, moreover, parodies innumerable moments of destiny, such as the scene in which Ann Rutledge indicates from the grave to Abe that he should be a lawyer in *Young Mr. Lincoln* (1939).

American Splendor is an example of the sort of postmodern biopic that makes irrelevant the body-too-much issue by either bringing it out into the open or going so far from the concept of embodiment that the issue is simply besides the point or, perhaps, besides the body. Also out in the open is the acting, which may be where the distinction in subject matter in *American Splendor* is actually made. Paul Giamatti, who plays Harvey, explained that the performance style needed to be a cross between realism and the comics (Fischer, 2003). One of the first things one notices about the acting of Giamatti and Hope Davis as Joyce is that their performances are busier than one expects in naturalistic acting. Giamatti employs scratching, grunts, growls and grimaces for Harvey, much more so than the real Harvey we see in the documentary portions. We can almost see Giamatti's concept of the character and chart its development, as the Yale School of Drama graduate takes us through a workshop on character construction. For her part, Davis creates a character mostly out of widening her eyes and then closing them, suggesting disbelief followed by resignation. Entering the film a third of the way through and with much less screen time overall than Giamatti, Davis is more Brechtian in her approach. Since her character is known mostly from her occasional appearances in comic book instalments, Davis acts her, appropriately, in episodes. Calming herself down after an initial tantrum over a missing comic book by drinking herbal tea and writing letters, this woman negotiates her way through a world she, like her new husband, finds stacked against the little person. This is suggested in the way Davis replies that she won't mind moving from Wilmington, Delaware to Cleveland because 'I find most American cities to be depressing in the same way,' her voice going up on the last word, indicating resigned acceptance rather than despair or self-pity.

Davis's impatient calm counterbalances Giamatti's more volatile Pekar. Joyce is given to frequent spates of withdrawal, which Davis suggests by deeply sighing and closing her eyes. Joyce is a female character in a story told by male narrators (Pekar and the mostly male artists who draw his comics). *American Splendor* is a film written and directed

4.1 Giamatti grimaces: 'a cross between realism and the comics'. *American Splendor*

by a husband-and-wife team *about* a husband and wife. Davis's Joyce gets opportunities to break through Harvey's mild 'can't live with 'em, can't live without 'em' misogyny. The issue of motherhood, made moot by Harvey's long-standing vasectomy, is expressed mostly in wordless reaction shots of Davis to a woman at an airport carrying a baby and later to her reactions upon first meeting little Danielle, the girl whose legal guardian they will eventually become. As Harvey, in foreground, sketches out with the artist *Our Cancer Year*, the graphic novel he and Joyce write about his ordeal with lymphoma, Joyce and Danielle make Play-Doh animals behind them. Thus Joyce's glares and sighs of quiet desperation literally and figuratively interrupt Harvey's monologue of howls and grunts. Joyce/Davis interjects a female presence into Harvey's little corner of the male-oriented world (at least in the 1970s and 1980s) of underground comics.

American Splendor is a rare biopic in which the subject and the actor are placed side by side. The actors are made to seem extraneous to the film's controlling point of view, that of Harvey Pekar. Employing the unusual device of having the subject narrate much of the film while the actors go through their naturalistic paces, the film at first achieves the expected disjunction, a recentring of the subject from the visual to the soundtrack. The voice-over narration of Harvey, whose vocal qualities run to the sandpaper end of the spectrum, seems to regard the actors as necessary pests. 'Here's me. Or here's the guy playin' me,' says the

4.2 Davis counterbalances with impatient calm. *American Splendor*

real Pekar in his voice-over, 'even though he don't look nothin' like me. But whatever.' Giamatti's Pekar is a little softer, a little less raw than the genuine article. *American Splendor* seems to remind us that film fiction renders life with an idealising touch that may be inevitable, and that we crave the sensitivity and expressiveness that good actors and a creative mise-en-scène can provide. Harvey Pekar doesn't quite have the skills, the depth of emotional and mental projection, to play Harvey Pekar.

American Splendor is not the first biopic to bring the 'body too much' issue out of the subtext and make it central to the text. *Yuen Ling-yuk* (*Centre Stage*, Stanley Kwan, 1992) features documentary sequences in which the director interviews Maggie Cheung, who plays the Shanghai movie actress Ruan Ling-Yu. Ruan committed suicide in 1935 at the age of 25 amidst sensational press coverage of her divorce from her first husband and her affair with an older, married man. While it first seems as if Kwan has simply cut into his film scenes from the standard 'making-of' documentary or perhaps has included videotaped conversations from the read-throughs with his cast, the effect is to make three 'bodies too much' – the actress Ruan seen in some clips and production stills, mostly from films which overtitles tell us have been lost; scenes of Cheung in 'street clothes' talking with the director about playing the character in early 1990s Hong Kong; and the character whom Cheung creates out of the synthesis of historical data and the resources of the present-day studio. Despite the very different political and cultural circumstances of

Shanghai in the 1930s and Hong Kong in the early 1990s,[1] Kwan's point is that filmmaking essentially does not change. Female biopics continue to seek out as subjects beautiful young women who suffered, and perhaps who were victimised and/or who died young. One of the actors remarks that 'If she had lived, we probably wouldn't be making "The Ruan-Ling Yu Story,"' with Kwan adding, 'Yes, we'd probably be interviewing her for some other film.' The Ruan-Ling Yu created by Cheung with a lot of assistance from the costume designer, the director and the cinematographer, is a perfect porcelain doll, a paragon of studio-trained deportment and culturally taught deference, who smiles politely to everyone who addresses her. Cheung's character not only is understood as a product of research, reflection and collaboration, all of which Kwan puts on screen for us to see. Her character also would be inscrutable, as a woman, as an Asian, as a personage from a remote past, without Kwan making his own film's production part of the story of an actress destroyed by publicity.

The conceit that Pulcini and Berman carry out in *American Splendor*, with scenes shot on naturalistic locations, is that the documentary scenes take place on a bare white soundstage. This stylisation seems a frank analogy for the relations of the actors towards the characters they are playing. This becomes clear when a scene in which Toby enlightens Harvey on the pleasures of piña colada-flavoured jelly beans wraps. The director signals the end of the take and the actors. Giamatti, still in character, does his Harvey walk off the set towards the real Harvey and Toby, whom Friedlander has already joined at the catering table. This begins Harvey and Toby on a discussion of jelly beans, and then a serious conversation on loneliness. Giamatti and Friedlander take their seats in the background and wait for the next setup as Toby and Harvey talk in the foreground. All remain in focus. Friedlander takes off his Toby sweater and his Toby glasses and looks a bit bored and bereft without his character to play; Giamatti leans forward, smiling, enjoying Toby and Harvey as if they were the entertainers. The two twains, actors and subjects, never meet or mingle.

The interest and enjoyment with which Giamatti regards Pekar reverse the expected relation, whereby ordinary people supposedly regard actors and celebrity with fixated concentration. This reversal is appropriate for the biopic, in which the actor serves as just a temporary outlet for the actual subject. Harvey's irritation and ordinary-guy haplessness, cartoon trademarks of an obviously more complicated person whose signature line is 'ordinary life is pretty complex stuff', appear as the more fixed concepts of the actor, whose idea of Harvey as he immortalised himself in his comic book stories shows the limits and depths of acting as compared with the actual person. The directors and the actor appear to challenge the spectator *not* to believe the illusion, since that illusion keeps being pulled out from under the spectator.

By the end of the film, however, the spectator has come to appreciate the warmer Giamatti. The curious effect is that Pekar, not Giamatti, becomes the body-too-much in the biopic about him. Don't call us, Harvey. We'll call you. We see so many different renditions of Harvey Pekar – we see him, inside and out, coming and going, but we still don't know him. This leaves a sense of the enigma that may always be the destination of the biopic in its post-*Citizen Kane*, postmodern stage (which in this genre is perhaps saying the same thing).

Cate Blanchett, Todd Haynes and the many faces of postmodern performance

Giamatti's challenge is unusual; the actor must play down the person and smooth him out while also exaggerating him. Two rightly celebrated performances by Cate Blanchett, as Katharine Hepburn in *The Aviator* (Martin Scorsese, 2004) and as the 1966-model Bob Dylan in *I'm Not There* (Todd Haynes, 2007), are of a different sort, and they differ from each other as well. Both are full-out impersonations that stand out from the films they are in. While Blanchett's Hepburn is in a realistic vein – she is Kate Hepburn at the particular time when Howard Hughes knew her – her 'Jude Quinn' is one of six facets, or historical phases, or personae, of Dylan. While gender is always a text in films, it is a disruptive text in *I'm Not There*. This gives Blanchett's presence and stardom, and those of her fellow actors Christian Bale and Heath Ledger, resonances that exceed the performances. *I'm Not There*, overall, involves all three biopic modes of performance, in unique and disjunctive ways.

The Aviator has to stretch to make the late 1930s liaison of Hepburn and Howard Hughes the grand romance that it probably wasn't and to portray the end of the relationship as the start of the tycoon's gradual mental deterioration. Accordingly, Blanchett, in order to suit popular memory, is more Hepburn than Hepburn. She accentuates the behaviours and mannerisms that spell Katharine Hepburn without caricaturing the star. All one has to do is look at a Hollywood-history film like *The Aviator* to see that for every performance like that of Blanchett, who makes Kate Hepburn endearingly human while duelling the body-too-much at least to a draw, there are Jude Law and Kate Beckinsale assaying puny imitations of Errol Flynn and Ava Gardner and providing unhappy reminders that early twenty-first century Hollywood produces less vivid and more undernourished-looking movie stars than it used to. Blanchett's art combines a talent for impersonation with a relaxation that negates the mimicry and makes the performance natural. Although Blanchett is slender and lithe like Hepburn, she does not have the star's high degree of angularity nor her high cheek bones and sharp features; the script does help the actress with Hepburn's line to Hughes just before they make love, warning him of 'sharp elbows and knees'. Indeed with Blanchett's soft features, she barely resembles Hepburn at all (which, amusingly, cannot be said of her as Bob Dylan). Yet one forgets after less than a minute that it is not Hepburn we are watching; even a mental check against the real Hepburn does nothing to dent the truth of *this* Katharine Hepburn. This may demonstrate the power of the voice in biopic acting of well-known people; once the actress nails one of the most instantly recognisable of twentieth-century voices, she could look like Ethel Merman and it might not matter.

This is an important point about the refinement of acting since the 1970s. Katharine Hepburn herself did not make biopics set later than the Middle Ages and the Renaissance (*Lion in Winter* [1968] and *Mary of Scotland* [1936], for example) because her well-known and eccentric voice and distinctive features would have turned any modern figure into Katharine Hepburn. Thus, aside from folksy American types like Stewart, Fonda and Cooper, the most successful biopic stars were those, like Susan Hayward, who had voices that listeners probably could not have picked out on the radio. Even as late as *Patton* (1970), George C. Scott's makeup, costuming and posture were exact. But vocally, the commanding, temperamental General is all George C. Scott, reportedly because the producers thought that if the gravelly voiced Scott imitated Patton's high-pitched voice he might sound 'unnatural' (Toplin, 1996: 167). Thus, Scott's performance seems less transformative than would become the standard after 1980.

Another advantage for Blanchett in this colour film is that nearly all films and photographs of Hepburn in the late 1930s period being portrayed are in black and white. Thus with the public record in black and white and this film depicting private lives in colour (and until the late 1930s sequences of Scorsese's film, it is a defamiliarised, two-strip-Eddie Cantor-in-*Whoopee!* [1930]-colour at that), there aren't many points of comparison. Scorsese heightens this advantage further by not depicting Hepburn in her films; a shot of Blanchett with the leopard in *Bringing Up Baby* (1938) or in the moth costume in *Christopher Strong* (1933) probably would have destroyed the illusion Blanchett works so hard to build. In *I'm Not There* Todd Haynes protects his actors in a similar way by never having them lip-synch to Bob Dylan's own singing, only to that of cover artists, with Dylan's recordings used only extra-diegetically.

Stephen Hopkins, who directed Geoffrey Rush in *The Life and Death of Peter Sellers* (2004), failed to protect his actor in this way. The film itself, coming out in the same season as *The Aviator, Ray* and *Kinsey*, is another perfect example of the neo-classical biopic revival of the 2000s. It combines warts-and-all, almost defiantly making its subject unlikeable, and the *Kane* paradigm, with the multiple perspectives all Sellers, who plays the other people in his life in outlandishly self-serving ways. It ends with Sellers presiding over the ending credits (a la *Man on the Moon* [1999]) and then ducking into his trailer, warning, 'You can't come in here.' Rush renders the maddening charm, cruelty, selfishness and almost feral quality of the frighteningly talented Sellers, playing him as a prodigious wild child who, if left in a room for five minutes, will harm himself and others. The brilliance and truthfulness of Rush's portrayal and of the film's concept are almost wrecked, however, by moments in which Rush competes with Sellers in movie scenes that many fans know by heart, such as President Muffley's phone call to the Soviet premier in *Dr. Strangelove* (1964) or Inspector Clouseau's 'Fact!' speech in *A Shot in the Dark* (1964). These scenes from movies are done perfunctorily and indifferently; did Rush want to put his own stamp on these roles? If so, he could have made his own Clouseau comedy (as nearly everyone else has, it seems). Allowing Harvey Pekar to break in on Paul Giamatti's performance is postmodern playfulness; to have Geoffrey Rush try out alternate line readings of universally known Peter Sellers performances is simply ill-advised mimicry, where the body really is too much.

The body-too-much concept has been parodied, pastiched and expanded beyond its limits by Todd Haynes. In *Velvet Goldmine* (1998), his *film à clef* about the glitter rock era of the mid-1970s, the director found in Jonathan Rhys-Meyers and Ewan McGregor reasonable facsimiles of David Bowie and Iggy Pop. Earlier, however, in his 'outlaw' biopic, *Superstar: The Karen Carpenter Story* (1987), he 'cast' as Karen Carpenter, the pop singer who died from effects of anorexia nervosa, a Barbie doll, whose face he cut to simulate the appearance of makeup to indicate her emaciation; the impossibly thin dimensions of the doll do the rest. Thus, in posing against the actual Karen 'a body too small', casting is metaphor, both for Karen Carpenter and for the body image superimposed onto women by consumer culture. An actress's voice emotes for Karen, while recordings of the Carpenters' songs, in the copyright infringement that rendered the film illegal, complete the illusion. Nonetheless, what could have been a sick joke takes on unexpected emotional depth and resonance. Haynes parodies the tour de force acting of the melodramatic biopic, as a poster to the film's page on Internet Movie Database recognised by writing: 'Barbie gives an Oscar-calibre performance!' With the substitution of Barbie for Karen, Karen Carpenter's music takes the place of the body of the real Karen, much the way that Raoul Peck turns his documentary camera into the ghost of Patrice Lumumba in *Lumumba: Death of the Prophet* (1992). The body was burned long before.

In *I'm Not There* Haynes displaced the body-too-much issue onto bodies-too-many, again allowing the subject, in this case Bob Dylan, to escape amid the confusion. Repeating what Mary Ann Doane has characterised as Haynes's tendency to indulge in the obvious (Doane, 2004: 13). Haynes makes a two-way mirror out of the one-way reflection whereby the actor plays the subject. Oliver Stone, for example, invites us to find Nixon in Anthony Hopkins, but we would not see Hopkins in the historical Nixon, except in the most clichéd 'Don Ameche invented the telephone' sense. *I'm Not There* invites us to see Dylan in Cate Blanchett, while also asking us to see Cate Blanchett, as a woman, in Bob Dylan, as well as asking us to see an African American 12-year-old (Marcus Carl Franklin) and Woody Guthrie in him. In his memoir, *Chronicles, Volume One* Dylan describes seeing the Denzel Washington film, *The Mighty Quinn* (1989), whose title came from one of Dylan's songs: 'Denzel Washington. He must have been a fan of mine . . . I wondered if Denzel could play Woody Guthrie. In my dimension of reality, he certainly could have' (Dylan, 2004: 187). Jude, in the pastiche of a sequence in *Eat the Document* (1971), even wears a drawn-on, handle-bar moustache, as if his masculinity, like his famous press conferences of the time, is a jest. The effect of this is subversive, opening Dylan to the gendered inquiry previously closed off by what Haynes refers to as Dylan's 'reputation as a "guys' artist"' (IFC News, 2007).

A publicity 'introduction' to *I'm Not There* calls Blanchett's Jude Quinn 'the only character who looks and sounds like Dylan'. Actually this both is and is not true. Blanchett's is the only full impersonation, but each of the other actors is at least suggesting elements of Dylan. Bale gives the impression of the awkward, painfully inarticulate Dylan who first became a star as a folk singer; Ben Whishaw suggests the adept, wily Dylan who might have wanted to be the poet, Arthur Rimbaud, and calls up the cadences and vocal rhythms of a more erudite Dylan. Richard Gere, who has never allowed a director to make him look this dishevelled on-screen before, plays Dylan as if the singer were starring in an 'outlaw whose time has passed' 1970s Western; of course the middle-aged Gere is named Billy the Kid, who was played by a young and clean-shaven Kris Kristofferson in Peckinpah's *Pat Garrett and Billy the Kid* (1973), in which Dylan also acted and for which he wrote the music. Kristofferson does show up, off camera like Dylan, as a narrator; and the actor (Heath Ledger) playing Bale's Dylan in a 1965 biopic conveys Haynes's awareness of the body-too-much effect, while in the scenes of his private life recalling the Kristofferson of 1970s domestic dramadies such as *Blume in Love* (1973) and *Alice Doesn't Live Here Anymore* (1974).

The idea that Blanchett is doing the only completely embodied, transformative portrayal in the film is intriguing, as if it takes a woman to be Dylan. 'The amazing thing' about her performance, says Haynes, 'is that she's just wearing a wig, eyebrows, a toothguard, and that's it' (Haynes, 2008: Ch. 11: 50:00). Blanchett is the only one with filmed record to work from; a number of her scenes are re-enactments of moments in the D. A. Pennebaker documentary, *Don't Look Back* (1967), which covered the 1965 British tour, which was largely a lovefest, and the little-seen *Eat the Document*, which covered the 1966 British tour when Dylan caught the fans' full venom at his having 'gone electric' and which occurred shortly before the July motorcycle crash that called a hiatus to his career. Haynes and his writing partner Owen Moverman had always had a woman in mind for Jude Quinn because of Dylan's performance and behaviour in 1966, 'the way he spoke, his gestures, everything about him . . . is not evident in *Don't Look Back* from a year earlier and would never return again . . . It was androgynous . . . like channeling Patti Smyth of a decade later . . . His flamboyance and foppery during that time is really profound' (IFC News, 2007).

'Jude', as in 'Judas', which Dylan was famously called from the crowd at the Manchester Town Centre in 1966, but also in 'Hey Jude', indicating the mutual influence between Dylan and the Beatles at this time: 'Remember to let *her* under your skin', write Lennon and McCartney. 'Quinn', is as in the song 'The Mighty Quinn', about Quinn the Eskimo, a cool customer. In *Superstar* Haynes performed an acute examination of the female biopic and its reliance on victimisation and the downward narrative trajectory, as if the woman is punished for her ambition. Jude has no private life; the black and white in which she/he is photographed has the effect of trapping her in a bubble, to be looked at by others. In a sense, she is in the same trap as Karen Carpenter, ruled by what others think and expect of her. Karen never recognises what is happening to her. Jude, like Brian Slade, the glam rock idol in *Velvet Goldmine*, fakes his/her death as the only way out. Because the Dylan of Pennebaker's Direct Cinema classic is mocking, self-effacing, arrogant, polite, cruel (to Joan Baez, whom he ignores and lets others in his entourage make fun of), focused (typing lyrics in the hotel room in the midst of all kinds of commotion), passionate, calm, passive-aggressive and direct, Blanchett plays all of these facets, but most of all the ducking, spinning-out-of-control Dylan who still tries to maintain at least her/his cool. Haynes audaciously portrays Jude Quinn the way Dylan's songs often portray women – as inconstant, unfaithful, shrill, flighty, unpredictable, deadly and betraying. Jude machine-guns the crowd at the 'New England Folk and Jazz Festival' ('Folk and Jazz?'), has flirtations with Beatles (even as he pokes fun at them in his lyrics, as in 'Some Englishman said "Fab"' in 'Bob Dylan's 116th Dream' [1965]), and is undependable – in short, 'Just Like a Woman'.

Moreover, Blanchett's Jude wanders through the film with the self-destructive cluelessness of many a female biopic subject, from Susan Hayward in *I'll Cry Tomorrow* (an antecedent for Haynes's *Superstar*) to Jessica Lange in *Frances* to Blanchett herself in the female biopic-as-victimology throwback, *Veronica Guerin* (2003). Jude is the out of control, despised, blamed, downward trajectory stage of Dylan (in one shot, set in Andy Warhol's 'Factory', he even peers into a long downward spiral). Haynes circumvents the 'body too much' issue. In casting six actors of, shall we say, diverse physiogamy, he is conceding that his Dylan is a representation, or rather multiple interpretations, and implies that there could be other ways to suggest 'Dylan' than what we see here.

Performance in the postmodern biopic, therefore, demonstrates a contradiction, in which in terms of the arts of cinema and of acting the expectations are of complete illusion. Reviews often refer to this or that actor having 'channelled' a subject. The ideal is a completely successful illusion, with space between the original body, the body of the referent, and 'the body too much' entirely closed. On the other hand, postmodernity rejects the unitary subject, for a host of reasons. These include a Brechtian attitude towards representation, a disbelief in objectivity or in 'reality' as anything other than a cultural and political construction, a psychological approach to the complexities of personality, and a multiperspectived approach to the telling of history and the events of lives. Memory, subjectivity – these have deepened and complicated the treatment of lives in the biopic. What we see in *American Splendor*, *Centre Stage*, *I'm Not There* and other contemporary biopics are a multiplicity

4.3 Male icon re-imagined as female biopic subject. Cate Blanchett as Bob Dylan (and vice versa) in *I'm Not There*

of viewpoints and a fragmentation of notions of unitary subjectivity. Attending these is a fluidity in approaches to performance, one that has always been part of the actor's preparation, but that more and more is visible in the performances of actors as they collaborate with directors in the proving ground of the biopic.

Notes

1 Julian Stringer (1997) has read *Centre Stage* as an expression of the myriad anxieties felt in Hong Kong into the years leading up to the 1997 'handover' of the city from British to Chinese rule.

References

Alexander, S. and L. Karaszewski (1999) 'Introduction', *Man on the Moon: The Shooting Script*, New York: Newmarket.

Comolli, J.-L. (1978) 'Historical Fiction: A Body Too Much' *Screen*, 19 No. 2 (Summer): 41–51.

Custen, G. F. (1992) *Bio/Pics: How Hollywood Constructed Public History*, New Brunswick, NJ: Rutgers University Press.

Doane, M. A. (2004) 'Pathos and Pathology: The Cinema of Todd Haynes', *Camera Obscura*, 19, No. 3: 1–20.

Dylan, B. (2004) *Chronicles, Volume One*, New York: Simon & Schuster.

Fischer, P. (2003) 'Paul Giamatti/*American Splendor*', www.femail.com.au/paul_giamatti_american_splendor.htm (c. January), accessed 20 April 2008.

Hagopian, K. J. (2006) 'Hollywood Restoration: Genre and the American Film Industry in the Culture of American Affirmation, 1936–45', PhD dissertation, University of Wisconsin.

Haynes, T. (2008) *I'm Not There*, DVD Director's Commentary, Special Features, Santa Monica, California: The Weinstein Company Home Entertainment.

'Heroine's Reel Life Outstripped by Real Version' (2000), *Times of London* 29 March.

IFC News (2007) 'Todd Haynes: Using 6 Actors to Play Bob Dylan in "I'm Not There"' (2007) Independent Film Channel (IFC) News, 3 October, www.youtube.com/watch?v=HBAsheMKy0s&feature=related, accessed 28 December 2007.

Inside the Actor's Studio (1997) Interview with Tommy Lee Jones, Bravo TV Network, US airdate, 26 March.

Rosenstone, R. (1995) *Visions of the Past: The Challenge of Film to Our Idea of History*, Cambridge, MA: Harvard University Press.

Rosenstone, R. (2007) 'In Praise of the Biopic', in *Lights, Camera, History: Portraying the Past in Film*, College Station: Texas A & M Press, 11–29.

Siskel, G. and R. Ebert (1993) Review of *Chaplin*, US airdate, 8 January, http://bventertainment.go.com / tv / buenavista / ebertandroeper / index2.html?sec=1&subsec=839, accessed 16 May 2008.

'Spotlight on Location: The Making of Erin Brockovich' (2000) *Erin Brockovich*, DVD Special Features, Universal City, California: Universal Home Video.

Stringer, J. (1997) 'Centre Stage: Reconstructing the Biopic', *CineAction*, 42 (February): 28-39.

Svetkey, B. (2008) 'Playing President' *Entertainment Weekly*, 16 May: 22–29.

Toplin, R. B. (1996) *History by Hollywood: The Use and Abuse of the American Past*, Urbana, IL: University of Illinois Press.

5

Borders and boundaries in *Deadwood*

Steven Peacock

The US serial drama *Deadwood* (HBO, 2004–06) charts the birth of an American frontier town at a time when 'the forces of social order and anarchy are still in tension' (Pye, 1996: 10). It is set in 1876, in Deadwood, an outlaw camp in the Black Hills. In focusing on the daily lives of the camp's inhabitants, on the founders, settlers and outsiders, the series explores the constantly shifting negotiations of changing ways. Following many prior examples of the Western from television and film, *Deadwood* is concerned with the fundamental theme of settlement, exploring the creation and closure of the frontier as a line between urbanised, civilised society and untamed wilderness and wildness. The series is distinctive in its sustained and intricate use of this thematic opposition to explore borders and boundaries. It achieves depth and complexity in its handling of established generic demarcations; in turn it is alert to the boundaries of roles performed within the Western genre, in the diegetic social enclave of Deadwood town. Through an expressive integration of performers and performances in this particular Western world's settings, the series also explores the boundaries of language, the physical border of setting and locale, and the limits of characterisation, as it embraces and breaches the boundaries of Western 'types'.

The richness of *Deadwood*'s involvement with the central syntax of the Western is inextricably linked to its status as a work of television. It uses the restraints and possibilities of television – or TV's own borders and boundaries – to develop the genre. A survey of previous TV Westerns, from the genre's heyday in the 1950s and 1960s, shows little evidence of similar qualities, of a richness of physical and verbal expression, a sensitive handling of locale, or complex characterisation. There are different pleasures to be found there, than in the murky, loquacious and layered world of *Deadwood*. Series such as *Gunsmoke* (CBS, 1955–75) and *Rawhide* (CBS, 1959–66) are bound by a tight economy of structure, language and movement that is at times taut, at others restricted and restrictive. Characters such as Rowdy Yates (Clint Eastwood in *Rawhide*) have a form and economy of gestures and words that is firm and stark, each act or oration being singularly purposeful. Coming before the multi-strand narratives of contemporary serial drama, these series channel their efforts into the constraints of a single line of action, encapsulated by *Rawhide*'s ever-rolling cattle drive. The series' also follow a clear-cut moral code, stripped of complexity or ambiguity. There is little expansiveness to these tales of Westward expansion.

As a further point of comparison, there are myriad cinematic Westerns that deal (with varying levels of skill) with the thematic opposition of civilisation and wilderness in an integration of performance, setting and scenario. To exemplify, this concern is captured in a moment from John Ford's 1946 film *My Darling Clementine*. Accompanied by his brothers Morgan and Virgil, Wyatt Earp (Henry Fonda) takes on the job of town marshal to avenge the death of sibling James. The film comprises Ford's retelling of the infamous Western feud between the Earp and Clanton clans, and the showdown at the OK Corral. Moreover, *My Darling Clementine* is alert to the *balancing* of a particular performer's attributes with a specific situation. In this respect, the moment in question is pivotal in more ways than one. About 30 minutes into the film, a long shot reveals Fonda-as-Earp rocking back on a chair outside Tombstone's hostelry; one foot rests against a solid vertical timber with the other on the ground. His tall frame crooks into a diagonal leaning position. A stagecoach arches around to stop in front of the seated marshal, blowing up some dust and trouble. The moment offers a good meeting point between this film and the later television text, as Earp asks the unwelcome visitor, 'How are things in Deadwood?' While emphasising the need for his villainous 'friend' to travel on ('Get yourself some flapjacks . . . the stagecoach is leaving in 30 minutes – make sure you're on it'), Earp remains stock still, sitting yet also suspended on the leaning chair.

In this moment, a complex of the performer's and scenario's leading characteristics hangs together. Fonda brings to the film a tall and statuesque figure, a looming yet delicate presence, grace combined with a gangling stiffness. In the sequence, in the world of this film, Fonda-as-Earp tries to find his bearings: bending into an awkward position as the rowdy town's marshal; expressing the firmness of his position with a sense of underlying uncertainty; testing the ground. The critic David Thomson hints at the expressive complications of the performer's situation in this instance as he states that, 'Fonda edged deeper into the American myth

5.1 A pivotal moment in *My Darling Clementine*

as Wyatt Earp, sat precariously on a veranda, his feet propped up on a post' (Thomson, 2002: 298). The film and Fonda perform a balancing act, deftly holding on the Western fulcrum point between civilisation and wilderness. In the framing of the sequence, a synthesis of cultivated and natural structures is sensed as the building's wooden strut (supporting Earp's foot) and the stalk of a cactus plant meet in line. As Deborah Thomas suggests, in reference to a neighbouring moment of the film (though equally pertinent here), *My Darling Clementine* achieves 'a perfect image of the reconciliation of East and West, town and landscape, artificial improvement and untouched natural beauty, with Wyatt at its centre as the focal-point and emblem of its harmonies' (Thomas, 2001: 19). Even as Earp squares up to an unwelcome visitor, in his physical position and performance, Fonda does not square off the town's boundaries: possibilities are held in suspension.

In contrast, there is disharmony and confusion in *Deadwood*. First, let us address the series' generic situation in terms of locale. The series immerses itself in the grimy intricacies of business in the world of the Western camp and, in doing so, muddies all clean *settlements*. In this way, *Deadwood* is akin to, and better understood by, certain considerations of Peter Stanfield in an essay on another settlement in another genre. In 'American as Chop Suey', Stanfield explores the cinematic portrayal of Chinatown found within examples of the Gangster film. He sees Chinatown represented in the Gangster genre as 'a country within a country, a city within a city', as a 'loose confederation that help[s] organise and exploit the illicit activities of gambling, prostitution and dope-peddling' (Stanfield, 2005: 241). Within this pocketed space, Stanfield discerns, time and again, 'a compelling image of an outlawed [culture] . . . which with ever-vigilant policing could be safely contained within the borders of Chinatown, located within, yet not part of, the United States' (2005: 239–240). These ideas are equally crucial to the situation of *Deadwood*. The Western outlaw camp exists as a self-governed cluster of dwellings set at once within America yet without the Unionised States. It is structured as a 'loose confederation' fuelled by 'illicit activities'. Moreover, the series is deeply concerned with the maintenance and rupturing of boundaries. The borders of this insular community are porous, allowing for the melding of primitive and civilised ways. Crucially, as the Union encroaches ever closer, the series questions which elements are primitive, which are civilised, putting the distinction under suspension. Deadwood camp is held together by its tight operation of vice, reckoning and retribution. There is order in anarchy. As representatives from the East and the Union cross borders into the camp, they bring the promise or threat of cultivation and regulation. At the meeting point of these forces, the notion of propriety is complicated.

Two further remarks by Stanfield encourage this understanding of *Deadwood* and lead us into thoughts on performing the spoken word. In Stanfield's analysis, the principal figures of Chinatown in the Gangster film genre are 'represented as hiding behind a veneer of respectability' (2005: 242). Equally, the permeation of borders between Chinatown and the outer world of America is seen to produce 'a potential collapse of the boundaries that separate self from other' (2005: 238). Both of these ideas are pertinent and pivotal to *Deadwood*'s performers' skilful handling of the spoken word. In its distinctive melding of arcane and profane language, the series explores the borderline meeting point of civilised and wild ways. Equally, in extensive monologues and involved exchanges, its performers explore the limits of verbal communication. The characters adopt and adapt cultivated forms of language, coming from beyond and through the porous boundaries of the camp, to shape their negotiations.

The expansiveness of television's serial form allows for a gradual and intricate development of these negotiations. In a long-running serial drama (and in a settlement on the edge of the frontier) there is an abundance of time for talk. *Deadwood*'s heightened language, at once florid and foul, achieves depth and complexity over the length of the series. At the same time, while *Deadwood*'s rich guttural scripts have been the subject of much prior scrutiny, the performers' work in delivering the lines (and not letting the words overshadow nuanced physical performances) has been overlooked.[1] Over time and in sustained, subtle yet striking acts of delivery, the primary shock of profanity and the disorienting flux of register give way to a sense of fluency, of rhythms shaped by arch or nuanced expression, flutters of gesture and fanciful patter, and timely terse jabs of curse words. In this television world, in this outlaw settlement, performers-as-citizens lay claim to permeations of high and low forms of expression. Certain performances reveal characters using language to hide 'behind a veneer of respectability' (Stanfield, 2005: 242), circumnavigating truths in distracting moves and circuitous conversations. Others use a mixed register to negotiate and enact 'the boundaries that separate self from other' (Stanfield, 2005: 238), to *manage* their situation. Some give and gain acknowledgement in body language; others use articulations of the spoken word to push meaning beyond the grasp of their company. Language is vital to the currency of information in Deadwood town. Public and private boundaries are often porous in the camp; in turn, information is overheard, circulated and exploited. The series is alert to the precise verbal and physical arrangements of each discussion, to how and when particular signs are revealed or sensed, and the shifting dynamic of control found in bodies and words in motion. Above all, *Deadwood* explores the way its performers shape gestures and words to overcome, or set in place, their characters' surrounding restrictions.

Many of these aspects, of the boundaries set, tested and crossed by body/spoken language, both vulgar and ornate, meet in a moment from Season Two. The moment comes in the closing stages of the second episode (2: 2). It marks the aftermath of a verbal and physical fight between saloon owner Al Swearengen (Ian McShane) and the newly self-appointed sheriff Seth Bullock (Timothy Olyphant). Following the fight and at the close of day, newspaper editor A. W. Merrick (Jeffrey Jones) visits the bruised Swearengen to take account of the brawl, ready for the press. Through close analysis of this sequence and these three characters' negotiations, the performers' and series' skilful exploration of recitative boundaries can be revealed. In particular, the moment illustrates *Deadwood*'s attention to the borders of physical revelations of emotion and knowledge; that is to say, inner thoughts and feelings hidden or shown in behavioural gestures, in speaking aloud, or in struggling to stay quiet. Arrangements of language, performance and positions both moral and physical mesh to form a micro-drama of (an) unsteady settlement.

The editor Merrick seeks testimony from saloon owner Swearengen. In his publicly aired insults and tussle with the Sheriff, Swearengen has physically crossed Deadwood's unspoken boundaries of social order, boundaries he himself has established as a leading figure of the camp. To encourage the anxious citizens of Deadwood to return to the streets, to conduct their daily business, Merrick requires personal acknowledgement from Swearengen that order has been restored. To reach settlement, the two men set and unsettle the defining lines of truth and the limits of decency. At the close of the day's business, Swearengen neatly packs away a sheaf of bank notes. In close-up, Swearengen's gnarled hands gather and tap the bundled money twice on the desktop. It is a gesture of sharp decision, in all ways economic. The collection and containment of moneyboxes the conversation, as it does all business in Deadwood. Money structures the negotiation and dictates the choice and route of words. Around this fixed standard, the other defining criteria of truth and decency become unfixed, yielding to the speakers' differing demarcations. As the two characters talk, Swearengen keeps close to the money: tapping the notes, slamming shut the moneybox lid, scooping the box to his chest. As well as expressing a firm kinship with wealth, the performer's concise gestures convey a tightening up, a packing down of emotion. Over the series, McShane's performance intricately compresses little acts of solidity, as if physically pressing down the character's explosive temperament. Occasionally though, in contrast, he suddenly releases all the carefully condensed anger on an unfortunate victim. Wary of such capacity, Johnson-as-Merrick delicately cajoles the fiery bar-owner. He stands stooped, haunches up, as if set for the sudden springing of Swearengen's temper. There is a further performative layer to acknowledge here. From his filmic pedigree, Jeffrey Johnson brings with him the markings of a supporting actor: typically, he attunes his performance of assuagement to blend in (with tone, surroundings, the ensemble cast) rather than stand out. In contrast, McShane (as the eponymous Lovejoy and as pivotal player Swearengen) offers a star television turn. In turn, Johnson can be seen to allow McShane the lion's share of dramatic space in which to move, speak and gesticulate. The series' handling of such positions is inextricably linked with the characters' own positioning and negotiations: the wily editor Merrick cow-towing with due reverence to Swearengen's grander orations and stance in the camp.

Called upon to present the facts, Swearengen tests the limits of decency in his descriptions. His initial words form a fusion of high and low language, of urbane and profane expression. Merrick is first cast by Swearengen as 'tenacious': a precise and eloquent report of the editor's behaviour. Yet, the eloquence of the expression is both troubled and made vivid in the addition of 'I'll fuckin' give you that.' The use of profanity, here as elsewhere in the series, is complex. Through a constant peppering of expletives, *Deadwood* tests the boundaries of television censorship. Equally, its use of profanity, although constant, is consistently meaningful. There is precision not only in the play and punctuation of swear-words in *Deadwood*, but also in the particular way they course from the actors' mouths, cherished and delivered with glee, coughed or spat out. For example, Swearengen, the 'swear-engine' of profanity and promises, curses for emphasis or release, to rouse, cajole or disarm his audience, to smooth or ruffle feathers. Swear-words comprise the keystones of Deadwood camp, markers of Western ways, opposed to the imported Eastern patter of refined speech. The series is alert to the fusion and confusion occurring when the two forms meet. Swearengen's phrasing in the moment under scrutiny is exemplary; the combination of 'tenacious' and 'fucking' forms a jarring imbalance of language, expressive of his desire to throw Merrick off balance in their negotiations.

The sense of Swearengen gaining the upper hand through base expression develops in the use of the word 'cunt', sounded as the moneybox snaps shut. Again, a tension arises as Swearengen couples and topples a passage of heightened prose with profanity. In answer to Merrick's invitation for a recount of the fight, Swearengen replies, 'after the conflict's genesis I'd laid at cunt's doorstep; now, has "cunt" one "N" and two "T"s or the other way around?' 'Conflict's genesis' is a grand opening to the tale, elevating the account, in its origins, to almost Biblical proportion. The sense of elevation is suddenly curtailed, in an abrupt fall from grace, by the violent reduction of language to 'cunt'. The impression of the word is enforced by Swearengen in wanting to spell it correctly for the newspaper; one conjures the image of the word marked in indelible form.

Further, Swearengen's querying of the correct spelling conveys his desire for just this word to be used, that his choice is precise. While shocking, it is also telling. While Swearengen's account of the brawl is indecent, it is also truthful. The vulgar word encapsulates the violence of the event, and echoes the language used in the moment. In turn, it also most precisely marks the reason for the brawl, as Swearengen accuses Bullock of being 'cunt-stricken' in his affair with the widow Garrett (Molly Parker), shirking his sheriff's duties for the pleasures of sex. The language of the gutter is also the true language of the street, of the camp's denizens, or 'hoople-heads', to use the parlance of *Deadwood*. In the series, swearing holds a claim to truth, whereas cultivated language is distrusted because it presents a 'veneer of respectability' that borders on falsehood.

Moreover, in truth the daily business of the camp is marked and informed by vulgarities of sexuality. To recall and assign one of Stanfield's remarks to *Deadwood*, the camp is 'a loose confederation that help[s] organise and exploit the illicit activities of gambling, prostitution and dope-peddling' (2005: 241). Prostitution is central to the social and economic order of the camp. A controlling figure of this primitive institution, Swearengen's choice of word strips the business of all and any claims to cultivation or decency, laying bare its truths. As the saloon owner reminds Merrick, 'you *solicited* a true account'. At base level, 'cunt' comprises the camp's bedrock. In reducing his language for impact, crossing the boundaries of decency, Swearengen broaches a truth that is everywhere visible but rarely acknowledged.

As the negotiations develop, the series is sensitive to the dynamics of gesture, words and setting. The characters climb the stairs to Swearengen's private quarters, shaping the public account of the fight. As they move upwards they elevate their choice of words. While truthful, Swearengen's guttural descriptions must be recast in heightened prose, to fit in line with the editor's definitions of decency. As Merrick claims, '[He] would define as true and decent in such endeavour the facts rendered fully, within social standards and sensibility, without bias and abridgement.' As both men work to settle on the boundaries of their testament, they negotiate a series of dividing planes, of what lies within and without the limits of truth and decency. Standing on the staircase, in the doorway between bedroom and balcony, the characters are suspended between levels.[2] As the men move across the landing, the terms 'truth' and 'decency' cross and re-cross in each character's claims to their meaning. Swearengen lays claim to the truthfulness of his account and the decency of his actions, against the deceitful indecency of Bullock's infidelity. Yet, a 'decent' or more tolerable truth will help restore the status quo, and re-state decent standards of behaviour, in turn assisting both men in their fidelity to matters of money. In their physical positioning, in particular the squaring and slumping of shoulders, the two actors conduct a tussle for control. Moving to set the moneybox down on his bedside dresser, the beaten Swearengen bends down, wincing with pain. Merrick seizes the opportunity to take the upper hand: back straight and arms outstretched, he entreats the barman to present a final clear account. Crucially however,

5.2 Merrick's brief gain of the upper hand in *Deadwood*

McShane-as-Swearengen regains control through a stance of declination. The painful flinch becomes a flick, as Swearengen shucks off his overcoat and dismisses Merrick's play for 'top dog'. He turns a momentary weakness into an underhand position of insidious authority, shrugging off coat and request, slipping onto his bed to deliver a final soliloquy:

> Tonight, through Deadwood, heads may be laid to pillows assuaged and reassured for that purveyor for profit of everything sordid and vicious Al Swearengen, already beaten to a fare-thee-well earlier in the day by Sheriff Bullock, has returned the implements and ornaments of his office. Without the tawdry walls of Swearengen's saloon, the Gem, decent citizens may pursue with a new and jaunty freedom all aspects of Christian commerce.

Again, words demarcate borders in the camp. There are lines drawn between spaces within and without: if you are 'without the tawdry walls of Swearengen's saloon' you are safe. Yet, crucially, in the development of the moment, Swearengen's words cross boundaries, permeating through the camp. Equally, McShane carefully toys with breaking (through) a staunchly observed principle of filmed dramatic performance. As he lays down his head and tale, his eyes come close to fixing the camera with a piercing gaze; the actor encroaches on 'talking heads' territory by threatening to rupture the fictional world's intrinsic workings in delivering a direct address. Yet, crucially, the gesture of acknowledgement is only

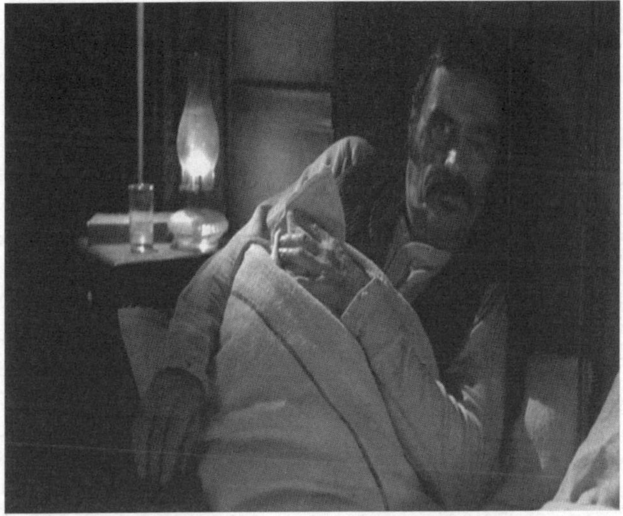

5.3 Swearengen's bedtime story in *Deadwood*

partially achieved; one eye remains bruised and swollen, and glares a little off-centre. The other flits and skims the camera's own eye, taunting in directness. As Swearengen's words blanket the camp, McShane tugs softly at his bedspread: while a gesture of childish comfort, it suggests how the saloon-owner's presence mantles the camp: when all is said and done, he has it at his fingertips.

Perhaps recalling the narrator's voice at the beginning and end of Dylan Thomas' *Under Milk Wood*, Swearengen's words drift across the settlement, enveloping the sight of Sheriff Bullock standing outside his home. Again, private boundaries are porous; Swearengen is positioned as the controlling agent. In turn, there is a sense that Bullock stands still, as if awaiting authority to move; the hushed low tones of Swearengen's voice magically usher him inside the home. There are more influences at work, too. The Sheriff's stance in this moment strongly recalls that of Fonda-as-Earp's in the earlier instance from *My Darling Clementine.* On the edge of his homestead, Bullock rests his foot on a wooden plinth suspended above a dividing stream; the situation, it seems, is rocky. Like his earlier filmic associate, the Sheriff stands at the meeting point of archetypal Western oppositions, of nature and civilisation. There are further adjacencies between the two actors. Olyphant-as-Bullock uses his tall and athletic frame in much the same way as Fonda in the earlier

5.4 Bullock's rocky situation in *Deadwood*

text. Whereas Swearengen is mostly confined to the Gem in the series, the Sheriff is often viewed striding around Deadwood camp. Olyphant walks with the wary purpose of a lawman in unruly terrain, channelling Fonda's lean, stiff grace: his eyes have a feline flash and his legs a nimble gait, yet he always swivels his neck and walks as if carrying a book on his head, always *poised*. Like Fonda precariously leaning on the chair, Olyphant the reluctant Sheriff expresses an attitudinal balancing point.

In this particular instance, his stance is also emblematic of another Western trope: the outside world of 'men and their doings' and the domestic space of the woman.[3] After suggesting Bullock's suspension on the meeting point of such set zones, the series sustains attention on the image of the foot to trouble this generic boundary. Entering the home, Bullock insists on bringing his boots inside. Subsequently, the Sheriff places his returned gun in the hearth for his son to see. Again, in line and action, *Deadwood* muddies the clean partitions of the television Western genre. Spaces in the series are not claimed by male or female characters, as domesticated or wild. All archetypes of role and theme are acknowledged, and then troubled, made complex.

The assignation and complication of generic roles are also conveyed in Swearengen's monologue. In the narration of his account, Swearengen proffers a view that appears to affirm the orderly roles of the civilised

Western community. The saloon-owner casts himself as 'that purveyor for profit of everything sordid and vicious', who has been castigated by the law-enforcing Sheriff. To restore order, Swearengen has 'returned the implements and ornaments of [Bullock's] office', namely the classic Western totem of a sheriff's authority, his gun. The form of the account reveals its complexity. Swearengen's words, initially crude and honest, are now presented with the 'veneer of respectability' offered by official reportage. They are designed to re-affirm the boundaries of respectable behaviour, demarking moral ground, separating self and other.

In tone and musical accompaniment, the monologue carries the airs of a bedtime story, of a fairytale starkly recounting the triumph of good over evil. Swearengen's comforting tale covers the camp. It casts the day's events in mythical form, as a myth of the binary world of the Western, of good versus evil, of forces set 'within' and 'without'. It counters the series' constant blurring of strict moral boundaries and the complexities of the characters' roles in the world of Deadwood. The series consistently adopts and adapts stock types. For instance, counter to the 'official line' of Swearengen's report, the generic Western convention of a close relationship between the hero and villain is ambiguous, a sense informed by the ambiguities of the characters' moral standing.[4] Bullock is forced into adopting the role of sheriff; he enters into an affair with the widow Garrett; Swearengen's Old Testament law offers unspoken protection to weaker occupants of the camp.

Deadwood achieves density and detail in its negotiation of roles, in its characters attempts to maintain, define or blur borders and boundaries of roles to their own advantage. Moreover, these attempts are explored across television's extended boundaries. That is to say, the longevity of the serial and the form of the ensemble drama allow *Deadwood* gradually to reveal tensions or facets of personalities, divided loyalties and the intricate workings of a community of characters. Crucially, the series explores its characters' efforts to test limits of prescribed roles to again engage in the fusion and confusion of civilised and primitive ways. The citizens of Deadwood take on multiple roles, playing games with official positions. For example, the insidious hotelier E. B. Farnum (William Sanderson) takes on the role of mayor, with increasing self-awareness that his position is mainly ceremonial. Equally, many of the characters are involved in double-dealing, in double-crosses, deception and disguises. Over time, the character of the schoolmistress shifts in disposition from a refined and respectable Eastern lady to reveal her manipulative and murderous nature. Perhaps most intriguingly, the same actor (Garret Dillahunt) is cast in two different roles. In Season One, he appears as Jack McCall, the feral killer of Wild Bill Hickok; in Season Two, Dillahunt returns as the cultivated Mr. Wolcott, right hand man to George Hearst. While apparently contrary – the former a stalwart figure of the Old West, the latter a man of Eastern manners with a 'veneer of respectability' – they form two sides of one treacherous figure of man, joining civilised and wild ways as indivisible.

Through agile performances shaped by a firmly established genre, *Deadwood* achieves a final blurring of boundaries: between the 'type' and the 'individual'. The television series is fully aware of the character 'types' that systematically inhabit the Western landscape; as we have seen, it revels in emboldening and complicating the traits of the Villain and the Sheriff. We can add to this list the 'types' of the Eastern lady, the camp's troubled Doctor, the Whore, the Housewife, the Drunk, the Prospector, and so on. It is a particular accomplishment of *Deadwood* and its performers to recognise the possibilities within the putative limitations of such 'types', as well as to inform such roles with rich and intricate personalities.

Whereas many modern Western films seek to overturn or invert conventional 'types' in revisionist or postmodern treatises (*The Quick and the Dead* (Sam Raimi, 1995); *Brokeback Mountain* (Ang Lee, 2005); *No Country for Old Men* (The Coen Brothers, 2007)), *Deadwood* holds true to the form of stock characters. Some critics of the series view this adherence to 'type' as a failing; Tim Goodman represents this camp as he suggests how, while 'ably re-creating Western characters blown into our memories over time – dangerous prostitutes, loveable drunks, sane bartenders, trigger-happy opportunists . . . the trouble with *Deadwood* is the trouble with most Westerns: the archetypes have become caricatures, people we don't necessarily believe in because they exist only at amusement parks and in hokey local parades' (Goodman, 2004). Rather, I would suggest that some performers in *Deadwood* (perhaps best represented by Olyphant and Parker) encourage a restraint of the kind of broad-brush actorly tics and mannerisms that normally pass for dramatic characterisation on television (see *24*'s streak of singular defining traits that are meant to transcend 'type' and inject a sense of pseudo-realism, for example). In place, they cast themselves in performative profile, distinguished by (and not against) their time-honoured 'type' in a similar way to classical Hollywood performers such as Fonda or Jean Arthur.

At the same time, *Deadwood*'s ensemble also comprises stalwart character actors, bringing their own feathering of 'type' to the series (such as Johnson and Brad Dourif as Deadwood's doctor); further still, there are those who test the boundaries of performative extremes of 'type'. This group (represented most strongly by McShane) is not only alert to the characteristic attributes, moves, gestures and expressions of their Western characters' filmic forefathers, but seek to push against the limits of 'acceptable levels' of dramatic performance. As in his remonstrations of Merrick the Editor, McShane-as-Swearengen often whoops and hollers his way around the Gem; yet there is a balancing act as precise as Earp's chair here - his supercharged expressive register never tips into parody, but adds a sad, pantomimic quality to the portrait of a man who refuses to accept the inevitability of change and more modern designs. Swearengen's revelry in his 'type' reveals a stubbornness to remain closed off from the world, even as Deadwood begins to open its borders.

It is in this respect that *Deadwood*'s handling of 'type' calls to mind remarks made by Stanley Cavell in *The World Viewed*. Speaking of film, Cavell notes that:

> Types are exactly what carry the forms movies have relied upon. These media created new types, or combinations and ironic reversals of types; but there they were, and stayed. Does this mean that movies can never create individuals, only types? What it means is that this is the movies' way of creating individuals: they create *individualities*. For what makes someone a type is not his similarity with other members of that type but his striking separateness from other people. (Cavell, 1979: 33)

Deadwood offers a rare instance of a work of television achieving this particular filmic quality, as Cavell understands it: a creation of 'individualities' in 'types' that express a 'striking separateness from other people'. Swearengen as a 'type' is most salient here, as that of a man surrounded by members of his 'gang' and the ghostly figures of Western villains past, manoeuvring the camp's denizens as pawns, twirling words in grand orations, and yet standing utterly alone. Equally, the series' total combining of genre and performance repeatedly offers other examples of separateness: the occasional extrovert delivery of an introspective monologue by Doc Cochran or E. B. Farnum (adroitly delivered and spiked by Dourif and Sanderson) is at once a celebration of their types' 'lot' in the world of Deadwood as camp and *Deadwood* as Western; at the same time it is a eulogy to separateness: acknowledging the bind between self and others, it is a private performance to no-one and everyone.

The series' handling of individuality in type and interest in isolation recall another extraordinary voice found in the neighbouring realm of film criticism: that of Manny Farber. More precisely, it encourages a return to Farber's notorious thesis 'White Elephant Art vs. Termite Art'. I would like to conclude by claiming that, in its acute understanding and its *own* intricate performance of a Western, *Deadwood* digs its way into the strata of termite art. There is not space here to pull apart the complexities of Farber's polemic; we could follow the writer's succinct summary of the two categories found in the introduction of *Negative Space* as a good starting point: 'white elephant and termite, one tied to the realm of celebrity and affluence and the other burrowing into the nether world of privacy' (Farber, 1971: 11). A further description leads more directly to the overarching tendencies in *Deadwood* set out in this chapter: 'Good work usually arises where the creators . . . seem to have no ambitions towards gilt culture but are involved in a squandering-beaverish endeavour that isn't anywhere or for anything. A peculiar fact about termite-tapeworm-fungus-moss art is that it goes always forward eating its own boundaries, and likely as not, leaves nothing in its path other than the signs of eager, industrious, unkempt activity' (1971: 135). The strange use of words like 'tapeworm', 'fungus', 'beaverish' seem peculiarly appropriate to *Deadwood*'s designs – the series flings us into the lairs and hideaways of a grubby world and rarely do we come up for air, let alone escape the confines of the camp. Unless elevated to survey the settlement from Swearengen's balcony (another position of perceived superiority and striking separateness), the camera keeps us close to the dark heart of a 'country within a country'.

More precisely, Farber offers examples of 'termite performances' in the Western film that strike me as comparable to some of the opaque, hard-to-articulate qualities to be found in *Deadwood*'s company. Farber interprets John Wayne's performance in *The Man Who Shot Liberty Valance* (1962) as:

> Infected by a kind of hoboish spirit, sitting back on its haunches doing a bitter-amused counterpoint to the pale, neutral film life around him . . . Wayne is the termite actor focusing only on a tiny present area, nibbling at it with engaging professionalism and a hipster sense of how to sit in a chair leaned against the wall . . . As he moves along at the pace of a tapeworm, Wayne leaves a path that is only bits of shrewd intramural acting – a craggy face filled with bitterness, jealousy, a big body that idles luxuriantly, having long grown tired with roughhouse games played by old wrangler types like Ford. (1971: 136)

A surprising and evocative description leads to the startling discovery that, in a shared generic context, McShane is able to offer a similar kind of termite performance. As Swearengen, his milky hungry eyes seem to rootle out a midpoint, ready for some 'nibbling'; as he moves slowly up the stairs with Merrick for instance, there are 'bits' of shrewd acting to be found: adjusting his gait to press his weight against the moneybox, using it as a support to his words and moves; the slump of the coat off his shoulder; the pointed glare and tugged bedspread as he lays down to rest. Above all, there is the same weatherworn leathery texture to his performance, whisky-steeped and sour.

A further example takes us back to Henry Fonda, and to a ready comparison with Olyphant-as-Bullock:

> Fonda's defensiveness (he seems to be vouchsafing his emotion and talent to the audience in tiny blips) comes from having a supremely convex body and being too modest to exploit it. Fonda's entry into a scene is that of a man walking backward, slanting himself away from the public eye. Once in a scene, the heavy jaw freezes, becomes like a concrete abutment, and he affects a clothes-hanger stance, no motion in either arm. (1971: 176)

An adjacent stance (in the scene, to acting in the scene) is adopted by Olyphant in moments across *Deadwood* – see, for instance, the gently stiff way he moves inside the house to speak with his wife at the end of the moment under scrutiny in 2: 2. Even while 'making up' with a loved one, in his lockjaw physical terseness, Bullock appears to silently withdraw himself from the experience of closeness. Aspects of isolation underline both of Farber's examples. In similar ways, the performances in *Deadwood* express the characters' remoteness from each other; at the same time, the bind across time and performative periods suggests an often overlooked form of *generic* conciliation. In seemingly moving far beyond the traditional conventions of the Western in its use of language, if Farber's interpretations are to be followed, then *Deadwood* appears to hark back to a classical mode of acting favoured by particular American stars (and, even more particularly, stars of the Western film). In its combination of individual performances, the series follows another set of boundaries, or recitative parameters, to achieve termite-art intimacy with its world.

Notes

1 Tim Goodman's (2004) critique summarises and tackles this pervasive analytical slant in his review of *Deadwood* for *The San Francisco Chronicle*, 19 March 2004.

2 The meeting points of space and sensibility in the relationship of these two characters is developed as the series progresses. As the connection between

Swearengen and Merrick grows closer, an inner door between their places of business is magically discovered. The is an open passageway between the machinations fostered in Swearengen's saloon and the newspaper's 'official line'. The doorway is a playful way for the series to take advantage of ongoing television drama's ability to change and adapt situations. A transitional space permits and ushers in the transitions of the series. It is also a physical expression of a central concern of *Deadwood*, of the forging and testing of alliances across natural boundaries.

3 John Saunders, in his analysis of the farmer's wife Marian (Jean Arthur) in *Shane* (George Stevens, 1953), states: 'The roles allotted to women in the Western are painfully circumscribed, and it is fitting that we should meet her indoors, the "Angel of the House", leaving the outside world to men and their doings' (Saunders, 2001: 16).

4 Saunders notes the archetypal relationship by making reference to Will Wright: 'Wright finds this [convention] sufficiently prevalent in the "classical" plot to warrant a separate category: "there is a strong friendship or respect between the hero and a villain" (1975: 45). Partly it suggests a professional respect which unites characters apparently separated by conventional moral criteria, or at least by social prejudice' (2001: 30).

References

Cavell, S. (1979) *The World Viewed: Reflections on the Ontology of Film*, Cambridge, MA and London: Harvard University Press.

Farber, M. (1971) *Negative Space: Manny Farber on the Movies*, London: Studio Vista Limited.

Goodman, T. (2004) '*Deadwood* Review', *The San Francisco Chronicle*, www.sfgate.com, accessed 7 September 2008.

Pye, D. (1996) 'Introduction: Criticism and the Western', in I. Cameron and D. Pye, eds., *The Movie Book of the Western*, London: Studio Vista.

Saunders, J. (2001) *The Western Genre: From Lordsburg to Big Whiskey*, London: Wallflower.

Stanfield, S. (2005) '"American as Chop Suey": Invocations of Gangsters in Chinatown, 1920–1936', in L. Grieveson, E. Sonnet and P. Stanfield, eds., *Mob Culture: Hidden Histories of the American Gangster Film*, Oxford: Berg Press.

Thomas, D. (2001) *Hollywood: Spaces and Meanings in American Film*, London: Wallflower.

Thomson, D. (2002) *The New Biographical Dictionary of Film*, London: Little, Brown.

Wright, W. (1975) *Six Guns and Society: A Structural Study of the Western*, Berkeley, CA: University of California Press.

6

The Colbert Report: performing the news as parody for the postmodern viewer

Gwendolyn Audrey Foster

While I still watch the 'news' on the three major American networks, as well as any number of other 'news networks', I have to admit at the outset that like most postmodern viewers I have a thorough distrust and mistrust of these 'news sources' which pretend at objectivity and deliver watered-down, safe, carefully crafted, carefully worded and carefully chosen news items. Increasingly, news agencies are compromised by allegiances to corporate sponsors such as pharmaceutical companies, automobile makers and other powerful marketing forces.

One could readily argue that the public's faith in official 'news' broadcasts is faltering to the breaking point; for many, the daily news, whether from the BBC or any of the three American networks (ABC, NBC or CBS), to say nothing of Fox News, Sky News, NPR and other news outlets, seems soft, pre-digested, and has all the authenticity of an Orwellian broadcast by Big Brother. Fox News is particularly egregious in its distortion of the facts, as noted in a number of studies by The Pew Research Center for the People and the Press and The University of Maryland. In his article on Maryland's research in this area, 'Survey: *Daily Show/ Colbert* Viewers Most Knowledgeable, Fox News Viewers Rank Lowest', on the website Think Progress, Nico Pitney reported:

> In 2003, University of Maryland researchers studied the public's belief in three false claims – that Iraq possessed WMD, that Iraq was involved in 9/11, and that there was international support for the U.S.-led invasion of Iraq. The researchers stated, 'The extent of Americans' misperceptions vary significantly depending on their source of news. Those who receive most of their news from Fox News are more likely than average to have misperceptions.' Fox News viewers were 'three times more likely than the next nearest network to hold all three misperceptions'.

Further, Ben Armbruster of Think Progress noted that the Pew Report of 17 August 2008 ('Key News Audiences Now Blend Online and Traditional Sources') found:

> Viewers of *The Daily Show* and *The Colbert Report* are more knowledgeable about current events than those who watch Bill O'Reilly, Lou Dobbs, Larry King, and the 'average consumers of NBC, ABC, Fox News, CNN, C-SPAN and daily newspapers.' Thirty percent of *Daily Show* and 34 percent of *Colbert* viewers correctly identified Secretary of State Condoleezza Rice, British Prime Minister Gordon Brown and the majority party in the U.S. House of Representatives, compared to the national average of just 18 percent.

These are just some of the reasons that programmes such as *The Colbert Report* and *The Daily Show* are becoming more and more pervasive; they offer up an alternative and arguably more honest version of the news in the guise of satire, which younger and more informed viewers – admittedly leaning to the left – find both more authoritative and more accessible; the reader is directed to the aforementioned Pew Report, cited below, for more details on Colbert's increasing influence among viewers seeking national news.

While younger viewers have tuned out the old news dinosaurs, many have drifted to 'infotainment' programmes that typically 'star' sexy but clearly uninformed 'hosts' who tell us about the latest mine collapse, horrific murder/suicide, college shooting spree and/or Britney Spears' latest personal meltdown as if they were equal in importance. After enough repetition, these events become part of a mind-numbing world of meta-news discourse, in which celebrity belly-bumps actually displace genuinely important international and national news events, to say nothing of reports from the warfront in Iraq. Repeatedly, audiences are told that we live in an exciting new age of access to information via news alternative sources and new media; that the truth is out there for all to see. But this really isn't the case.

We live in an era in which many seem to accept the axiom that 'too much information' is just enough information; or, more accurately, that scandal leads the daily news cycles. We need, or supposedly need, a layer of pundits and screaming, cajoling outsized news personalities from Nancy Grace to Bill O'Reilly to distil all this information. News has become an entertainment industry; it is no secret that the right wing is much better at producing talented, loud, seemingly informed, highly provocative personalities.

These pundits rail and seduce their audiences with their bullying styles, their refusal to play by the rules of objective reporting, their outrageous speech-acts in defiance of political correctness, their reduction of the news to the stories that suit them, privileging stories of sensation around the threat of Otherness (illegal immigration, the 'war' against marriage, the 'war' against the middle class, the threat of the liberal, and so on). Their programmes centre not so much on the news, but rather messianic figures of judgement such as Bill O'Reilly, who himself performs defiance, anger, a raised voice, mechanical performative gesticulations such as finger pointing, slamming of body parts on desks and verbal abuse of his guests, to the apparent delight of O'Reilly's audience.

Similarly, radio personalities such as Rush Limbaugh have found mass audiences who follow their every word as they spew malicious lies and distortions, and play into the fears that audiences have of a world gone to hell in a hand-basket. It is against this backdrop that left-leaning comics such as Jon Stewart began to develop a backlash of sorts with the rise of 'fake news' shows such as Jon Stewart's *The Daily Show* and Stephen Colbert's *The Colbert Report*. It isn't as if left-leaning news correspondents haven't tried to outmanoeuvre the O'Reillys and Limbaughs. They have tried, for example, with Air America, a leftist answer to powerful right-wing conservative radio; there are also myriad left-of-centre blogs and bloggers on the web. But for a postmodern audience, Stewart and Colbert's use of postmodern humour is much more successful, especially with young audiences.

Postmodern humour is deliberately ironic, self-referential, and partakes of a shared knowledge between performer and viewer that much of what we see and experience in contemporary society is inherently absurd. Audiences want entertainment, humour, with their news, but what makes Stewart and Colbert so wildly popular is their embrace of parody, pastiche, zany ideas taken from a page from the Marx Brothers' films, and plenty of 'wink–wink, nod–nod' from the playbook of Monty Python. Stewart and Colbert have elegantly tapped into the audience's desire for meta-discourse in all things. They have respect for their audiences, and acknowledge their intellect and postmodern approach to knowledge and 'fact'. The facts don't matter at all; opinion, masquerading as reportage, is the key ingredient of their respective shows. The forbidding anchor desks, hyperbolic graphics and equally fake news analysts employed by Stewart and Colbert perfectly mimic the style not only of mainstream newscasts but also of the 'news' programmes produced by Fox, CBN and other right-wing alternative news outlets.

As Alan Dale writes in *Comedy is a Man in Trouble*, satire, parody, pastiche and send-ups figure in a long line of 'festive abuse' from the days of the Medieval and Renaissance period that are themselves recalled in the Marx Brothers' *Duck Soup* (1933), wherein 'the Brothers demolish various upper-crust institutions and figures – government, high society, art collectors, academia, grand opera – and stand tall in the rubble, having freed, in the manner of the older holiday festivals' (2000: 132). But like those older festivals and the parodic performances of the Marx Brothers, the satire of Colbert and Stewart is not merely nihilistic or destructive. Quite the contrary. Writing on the power of satire on the citizen, Dale notes that 'satire is purposeful and usually compares its objects of ridicule to a norm of better behavior. *It hopes to ameliorate*' (2000: 132, my emphasis). Stewart and Colbert hope desperately to ameliorate the postmodern condition of praxis in the news industry.

Stewart and Colbert are very seriously engaged in a postmodern 'take back the nightly news' strategy of sorts. Jon Stewart himself is so obviously appalled at the lack of hard news reporting that he seems genuinely sad to report on the reporting (or lack thereof) of current news events, such as the failures of George W. Bush's presidency, inadequate news coverage of events such as the falling economy, the lack of government response to Hurricane Katrina, Darfur, the war in Afghanistan, and government waste and mismanagement, to name just a few of many possible topics. Stewart has been the host of *The Daily Show* since 1999, and he seems less able to keep on joking about world events; the whole thing is becoming too tragically serious. With his built-in ironic distancing, Colbert manages to make fun of himself, the right-wing media and our shared tendency to 'catastrophise' the news.

A lot of the laughs Stewart gets are at the expense of himself. Stewart plays himself as a well-informed Jewish intellectual who actually cares about the news and desperately wishes to ameliorate. He imbues his performances with much eye rolling, wringing of the hands, beating of his head on his 'news desk', and seems to be stepping in and out of character more and more as if he can't go on playing and needs to express his genuine anger, discomfort and hostility towards the lies and distortions of the mainstream media, especially as they are rehearsed and performed by the staff and public relations staff of the Bush administration. Audiences are drawn to Stewart because of his use of self-deprecating humour, his continual referencing of his Jewish heritage and his relatively small physical stature, which perversely only serves to buttress his persona as a sort of postmodern superhero of the meta-news generation.

Numerous studies demonstrate that many Americans actually get their 'news' from *The Daily Show* and *The Colbert Report*; they trust it more than the 'real' news. This is especially true of younger viewers who are very postmodern in their approach to news, news commentary and infotainment. Cognizant of the fact that they are immersed in an environment of spin and distortion, younger viewers are eager for truth. But because they are so used to reading through the prisms of meta-narrative, they generally reject systems that seek to sell them facts as if they were children of an earlier, more naive age. When people say they 'get their news' from Colbert and Stewart, what they really mean is that they distil, from these comic fake news programmes, what is important in the news. Then they go to the web and do some Googling, look at a variety of news sources, read their favourite blogs, and attempt to make informed choices about what sources are credible and what stories really are 'news'.

I know this to be true because if I have a question about recent political events I have only to ask my students, who either have an answer at the tip of their tongue, or at the tip of their fingers on their laptops or Blackberries. Though they may not be aware of the jargon of theorists of postmodernism, they are involved in a postmodern critique and reception of mass media. They reject conventional news sources that treat them like children; objects in which to inject meaning. In doing so, their actions seem to answer these questions posed by Jean Baudrillard:

> Are the mass media on the side of power in the manipulation of the masses, or are they on the side of the masses in the liquidation of meaning, and in fascination? Is it the media that induce fascination in the masses, or is it the masses who direct the media into a spectacle? (1994: 84)

Audiences who play the game of news in a postmodernist search for meaning seem to supersede these important questions posed by Baudrillard. The strategic resistance to non-parodic mass media on the part of such audiences manifestly rejects becoming an object of conformity, passivity, idiocy and vulnerability. If mass media is involved in rejecting meaning, hiding truths, blatantly distorting facts about the Iraq War, the elections, the economy and all the major news events of the day, the postmodern viewer is almost forced into an active and participatory role in finding news, much less reality, that seems credible, negotiable. In a world of supposed excess of meaning, excess of news sources and excess in general, audiences as individuals can and do reject the consensus that information devoirs the subject. Postmodern communication, especially in the more mainstream media, does not conduce communication. As Baudrillard observes:

> Information devoirs its own content. It devoirs communication. *It exhausts itself in the act of staging communication*. Rather than producing meaning, it exhausts itself in the staging of meaning. A gigantic process of simulation that is very familiar. (1994: 80, my emphasis)

But while Baudrillard is busy decrying the loss of communication in the postmodern condition, humorists and their audiences in the guise of 'fake news' have ironically found a place to negotiate meaning through simulation, especially the simulation of such puffed-up newspeople as Sean Hannity, Shepard Smith and their Fox News cohorts, who are the clear targets of *The Colbert Report*.

The Colbert Report exemplifies a postmodern pastiche that rejects Baudrillard's thinking about the exhaustion of communication, instead injecting meaning in meta-humour. The gap between Stephen Colbert the humorist and writer and actor, and Stephen Colbert the persona, his Shellyian monster of id, a right-wing egomaniacal buffoon, would seem to be easy to negotiate, but sometimes the wedding of the artifice and the real is amazingly small. As CBS News commentator Morley Safer noted:

> If there is such a thing, he is your humble egomaniac. On his first broadcast, Colbert announced, '. . . This show is not about me. No, this program is dedicated to you, the heroes. And who are the heroes? The people who watch this show, average hard-working Americans. You're not the elites. You're not the country club crowd. I know for a fact my country club would never let you in. You're the folks who say something has to be done. And you're doing something. You're watching TV.' (Safer, 2006)

Ironically, they are watching a programme on which Stephen Colbert performs himself to more than one million viewers nightly. Colbert, or the two Colberts, demonstrate that 'to be photographed is to be transformed' (Shaviro, 1993: 212) and 'we are always acting, even if our performance is usually unconscious or involuntary' (Shaviro, 1993: 213). It may help to look at *The Colbert Report* as a drag act of sorts. As Steven Shaviro, writing about drag performers in Andy Warhol's epic film *The Chelsea Girls* (1966) notes, drag can be a mode of empowerment:

> Drag performers exteriorize themselves so completely, they exalt visibility and artificiality so ostentatiously, . . . they so utterly give themselves over to the mystique of the aura, that they disrupt the very models . . . that they are ostensibly imitating. (1993: 228)

In conjuring a drag act, Colbert gives himself over to the transformative aspects of spectacle completely. He goes into his character and remains there. While gender is not his main concern, his act involves a complete transformation, minus the heels and dresses of the drag acts of Warhol's drag superstars, or the multi-gendered protagonists of Jack Smith's notorious film *Flaming Creatures* (1963). Instead, Colbert's drag act includes a shellacked waxen hairdo, the kind that only politicians, newsmen and other professional liars don. He pimps himself out in expensive Brooks Brothers suits (that he often comments on), and brandishes his frameless glasses like a weapon of destruction not entirely unlike Harpo Marx's scissors.

Colbert uses his ability to arch one eyebrow in the way a great drag 'Cher' might purse her lips and he jabs his fingers in the air like a drag version of the macho swaggering men he parodies. He swaggers around the stage like a preening peacock in a clearly exaggerated send-up of the staged masculinity found on actual news programmes. His *sprezzatura* delivery style of the news is imbued with a gravitas and masterly quality that is such a terrific parody of the self-importance of news jockeys that one of the pleasures of the show is to wait for the occasional moment when even he himself breaks with his own drag act and once in a brief while bursts that fourth wall and can't help but enjoy a quick smile or laugh on himself (or actually his parody of himself).

As a drag act, Colbert is frighteningly competent. Because we all know he is playing a part, he can get away with saying any number of outrageous and politically incorrect things; in short, his nightly presentation is a pastiche of the real and the constructed; the false, and the factual Colbert reminds me now and then of Groucho Marx or Jack Benny, comics who also used their respective personas to utter things they would never be able to say in any other context. Above all, Colbert is cognizant of his public persona, and of his relationship to his audience, which he continually refers to as his 'nation'. As any competent parodist knows, irony is inevitably co-produced by the audience. Richard Dyer aptly summarises this relationship:

> Pastiche intends that it is understood as pastiche by those who read, see, or hear it. For it to work, it needs to be 'got' as a pastiche. In this sense, it is an aspect of irony. This implies particular competencies on the part of audiences and, to this extent, pastiche may be seen as elitist, including those who get it, excluding those who don't. (2007: 3)

Clearly, part of the postmodern fun of watching *The Colbert Report* and being part of his select audience plays upon our desire to live in the Colbert playhouse. He has even given us a name: we are 'the Colbert nation'.

The pleasure of watching the show is also that the drag act goes beyond clothes and performance. Every element of the set is a drag act or pastiche of that which has been usurped as the symbol of 'freedom' and 'America'. The set and the visual graphics are strewn in red, white and blue in a manner that is so blatant as to make even a cross-dressing version of Liza Minnelli blush. The set is frenetically busy to the eye, carefully designed to bring all attention to the beautifully lit Colbert persona. Everything is covered with the Colbert logo or American flags, eagles, 'patriotic' busts and swirling canopies of freedom-licious reds, whites and blues. It is dizzying and completely over the top, but no more so than that which it parodies, those shows that drag out the corpses of patriotism, flag waving and performed nationalism, imperialism and corporatisation of 'traditional American values'. The opening of *The Colbert Report* is an almost hallucinogenic display of exaggerated patriotism, underscored by a compelling rock and roll main theme, written by and performed by Rick Nielsen and his band, the classic rock act Cheap Trick. But Colbert is not simply making a travesty of the iconography of American patriotism, he and his creators and writers are carefully critiquing those who routinely appropriate and violate the iconography of patriotism itself.

The meta-humour of the set, the graphics, the insane and riotous use of patriotism are other examples of 'festive abuse' of the kind employed by the Marx Brothers. It ultimately hopes to ameliorate the tension of the moment. As viewers, we may be laughing but we certainly miss a time when the iconography of America and America at least attempted to actually represent good things and freedoms. This use of pastiche is a simultaneous homage to a time when presidents at least attempted to respect the constitution, freedom of the individual, freedom of the press, and so forth. Colbert constantly reminds us that we are living through a time much like the 1950s, when flag-waving zealots used the iconography of patriotism to defeat the constitution and distort and destroy the freedoms promised by democracy. None of this happens, of course, by accident. As Colbert told Nathan Rabin:

> One of the things I said to the set designer – who has done everything, I mean even *Meet The Press*, he does that level of news design – was 'One of your inspirations should be [Da Vinci's painting] *The Last Supper*. All the architecture of that room points at Jesus' head, the entire room is a halo, and he doesn't have a halo.' And I said, 'On the set, I'd like the lines of the set to converge on my head.' And so if you look at the design, it all does, it all points at my head. And even radial lines on the floor, and on my podium, and watermarks in the images behind me, and all the vertices, are right

behind my head. So there's a sort of sun-god burst quality about the set around me. And I love that. (Rabin, 2006)

This egomaniacal design concept goes even further; except for the 'patriotic' trappings of the show's main anchor desk, there are no competing sources of information allowed. If it doesn't come from Colbert, it simply isn't 'the truth'. Again, speaking to Rabin, Colbert commented on the absence of TV monitors on the set (as carried to absurd extremes in CNN's 'real news' programme *The Situation Room* with Wolf Blitzer), noting:

There are no televisions behind me, like the way [*NBC Nightly News* anchor] Brian Williams has, or even [*Daily Show* host] Jon [Stewart]. At certain angles, there are monitors behind Jon that have the world going on, which implies that that's where the news is, and that's where the information is, and the person in front of it is the conduit through which this information is given to you. But on my set, I said, 'I don't want anything behind me, because I am the sun. It all comes from me. I'm not channeling anything. I *am* the source.' (Rabin, 2006)

In his choice of guests, Colbert often invites people with whom he would normally (out of character) agree. Highly educated historians, civil rights activists, scientists and left-leaning types of all professions are guests on the show. But instead of an agreement-machine, Colbert subjects these folks (in persona) to the types of verbal assault they might expect to find on *The O'Reilly Factor*. He 'debates' evolution, he 'debunks' racism, he argues against the constitution with constitutional scholars, and because we know these attacks are fake we can see how Colbert and his writers are skewering the rest of the media, particularly egotistical pundits such as Lou Dobbs, who has made a career out of attacking immigrants, or any number of self-appointed 'experts' who spend their shows acting the part of shocked and scolding upholders of the constitution.

Central to the parodic nature of *The Colbert Report* is the concept of 'truthiness', a word Colbert coined for his first 'Word of the Day' segment and has since been included in Webster's dictionary, as well as named 'word of the year' by the American Dialect Society. In an interview with Nathan Rabin, Stephen Colbert, out of his usual character, spoke about 'truthiness':

Truthiness is tearing apart our country and I don't mean the argument over who came up with the word. I don't know whether it's the new thing, but it's certainly a current thing, in that it doesn't seem to matter what the facts are . . . Facts matter not at all. Perception is everything. It's certainty. People

> love the president because he's certain of his choices as a leader, even if the facts that back him up don't seem to exist. It's the fact that he's certain that is very appealing to a certain section of the country. I really feel a dichotomy in the American populace. What is important? What you want to be true, or what *is* true? (Rabin, 2006)

Ironically, Colbert's show is an outright exposé and attack on 'truthiness' in the media, and in politicians, as it points to the double-speak, distortions and outright lies that audiences have come to expect from news sources, corporations and politicians. Colbert and his writers constantly play with the ways 'truth' is seen as negotiable, violable and subject to postmodern scrutiny, even as the show and Colbert, at their core, seek to expose all the manifestations of truthiness and the truth.

One of Colbert's routines, to which he continually returns, is his feeling that truth is not presented in facts but 'in your gut'. In drag, Stephen Colbert would appear to believe this absurd idea. It is a delicious irony that even before *The Colbert Report* became so wildly influential and successful, Colbert had terrific success when he lampooned President George W. Bush, in his actual presence, in full drag as Stephen Colbert, at the White House Press Correspondents' 'Dinner in 2006. Though those present didn't seemingly know how to react to Colbert's remarks aimed directly at the President, millions of viewers watched it on YouTube and through various Internet sources, and the performance bumped up the ratings of the new show considerably.

In a scathing faux homage to Bush, staged before the President and the nation's news media during the 2006 White House Press Corps dinner, Colbert famously skewered the President with a searing, controversial and amazing performance that was breathtaking in its sheer nerve and stamina. Gesturing to the President, Colbert (in character) delivered devastating blows, damning him with distinctly faint praise:

> I stand by this man. I stand by this man, because he stands for things. Not only for things, he stands *on* things, things like aircraft carriers and rubble and recently flooded city squares. And that sends a strong message, that no matter what happens to America, she will always rebound with the most powerfully staged photo-ops in the world. (Colbert, 2007: 224)

Colbert's speech went on for some time, but just this small tidbit cuts to the quick in exposing the President's use of 'truthiness', his famous photo-op on the stage of an aircraft carrier, his lack of a complete response to the Katrina disaster, and it makes an allusion to the rubble of Iraq. The complete text of the Colbert performance at the White House Correspondents'

Dinner is reprinted in Colbert's book, *I Am America* (*and So Can You*!). It is annotated, in a nod to postmodernism, or perhaps a nod to the Bible, in red along the margins.

After applauding Fox News for giving both sides of the story, 'both sides of every story: the President's side, and the Vice President's side' (Colbert, 2007: 224), Colbert launches into an attack on wiretapping, secret prisons and the implied torture that happens in overseas 'rendition houses':

> The rest of you [news organisations], what were you thinking? Reporting on NSA wiretapping or secret prisons in Eastern Europe? Those things are secret for a very important reason: they're super-depressing. And if that's your goal, well, misery accomplished. (Colbert, 2007: 224)

In a *Rolling Stone* piece on Stewart and Colbert, Maureen Dowd refers to them as the 'Cronkite and Murrow for an ironic millennium' (2006: 4), but the irony around the success of both *The Daily Show* and *The Colbert Report* is perhaps that it is in embracing irony – Brechtian irony, distancing irony – and using an array of the tools of humour, in-jokes, parody, pastiche, imitation, repetition, illogic and revelling in 'untruthiness' – that these two shows speak truth to a postmodern audience. Colbert in particular performs circles around his 'guests' (read victims) and audiences enjoy the privilege of being 'in on' the joke.

While Stewart employs the self-deprecation we are accustomed to seeing in Borscht-belt comics, Colbert badgers and struts around his set barking orders and inspiring his audience to play along with his mutual admiration society. His postmodernity is reflected in his meta-performance as well as his well-known pranks. For example, the Colbert character ostentatiously had his portrait done in the style of someone of the stature of a great president. Then he had a portrait commissioned of himself with the original portrait hanging behind him. He did this again and again, until he finally had a meta-portrait of himself within a portrait to the third power. As a neat ironic gesture, Colbert pulled off a stunt in which he visited Washington and went to various museums, including the Smithsonian Institution, seeking to have his portrait hung in a prominent place. The National Portrait Gallery's head curator Marc Pachter decided to go along with the prank and hung the portrait-within-a-portrait-within-a-portrait-within-a-portrait for a limited time only outside the men's bathroom at the Gallery. The stunt proved wildly popular and, as a result, attendance at the Gallery spiked considerably. Neither Colbert nor his alter ego could have planned it better. As he told Nathan Rabin:

> Sometimes I feel like maybe we should cut back on the burlesque, and really try to do that in a more sincere fashion, and it would really make it stronger. I find the branding that goes on in real news at times is funnier than what I do. It's just so shocking to hear descriptions of [*Fox Report* anchor] Shepard Smith, you know: 'Changing the world! He gives 110 percent!' Our problem is, there's no level of hyperbole that can be associated with me that hasn't at least been approached by the real thing. (Rabin, 2006)

Some of the funniest performances on the show are completely unplanned, as when Jane Fonda unexpectedly sat on his lap and visibly unnerved Colbert with her parodic professions of love and desire for him. Even though we know he is just putting on a performed self, we can't help but invest in this artificial self and at some level we believe in his simulacrum. Stewart and Colbert have spoken many times about how they conceived of him as 'a jerk' but 'not an asshole'. He is ill-informed, not a bad person. It is a bit frightening to think that one of the manifestations of the postmodern drag act is that at some level we identify with him or even like him. On camera, Colbert rarely even performs his 'real' self any more. He is so identified with the character he has created that, in a sense, he has come to 'be' him. He famously won't let his children watch the show because he thinks kids don't understand parody, but one wonders if he is really worried that his own kids might actually believe in this alter-ego.

Yet even Colbert's alter-ego has an alter-ego; Tek Janssen, an animated super-hero who rushes about in self-righteous fury, saving the planet from liberal infidels; he has also hosted a 'green screen' competition, in which he uploaded live footage of himself in front of a 'green screen', battling an imaginary foe with a *Star Wars* light sabre. Viewers were asked to complete the scene by compositing the live footage of Colbert with computer-generated imagery of his imaginary, 'anti-American' adversaries. In response, thousands of viewers sent in brief video clips of their home-brewed results, many of them surprisingly sophisticated. Ever the ironist, Colbert invited *Star Wars* director George Lucas on the show, with his own version of Colbert's green screen battle, pretending not to recognise Lucas, and identifying him only as 'George L'. In a final touch, after screening several runner-ups, Colbert awarded the prize for best entry not to Lucas, but to a young woman who had created a particularly inventive entry. Lucas, obviously in on the joke, displayed mock annoyance and left in a huff.

The very, very thin line between reality and fantasy was also tested when Colbert attempted a run for the Presidency by registering in the Republican primary in South Carolina; when apprised of his actions, the state responded by rescinding his certification as a candidate on the grounds that his run for the White House 'wasn't real' (which, of course, was absolutely true). Colbert's personality even extends to his 'warm up' routine before the show; unlike most other comedians, who rely on the services of a professional 'warm up' person to whip the crowd into a frenzy right before taping, Colbert regularly performs this chore himself. On one particular night, he was more animated than usual, and while running around the studio high-fiving his guests, slipped on the floor and fractured his wrist. Ever the professional, Colbert continued with the taping but made continual references to his 'grave injury', appearing the next day in an elaborate cast that he wore for weeks and giving out bright red 'Wriststrong' bracelets to his audience members to commemorate his historic injury.

As Colbert told *New Yorker* columnist David Remnick when the show first aired, 'the focus will be me, lots of me. Occasionally, we'll turn the camera elsewhere, but only for pacing. My ambition is to have Stone Phillips' neck and Geraldo Rivera's sense of humor . . . it'll be like Bill O'Reilly segueing into [Fox News anchor Sean] Hannity, Hannity into [Fox News personality] Greta [Van Susteren], Larry King into Aaron Brown' (Remnick, 2005). In short, Colbert's on-screen persona is an amalgam of all right-wing TV pundits combined into one toxic know-it-all, reeking of self-righteous ignorance, arrogance and self-importance.

Because of this, Colbert is, of course, an expert on 'anything', offering his viewers helpful suggestions in an article in *Wired* magazine (co-written with John Hockenberry), such as 'pick a field that can't be verified. Try something like string theory or God's will: "I speak to God. I'm sorry that you can't also."' Or, 'In the media age, everybody was famous for 15 minutes. In the Wikipedia age, everybody can be an expert in five minutes. Special bonus: You can edit your own entry to make yourself seem even smarter.' Or the ultimate fallback position, 'Don't be afraid to make things up. Never fear being exposed as a fraud. Experts make things up all the time. They're qualified to' (Colbert and Hockenberry, 2006).

Colbert's persona on the show is an entirely fictitious construct; why not make up all the information that goes with it? He often performs the persona of an opinionated conservative commentator so well that some of his guests, many of them genuine supporters of the Bush regime, momentarily forget they are engaging in mock combat with a completely fictitious adversary. During an interview with Judge Andrew Napolitano, author of the book *A Nation of Sheep*, a diatribe against the Patriot Act in which Napolitano argues passionately that the President must honour the constitution, Napolitano inadvertently addressed Colbert as 'Bill' in his haste to make a particular point, referring to real-life pundit Bill O'Reilly. Colbert was thrilled by the error, and immediately wrapped up the interview, telling Napolitano 'it's not gonna get any better than that' (31 January 2008).

Colbert actually had O'Reilly on his show as a guest and he has been, in turn, a guest on *The O'Reilly Factor*, where the two men duelled to a standoff, each trying to outdo the other in portraying the image of hyperbolic televised 'patriotism' (18 January 2007). Colbert also has a regular segment entitled 'Better Know a District', in which he interviews state legislators and usually leads or re-edits them into saying outrageous and/or embarrassing things; the 'interviews', like everything else on *The Colbert Report*, are constructs, both in the questions and the subsequent editing of the final segment. The "Better Know a District" segment was so successful in lampooning those in power that many representatives now refuse to be guests on this segment. Lately, Colbert has a spin-off segment, 'Better Know a Lobbyist', in which he debates the issues of Washington lobbying with actual lobbyists. Used to softballs and mutually agreed-upon questions in 'real' news shows, lobbyists, legislators and others in power are increasingly afraid to have a sit-down with Colbert; the results can be catastrophic to their careers, and as Colbert has continually demonstrated, no topic is off limits.

As media critic Seth Mnookin recently wrote, Colbert keeps upping the ante with each new episode of the show. As Mnookin notes:

> Last March, [former United States Ambassador to the United Nations] Richard Holbrooke drew on his experience brokering peace in Bosnia to mediate a truce between Colbert and Willie Nelson over who had the better flavor of Ben & Jerry's ice cream. (Colbert's is called AmeriCone Dream.) In April, former United States poet laureate Robert Pinsky judged a 'Meta-Free-Phor-All' between Colbert and Sean Penn. (Sean Penn won, 10 million to one.) In December, New York governor-elect Eliot Spitzer and Henry Kissinger appeared on the show to preside over a guitar contest between Colbert and members of the Indie-rock group the Decemberists. (Mnookin, 2007: 345)

As Jon Stewart admiringly told Mnookin, Colbert is 'able to create a universe where something surreal happens on the program that seems ordinary, and all of a sudden the absurd appears not mundane but expected, organic . . . he can have a conversation with Richard Holbrooke and Willie Nelson and it all makes perfect sense and yet it couldn't appear anywhere else without appearing [like] burlesque. Somehow he has managed to create a fake world that has impacted and found standing in the real world' (Mnookin, 2007: 345).

On more than one occasion, Colbert has been able with surprising ease to uncover the mendacity and ignorance of those who profess to uphold 'American' values but, as Mnookin notes, 'the best-known segment to date is likely one with Georgia Republican Lynn Westmoreland that included this exchange:'

> Stephen Colbert: You co-sponsored a bill requiring the display of the Ten Commandments in the House of Representatives and in the Senate.
> Lynn Westmoreland: Um hum.
> S. C.: Why was that important to you?
> L. W.: Well, the Ten Commandments is not a bad thing for people to understand and to respect.
> S. C.: I'm with ya.
> L. W.: What better place could you have something like that than in a judicial building or in a courthouse?
> S. C.: That is a good question. Can you think of any better building to put the Ten Commandments than in a public building?
> L. W.: No. I think if we were totally without them we may lose a sense of our direction.
> S. C.: What are the Ten Commandments?
> L. W.: What are all of them? [Colbert nods.]
> L. W.: You want me to name them all?
> S. C.: Yeah, please.
> L. W.: Ummm. [Colbert holds up two fists, waiting for Westmoreland to count them off.]
> L. W.: Don't murder. Don't lie. Don't steal. Uhhhhh . . . I can't name them all.
> S. C.: Congressman, thank you for taking time away from keeping the Sabbath Day holy to talk to me. (Mnookin, 2007: 384)

Later, Colbert mused off-camera that given the topic the two men were to discuss, Westmoreland might well have familiarised himself with the Ten Commandments, just to be prepared. But as Mnookin points out, the answer is simple: 'He'd never encountered a reporter who'd had the temerity – or, as Colbert would put it, the balls – to ask such an obvious question' (Mnookin, 2007: 384).

On another episode, Colbert assumed the identity of 'Estaban Colberto', in an interview with CNN host Lou Dobbs about undocumented workers, immigration and related issues. Clad in a loud purple jacket with an outrageous yellow tie, Colbert 'performs' Estaban Colberto completely in Spanish (subtitled in English) and asks all his questions in Spanish as well. Lou Dobbs attempts to play along and not make too much of a fool of himself, but Colbert ups the ante by entering the 'set' through barbed wire, underscoring the plight of the undocumented worker. This opening is shot in 'night-vision' as if captured by the border patrol.

As 'Colberto' plugs Lou Dobbs' book *War on the Middle Class*, it becomes clear that Dobbs agreed to appear on *The Colbert Report* for one reason only: he is just another author hawking a product. So even as the oily, smarmy, completely fake Estaban Colberto, Colbert wields the upper hand, as he pretends to be solicitous to his guest. 'Colberto' asks crazy questions. He begins with, 'let's talk about the middle class', adding, 'how do we beat those bastards?' Dobbs, trying to retain a shred of dignity, attacks both political parties for being in the service of corporations. 'Colberto' takes the tactic of arguing for the 'rights of corporations. They have their rights to the American dream . . . to outsourcing jobs.'

Dobbs tries to restrain himself and stays on point, continuing his message that corporations are waging war on the middle class, but Estaban Colberto punctures Dobbs' speechifying by saying he is against anything 'middle', including the 'Middle Class, the middle ages, Middle East, they're trouble . . . pick a side'. As the interview ends, the camera pulls back to reveal that both guest and host are imprisoned behind a chain link fence (17 January 2008). Middle America loses jobs, yet middle Americans don't wish to support a system of fair wages and unions. The debate on immigration reform is hopelessly mired in the egos of pundits who are themselves working for corporations that take full advantage of poorly paid undocumented workers or actively move jobs overseas and over borders.

At the core of his performances, the real Colbert has a very strong ethos. Clearly he values education and he values his audience. He implores them to seek out truth and reject 'truthiness'. A devout Catholic who teaches Sunday School each week, he nevertheless questions everything around him, a meta-critic who finds and exposes 'truth' in fake news and fake punditry, by cross-dressing and dragging pundits and self-appointed 'experts'. Who would have believed that this postmodern drag act of festive abuse would find such an immense following and help us sort out the truth from the truthiness? In an age where parody has become more authentic than officially sanctioned news reports, Colbert's show is just one indicator of how badly the press, as well as politicians, need intelligent criticism and satire as some sort of a compass point in a world where opinion masquerades as fact. Colbert, at least, acknowledges the masquerade, which is more than many of his serious colleagues manage to do. In 2008, this seems to be the most we can hope for.

References

Baudrillard, J. (1994) *Simulacra and Simulation*, trans. Sheila Faria Glaser, Ann Arbor: University of Michigan Press.

Colbert, S. (2007) *I Am America* (*and So Can You*!), New York: Grand Central.

Colbert, S. and J. Hockenberry (2006) 'Be an Expert on Anything', *Wired* 14.08 (August), www.wired.com/wired/archive/14.08/colbert.html (accessed 18 March 2008).

Dale, A. (2000) *Comedy is a Man in Trouble*, Minneapolis: University of Minnesota Press.

Dowd, M. (2006) 'America's Anchors' *Rolling Stone* (31 October), www.rollingstone.com / news / coverstory / jon-stewart-stephen-colbert-americas-anchors (accessed 18 March 2008).

Dyer, R. (2007) *Pastiche*, New York: Routledge.

Mnookin, S. (2007) 'The Man in the Irony Mask', *Vanity Fair* (October): 342–345, 382–386.

Napolitano, Judge A. P. (2007) *A Nation of Sheep*, Nashville: Thomas Nelson.

Rabin, N. (2006) 'Interview with Stephen Colbert', *The Orion A. V. Club* (25 January), www.avclub.com/content/node/44705 (accessed 18 March 2008).

Remnick, D. (2005) 'Reporter Guy', *The New Yorker* (25 July), www.newyorker.com/archive/2005/07/25/050725ta-talk-remnick (accessed 18 March 2008).

Safer, M. (2006) 'The Colbert Report', *CBS News, 60 Minutes* (13 August), www.cbsnews.com/stories/2006/04/27/60minutes/printable1553506.shtml (accessed 18 March 2008).

Shaviro, S. (1993) *The Cinematic Body*, Minneapolis: University of Minnesota Press.

7

Contemporary comedy performance in British sitcom

Brett Mills

To explore comedy performance is to acknowledge that there is something that defines a performance as 'comic'; that is, that comedy performance is of a particular type which is distinct from other, more serious and/or tragic texts. Furthermore, it is to acknowledge that comedy performance requires being read as such in order for its aims to be achieved; that is, comic acting must not only be funny (however that is measured) but try to ensure that audiences understand that it is intended as funny. This means that comic performance must not only be funny in and of itself, finding humour within its relationship to character and narrative, but that it must also signal its intended 'funny-ness', creating an interpretive space for audiences in which the kind of performance makes sense relative to other aspects of the text. While acting and performance are always textual components that signal their function alongside those other aspects of texts, it will be argued here that, traditionally, comic performance has displayed its intentions more obviously than performance for serious/tragic narratives. This is primarily because, in societies where being serious is an assumed norm, the realm of the comic is a 'special world' (Mulkay, 1988: 8) that requires clear contextual cues in order for it to be 'permitted' (Purdie, 1993: 13). While individual audience members might disagree over whether a comedy is actually funny or not, it is rare for disagreements to arise over whether a text was *intended* to be funny or not.

The signals associated with comic performance are consequences of the necessity of signalling humorous intent (McGhee, 1979: 71; Palmer, 1994: 22). That is, a joke can only be found funny if there is a 'framing system' (Whitmore, 1994: 65) that signals its desire to be read as humorous. This is not to deny that events can be unintentionally funny; but it is to note that while such events might not contain comic intention, they must exist within a discourse that allows laughter to be an appropriate response (Lynch, 2002: 423). Social restrictions on comic content – whether formalised through broadcasting regulations or laws, or personalised as offence – demonstrate the assumption that there are things that should not be laughed about (Lockyer and Pickering, 2005). The movement from a serious discourse into one which allows – or even requires – a comic response must be carefully negotiated, and the distinctions between the serious and the comic have been developed within societies for centuries (Davies, 2002). Anthropological studies show that successful comedy rests on negotiating an appropriate 'joking relationship' (Radcliffe-Brown, 1952: 90–116) between performer, audience and butt, all of whom must understand, and accept, the comic mode in order for offence to be avoided. While this is complicated for social humour between small numbers of people, broadcast comedy, in which the act of communication is more distant and the relationship between participants is more various and complex, offers particular problems for comedy to avoid misinterpretation, offence and upset.

It may come as no surprise, then, that recurring within analyses of comedy performance – whether in film, on television, on stage, or in any other medium or cultural form – is the assumption that it is 'excessive' (Naremore, 1988: 63; Mills, 2005: 33). Defining what is meant by 'excess' is obviously problematic and cannot escape the fact that individuals are likely to measure it in different ways. Perhaps the most useful way to think about 'excess', then, is to measure it against performance styles that are not seen as excessive, and to see what makes the distinction. For quite some time British culture has measured performance appropriacy via notions of realism and naturalism, even though these are themselves cultural conventions. Furthermore, 'Each age has its own idea of what is natural and lifelike' (Davis and Postlewait, 2003: 20), and the development of performance styles is at least partly a consequence of the range of media in which acting can now take place. Comedy acting – and television sitcom acting that arises from it – is marked by its distinctiveness from such naturalist or realist performance, often employing larger movements, a wider vocal range, and more common stresses on the rhythms of language than would be the case for the majority of 'straight' drama. Such performance foregrounds the physicality of comic acting, making the body a key site of comedy (Féral, 1997). In doing so, comedy acting signals its comic intent, ensuring that the aim of such performance can be easily understood, even if particular audiences find specific comic moments unfunny. Simultaneously, such performance distinguishes comedy acting from serious drama. In societies that value the social import of serious acting, and marvel at the 'believability' of realistic acting, comic acting therefore occupies a position that is less valorised, its excesses seemingly a bar to psychological realism and cultural value (Wright, 2006: xii).

The question to be asked, then, is why comedy acting has maintained such a style. For many, comic acting can be traced back to its theatrical origins, with institutions such as vaudeville and the music hall the training grounds for many of television's early comic stars (Pearson, 1992; Mayer, 1999); in America this includes people such as Jack Benny and George Burns, while in Britain Tony Hancock moved from theatre to radio and television, bringing a range of performers with him. While music hall and vaudeville are virtually non-existent now, a large number of comic performers still carry out their training in theatrical arenas, though these days this is much more likely to be in stand-up comedy clubs. For decades America has taken stand-up comedy stars and given them their own sitcoms, in series such as *Roseanne* (ABC, 1988–97), *Seinfeld* (NBC, 1989–98), *The Sarah Silverman Program* (Comedy Central, 2007–) and *Flight of the Conchords* (HBO, 2007–). The same occurs in Britain, with recent series based around stand-ups' routines including *The Mighty Boosh* (BBC3, 2004–) and *Not Going Out* (BBC1, 2006–). Noticeably, comic actors are often keen to return to the theatre after success in radio or television, as the stage versions of comedy programmes such as *Little Britain* (BBC3/1, 2003–05), *The Fast Show* (BBC2, 1994–97), and *The League of Gentlemen* (BBC2, 1999–2002) attest. This means that the relationship between the theatrical and the televisual remains upheld in comic acting, and while 'serious' actors may also move between media it is unlikely they would do so when playing the same part; for comedy, on the other hand, this is a norm, showing how characters and performance made popular on broadcast media remain comprehensible and funny when transferred to the quite different arena of theatre.

As many theorists of theatre have pointed out, what distinguishes live performance from that of film, television and radio is the existence of the actor as a physical being in the same space as the audience (Carlson, 1999: 3; Meyer-Dinkgräfe, 2001: 58). This is likely to affect the performance made by the actor, who can respond to the reactions of the audience as a performance progresses. The interplay between audiences and performers in comedy is demonstrated by the shooting style of many television sitcoms, which garner a real audience to watch the recording, re-creating the theatrical experience within a television studio. This audience is seen as so vital to the comic performance that its oral responses are recorded, resulting in the laugh track which accompanies many sitcoms. It is significant that many contemporary sitcoms have abandoned these conventions, with series such as *The Office* (BBC2/1, 2001–03) and *Marion and Geoff* (BBC2, 2000–03) having no live audience and no laugh track; I shall return to this later. The question, remains, however, why it should be that getting an audience in the same location as the performers has been seen as important for decades for television comedy, when straight drama, or soap opera, has resolutely refused to do the same; emotional scenes on soap operas, for example, do not come with crying tracks, and it is assumed that the audience at home does not need to hear an audience at the performance in order to understand how to make sense of a broadcast.

This physical presence of the performer can also be read in terms of analyses of comedy which highlight the relationship between humour and the body. Sigmund Freud (1960 [1905]) argues that humour often refers to the physical because in 'civilised' societies we are repressed about our bodies' corporeality, and their functions, which, while inescapable, are commonly downplayed in relation to the spiritual or intellectual aspects of our character. As Freud suggests that all humour is a response to repression, it is unsurprising he would argue that comedy should draw on physical behaviour which societies commonly categorise as 'disgusting'. A similar approach can be found in Bakhtin's notion of the 'carnivalesque' (1968 [1965]), where comedy is seen as a communal activity which pushes against the institutionalised social structures which condemn the physical. Whether or not such approaches are appropriate is up for debate, but it is clear that there are only three cultural forms of fiction for which the body is an integral site of meaning: horror, comedy and pornography. Each of these finds interest in the workings of the body, displaying the 'abject' (Kristeva, 1982) for revulsion, shock and pleasure; it is also noticeable that these three are usually categorised as of less social worth than most other cultural forms (Cohen, 2005: xiv). Much comedy draws on the physical, whether it be a joke about sexual behaviour, the pain of slapstick or laughter at fat people, even if 'civilised' societies condemn such humour (Bristol, 1989 [1985]). What is of note here is the importance of *presence* within comedy; comedy has repeatedly drawn on, and demonstrated, the physical proximity of performer and audience partly because such a relationship allows the performer to respond to the audience, but also, it seems, because the corporeal matter of the living body is a ripe site for humour. Television comedy, then, must find ways of signalling that presence within the technology of broadcasting in which there is an essential distance; laugh tracks have been the traditional way of doing this but, as will be explored later, newer comedic conventions have recently been adopted in response to generic developments.

This presence is also important because comedy performance often foregrounds the performer in a manner unlikely for serious acting. As Richard Dyer (1979) notes, film stars' meaning arises from the interplay between the characters they play and the personal qualities their constructed identity brings to them, so that audiences are watching a character and an actor simultaneously. The pleasures of such stars rest on the star quality an actor brings to a performance, meaning that 'Star images are always extensive, multimedia, intertextual' (Dyer, 1986: 3). A similar analysis has been put forward for comic acting, in Steve Seidman's notion of 'comedian comedy' (1981). Seidman notes that while the production process for the majority of serious fiction begins with the script, film comedy has instead often begun with the comedian themselves. To be sure, the star system in Hollywood developed scripts with stars in mind, but the narrative requirements of every film necessitated different kinds of performances from the stars involved, and there was an assumption that a star's skill rested on the ability to be someone slightly different in every text. For comedian comedy this is not the case; scripts and narratives are developed purely around the skills and abilities of the comedian, often resulting in episodic narratives whose structure exists merely to join together a series of comic moments.

As noted earlier, contemporary comedy continues to construct programmes around successful comedians and comedy performers, who often play versions of themselves. It is significant that in many such sitcoms the title of the programme is the name of the performer, even when, as in *Cosby* (CBS, 1996–2000) and *The Cosby Show* (NBC, 1984–92), Bill Cosby played characters whose surnames were not 'Cosby'. In doing so, such programmes promote themselves through their star, and while the majority of media texts employ stars in order to entice audiences, the system is not quite as blatant as it is for comedy. The conflation between the 'real' person and the comedy persona employed by stand-up comedians is also shown by the fact that comedians routinely use their own name when performing; Chris Rock is 'Chris Rock' when he is on stage, just as Victoria Wood is 'Victoria Wood'. While there are some comedians who employ personae with different names – such as Graham Fellowes as John Shuttleworth and Steve Coogan's characters such as Alan Partridge, Paul and Pauline Calf, and Tony Ferrino – these are much less common than in serious acting, and are noticeably categorised as 'character comedy'. In these ways, comedian comedy remains an important part of the ways in which comedy makes meaning, offering to audiences 'performance [that] does not demand that we forget the presence of the actor within the guise of the character' (Butler, 2007: 69).

Very early in its history, television sitcom therefore developed a shooting style which aimed to capture such presence and capitalise on the pleasures on offer in comedian comedy. Histories of sitcom note how it (and, for that matter, all television comedy) began as transfers from the theatre and vaudeville, and therefore commonly had a theatrical style. In Britain Morecambe and Wise performed to audiences as if they were in a theatre well into the 1980s, with the proscenium arch and the theatre curtain an important part of their mise-en-scène; in America, *Saturday Night Live* (NBC, 1975–) continues to be performed in a theatrical manner, even promoting its theatricality in the use of the word 'live' in its title. Yet theatrical performance is quite different from that which could be employed by television, with multiple cameras able to capture specific parts of the action and editing able to structure the rhythm of comedy scenes in particular ways. Because of this, it soon became clear that filming comedy as if it were on stage failed to capitalise on the abilities television technology offered. It was Karl Freund's work on *I Love Lucy* (CBS, 1951–57), developing a shooting style that became known as the 'three-headed monster' (Mellencamp, 1992: 322), that is seen as the aesthetic and technological breakthrough that bought television comedy into its own. Freund employed three cameras for every scene; in a scene incorporating two actors, one camera covered a mid-shot of the characters while the other two had closer shots of each actor. The wide shot was used to establish the situation, placing the characters within the mise-en-scène; the other two cameras could be cut between as part of any comedic exchange, offering a fast editing style that helped structure the rhythm of the comedy. Furthermore, Freund discovered he could get two laughs from any one joke; a close-up on a character saying something funny would get a laugh, and then a cut to the other character reacting to what had been said would get another. While reactions have always been important to comedy, television technology allowed directors to point audiences towards such reactions, and the reaction shot has since become a vital part of filming comedy. This shooting style has remained pretty constant for decades, and continues to be employed in *Will and Grace* (NBC, 1998–2006) and *The Big Bang Theory* (CBS, 2007–) by perhaps the most successful sitcom director in the world today; James Burrows.

That said, much sitcom has begun to move away from the 'three-headed monster' shooting style, and has instead adopted the aesthetics of a number of other forms. In America, this has mostly consisted of a more fluid camera style, with hand-held shots and editing that less obviously foreground the comic rhythm outlined above; this can be seen on *Arrested Development* (Fox, 2003–06), *30 Rock* (NBC, 2006–) and *The Sarah Silverman Program*. This development is much less apparent in British sitcom, though it can be seen in series such as *Ideal* (BBC3, 2005–), *Pulling* (BBC3, 2007–), *Nighty Night* (BBC3, 2004–05) and *Gavin and Stacey* (BBC3, 2007–); it may be significant that all of these series are on one of the BBC's less mainstream channels with a remit to invest in 'new, risk-taking ideas' for 'younger audiences' (BBC, 2008a: 19). These series have yet to be seen as a definitive movement in sitcom, and there has been little written – by academics, critics or the industry – on this development.

More vocal has been the response to another way in which sitcom has developed a new shooting style; the form known as 'comedy vérité' (Mills, 2004). Programmes such as *The Office*, *Marion and Geoff*, *Human Remains* (BBC2, 2000) and *People Like Us* (BBC2, 1999–2000) all have the visual characteristics of factual forms, especially those of the popular documentary or docusoap. Indeed, the comic conceit of each of these series is the relationship between the subjects of factual television and the production crews that make it, questioning the ability of documentary to 'capture' the truth of the world in the manner the format suggests. Considering sitcom's primary task is to signal its comic intent, adopting the characteristics of a factual form might cause problems, and there is certainly apocryphal evidence to suggest that some viewers were fooled, at least for a short while, into thinking series such as *The Office* were 'real' documentaries (Walters, 2005).

These series signal their relationship to factual forms in a number of ways. First, hand-held cameras result in wobbly camerawork that is one of the norms of the docusoap, and action is choreographed in order to suggest that it is being captured as it happens, rather than the clear and functional choreography commonplace in traditional sitcom. Second, the camera crews shooting the series are often acknowledged; *The Office* contains scenes of the characters talking directly to the camera crew in response to questions asked by the filmmakers, while *Marion and Geoff* consists of nothing more than its protagonist's monologues to the camera as he goes about his daily business. *People Like Us* takes this a step further, as the programme's only recurring character is the documentary maker, who visits a different workplace every episode in an attempt to make a documentary about it, but whose incompetence infuriates participants and results in a text that resolutely fails to conform to expectations for serious documentary. Third, the acting style adopted in each of these series is noticeably less excessive than that in traditional sitcom, and instead treads a careful line between the kinds of naturalism necessary in order to carry off the mock-documentary (Roscoe and Hight, 2001) conceit and the traditions of comic acting required in order for jokes to 'work'.

It is worth thinking about this in some detail, and the lengths these series have to go to in order to pull this off. Central to the success of *The Office* is the character David Brent, the boss of the eponymous office, who is played by Ricky Gervais, who also co-wrote and co-directed the series. Brent is the manager of a stationery distribution office, whose workers are demotivated and uninspired by their work, and the programme has been applauded for its 'realistic' depiction of the tedium of office work (Walters, 2005). Brent has plans for an alternative career, however, and is convinced he is a hilarious comedian, who motivates his employees through jokes, pranks and songs. The comedy in the series arises from the disparity between Brent's certainty of the value of such performances and his inappropriate actions; another disparity lies in Brent's poor abilities as a comedian, and he is routinely upstaged by other characters whose relaxed demeanour means the office staff are much more comfortable with their comic routines. Central to Brent, then, is a duality, for his job requires him to behave in particular ways, which conflicts with his desire for other forms of behaviour. This has significant implications for the acting in the series because this duality requires Ricky Gervais to signal the various roles Brent plays through different acting styles; the fact that Brent repeatedly plays up to the camera crew, giving them moments that he believes will make great television, only adds to the multiple performances on offer.

For example, *The Office* signals its 'vérité' characteristics by including moments where the characters are unaware they are being filmed, as if the camera crew just happened to come across a piece of action. These are often shot from a distance and extraneous objects are commonly in the way, such as office equipment or plants. The implication in such shots is that the characters are behaving 'naturally' and not performing for the camera; hence the acting style used is often muted. Brent's actions in these scenes are slow, with little bodily movement, and such scenes are as far away from the comic excess of traditional sitcom as can be imagined. In Erving Goffman's terms this is 'backstage' (1971 [1959]) behaviour, and the adoption of a naturalist acting style clearly has implications for notions of authenticity in character behaviour.

When Brent is 'frontstage' (Goffman, 1971 [1959]), however, Gervais adopts a noticeably different acting style. His desire to offer the camera crew the footage he feels would make good television requires Brent to dominate scenes and clearly signal his comic intent. In a number of scenes Brent employs silly voices, signalling the comic intent of his behaviour through traditional comic cues. His willingness to use his body is also clear, and his physical excesses and large gestures similarly match the acting style that sitcom has commonly adopted for decades. All of this behaviour can be seen in the opening, pre-credit sequence of the first episode of the second series of *The Office*. Shot all in one take, the scene begins with a number of the office employees absent-mindedly singing the 'Mah Nà Mah Nà' song from *The Muppet Show* (ATV, 1976–81), not as a comic performance for the cameras but instead as one of those activities employees often carry out merely to pass the time. Brent's office door is at the back of the shot and, some way through the song, he excitedly appears, joining in the song, walking towards the other characters who are nearer the front of the frame. As he does so, Brent carries out a little dance, expressing his desire to join in, and signalling in his bodily behaviour his awareness that this is a comic moment in the office. As the song ends, the characters stand rather bewilderedly, aware that they have just engaged in a piece of behaviour without a function, and not really knowing what to do next. Brent, like the other characters, turns and slowly walks away, returning to the drudgery of work. What is noticeable is the distinction between his movement in this return to work as compared with the movement when he entered the scene; while his dance is not excessive, it is clearly coded as 'abnormal' behaviour for an office and therefore beyond the bounds of what is accepted in this situation. His return to work, however, is signalled by a denial of the body, as his gestures become small and his movements insignificant. The scene clearly demonstrates the character's awareness of the performative requirements of comedy; in doing a little dance as he sings, he offers a small moment of excess which cues comic intent to the characters in the diegesis. What this suggests is that while comedy vérité is a clear interrogation of the conventions of factual programming, it also critiques the ways in which comedy is conventionally signalled, offering up David Brent as laughable because his comedy is based around such obvious and traditional cues. As Brent's humour is quite often derogatory, with unintentional insults hurled at people based on their race, class or physical characteristics, the programme suggests his humour is outdated and ignorant of contemporary debates about the appropriateness and power of comedy; in using a performance style resonant of traditional sitcom, the programme therefore aligns such humour with those excesses which have cued sitcom's comic intent for decades.

Yet it is important not to overstate the distinctions between these newer forms of comedy and the characteristics of those traditional forms from which they so actively distance themselves. In abandoning the live audience and the laugh track that have served sitcom for decades, newer forms of sitcom have instead adopted different techniques in order to maintain the presence of their performers. The most successful of these newer forms have been those that have adopted the comedy vérité format, for this is a technique that acknowledges a relationship between the characters within the diegesis and the audience at home who are watching such characters. That is, traditional sitcom has maintained the relationship between performer and audience by incorporating the audience's reaction into the programme, and this means that the text repeatedly reiterates the audience for whom the programme is made: in comedy vérité the audience is once again acknowledged and, in the conversations between the characters and the camera crew filming them, the production process is similarly apparent. Of course, this is actually more complicated than that; it is not as if 'real' people are talking to a 'real' camera crew, as would be the case in a traditional documentary or docusoap. Instead, what the audience is presented with are scripted and directed conversations between an actor playing the role of a character in a pretend docusoap and the camera crew who are actually filming those actors but who are purporting merely to record activities that would have occurred even if the camera crew was not there. So, while the actor plays a character, the camera crew plays a 'camera crew', and while this does not signal the fictive nature of sitcom, it *does* signal the production process that lies behind factual formats. These levels of the fiction and the real would appear to be highly complex; yet the fact that, on the whole, audiences have not been confused about such constructions demonstrates not only the pervasive characteristics of popular factual television in British broadcasting but also that these contrivances, and the ability to read a text as both real and fictional simultaneously, have always been strategies necessary to make sense of comedy on television.

Of course, this has significant implications for the kind of acting that is required. That is, in such programmes the performances must both make sense within the conventions of documentary realism in order for the factual characteristics that are being investigated to be adequately maintained: simultaneously, though, the performance must signal its comic intent and offer clearly defined moments of humour that audiences can unambiguously read as comic. Sitcom writers, producers and performers have always had to balance the needs of comic moments with the desire to create psychologically believable characters within recognisable worlds, if only because the pleasures of comedy are seen to be heightened if they relate to aspects of the world that an audience can relate to its own experiences. In the commentary on the DVD for *Marion and Geoff*, for example, the writer/producer/director Hugo Blick repeatedly discusses with the performer/writer Rob Brydon his tendency to abandon the 'truth' of his character for the sake of jokes, and Brydon's co-star Julia Davis does the same in the DVD extras of *Human Remains*. What is significant here is that such debates prioritise the 'realism' and 'truth' of a comedy character over their funniness, and, considering the BBC has a website on which office workers can discuss how much their boss is like David Brent (BBC, 2008b), it is clear that the promotion of such comedies encourages audiences to read the programmes relative to their own lives. What is going on in these debates is a battle over certain kinds of comedy, and it is one that led to Tony Hancock requesting that Sid James and Kenneth Williams ceased to be employed on *Hancock's Half-Hour* (BBC, 1956–60) because their performance style and vocal delivery were too obviously comic (Goddard, 1991). Contemporary comedy performance continues this debate; in using the mock-docusoap format, however, *The Office* constructs a text in which *both* forms of performance are diegetically legitimate, as Brent can be performed naturalistically when he does not know he is being filmed and can engage in more obvious comic material when he does.

Indeed, it is significant that many of the most memorable moments in *The Office* are those that are the most 'traditional'. In the fifth episode of the second series Brent is upstaged by new colleagues who engage in a well-choreographed dance routine for Comic Relief. Spurred on by his colleagues, Brent improvises a solo routine, full of odd and inappropriate movements, and, as the audience's enthusiasm wanes, he grunts his own rhythm, encouraging himself to continue the performance. The sequence can be seen as indicative of the programme's humour, as it is both funny and embarrassing at the same time. It can be read in a realist manner, for the psychological motivation behind Brent's behaviour is clear and, before he does the routine, there are a number of shots of his annoyance that others in the office are taking the spotlight away from him. The programme, therefore, goes out of its way to narratively and realistically justify the comic event, offering it not merely as a funny dance routine, but instead desiring it to be read as a moment that arises out of the psychology of the character involved. In that sense, it can be read as antithetical to the idea of comedian comedy outlined above.

Yet it is also clear that this moment does not have to be read in this way. Indeed, the fact that that sequence has often been shown removed from its context demonstrates how it makes sense without knowledge of the narrative event which led to it; it quickly became a hit on YouTube (BBC, 2005), and the BBC used it in promotional material for the licence fee. Someone doing funny dancing – if skilfully done by a talented comic performer – is humorous in and of itself, and contains the cues which suggest the ways in which it should be read, even if the diegetic information which surrounds it when seen within the full episode might add to its pleasures.

Therefore, I want to argue that it is a moment of comedian comedy, even if it is pretending not to be. While there is a psychological motivation to Brent's behaviour, it seems unlikely that Gervais, as the person who would have to perform the comic dancing, would agree to it being part of the script unless he felt it was within his comic ability. Indeed, in interviews and promotional appearances, Gervais has been requested to re-create the dance, just as John Cleese is often requested to do one of his silly walks. Such a request could only be made if the comic moment is understood through Gervais rather than Brent, and audiences would only be able to get pleasure from this de-narrativised event if its comic meaning was not reliant on factors outside of it.

This means that such performances can still be read as 'comedian comedy' even if there is perhaps an attempt to avoid the episodic nature of much comedy produced in this way. Rob Brydon's performances in *Human Remains* and *Marion and Geoff* work in this way too, especially as the latter programme consists of nothing more than an improvised to-camera monologue by Brydon, with the final episode a distillation of many hours' worth of footage. Chris Langham's performance in *People Like Us* works similarly, even though he never visually appears in the series. As the character Langham plays – Roy Mallard – is the filmmaker and cameraman for the documentaries he is producing, he is forever behind the camera and we only ever hear his voice. Langham's acting, then, rests on his vocal skills, and his performance in the series is one in which his slow, dull voice signals a disparity between a filmmaker's required enthusiasm in his subject and Mallard's inability to keep his mind focused on the job or encourage participants to behave in ways that would make a good film. While Langham is not the writer or creator of the series, it is clear that sequences are structured to encourage him to draw on the vocal skills evident throughout his career, and the comic meaning of much of the dialogue is heightened by his use of his voice.

Yet while I would argue that these performances can be equated with 'comedian comedy' it is apparent that there is unease within the programmes for such a categorisation. As has already been noted, the shooting style of these series carefully masks those moments that are most obviously comic, and the structures of the programmes attempt to suggest that the comedy instead arises from a naturalistic notion of character. Problematic for the idea of 'comedian comedy' here is that, as Seidman (1981) has noted, the fame and renown of a comic star create expectations from a text before the audience has encountered it; that is, the performer cues audiences into reading strategies. Yet all of the actors under scrutiny here were resolutely *not* stars before these series: Ricky Gervais was a virtual unknown before *The Office*, with only a few appearances on *The 11 O'Clock Show* (C4, 1998–2000) to his name; Rob Brydon had had a long and successful career on BBC Radio Wales and was much in demand as a voiceover artist for adverts, but *Marion and Geoff* is likely to be the first time national British audiences had come across him; and while Chris Langham has worked in comedy for decades, including being one of the original cast of *Not the Nine O'Clock News* (BBC2, 1979–82), he similarly never became a household name. This certainly helps support any sense of naturalism in the series, for if you are ignorant of who Ricky Gervais is, then you are not always aware that he is 'there' when watching him perform as David Brent. There seems, then, to have been a development here, in which comedian comedy remains a structuring force within successful comedy, even if there is an attempt to avoid drawing on the connotations of stars as one of the advantages of the comedian comedy system.

This avoidance of stardom can be seen by the short runs each of these series had; none of them lasted for more than two full series. While there is a question over whether any of them were massive ratings hits, their critical kudos and devoted (if small) audiences mean it is likely that they would have been recommissioned if their creative teams had desired. It has been noted that bowing out after a couple of series is a way of signalling 'quality', with the writers/performers of programmes that only ran for two series, such as *Spaced* (C4, 1999–2001) and *Gavin and Stacey*, referring back to *Fawlty Towers* (BBC2, 1975–79) as the exemplar. While this is often suggested to be because of running out of plots and ideas for certain characters, and not wanting to keep a series going beyond its peak, there is also a sense in such statements that keeping programmes running for years has certain consequences for performance and performers. Once an audience gets to know what to expect from an actor, the reading strategies bought to bear on a text change, and the actor starts to mutate into a star. While for an actor this can be limiting, it also clearly has consequences for the comedy on offer in such series. Many long-running comedy series develop catchphrases, and the times when these are used make clear the contract between audience and text at the heart of comedy. Victor Meldrew's cry of 'I don't believe it!' in *One Foot in the Grave* (BBC1, 1990–2000) occurs in most episodes, and the pause given by the actor, Richard Wilson, before delivering it cues the audience into expecting it. The pleasure an audience may gain from a catchphrase is not one of surprise, nor one of acting skill, but instead one of encountering that which is expected. Such catchphrases undermine any notion of naturalism or veracity that a text may have constructed, and actors who deliver them do so knowingly. Running throughout contemporary comedy performance is a desire to avoid such moments, and while this may be because of a wish to construct comedy that has links to naturalism, I want to suggest there may be another reason too.

A distinction which must be drawn here is that between 'acting' and 'performance'. The term 'performance' has been used in a variety of ways, especially since Goffman (1971 [1959]) and it is a word that is now 'so broad-ranging and open to new possibilities, no one can grasp its totality' (Schechner, 2002: 1). Acting is a little easier; for Naremore it is 'nothing more than the transposition of everyday behaviour into a theatrical realm' (1988: 21). In that sense, acting is behaviour that is not marked as such, and its success is commonly measured against an 'authenticity' (Burns, 1972: 106) that relies on the audience's lack of awareness of the production processes and interpretive intentions behind it. Performance, on the other hand, instead displays the skills, techniques and intentions within it, offering meaning and pleasure in its 'informal festive character' (Yi-Fu, 2001 [1990]: 161). In this way, comedian comedy is performance rather than acting, for an audience is not invited to enjoy comedian comedy as a 'truthful' re-creation of real-world activity, but is instead offered the pleasure of the mastery and skill of the performer who may 'stand outside' (Seyler, 1990 [1939]: 3) the character they play.

Of course, performance and acting cannot be neatly separated and it is likely that texts move between the two; I have argued elsewhere that this is the case in *Friends* (NBC, 1994–2004), where much of the comedy is presented as performance but the serious emotional moments are instead acted (Mills, 2005: 70–71). That said, it is clear that the history of television sitcom has been one in which performance predominates; the shooting style outlined above is the most suitable response to such performativity. The problem with this is that the consequence of such textual strategies is the marginalisation of the comic discourse as one unrelated to, and unable to comment on, the 'real' world outside of broadcasting. That is, in societies in which realism is valorised as *the* technique for representing the world around us, texts in which performance is foregrounded appear artificial and therefore of less serious import. Indeed, many critics have complained that, while comedy has for centuries been a powerful tool for critiquing and investigating social processes (Davis, 1993; Jenkins, 1994), its industrial forms within broadcasting – especially sitcom – have abandoned those aims in the name of pleasure, profits and consensus (Grote, 1983).

It is clear that the newer sitcoms examined above, while not completely abandoning performance, make moves towards encompassing acting as a suitable representational strategy within mainstream comedy broadcasting. Furthermore, many of them take Goffman's notion of 'performance' as the starting-point for their comedy; *The Office* is all about the different ways in which people 'perform' in front of, and behind, the camera, while *People Like Us* finds comic terrain in the disparity between actual performance and that required by Mallard's occupation. And a movement between performance and acting is a useful way to signal between frontstage and backstage (Goffman, 1971 [1959]) actions of the characters within such comedy. Running through these comedies is an awareness of the duality of character, and the ways in which individuals are required by social norms to behave in particular ways in certain circumstances; in that sense, 'culture is unthinkable without performance' (Striff, 2003: 1). In colonising acting – which has traditionally been the domain of serious/tragic texts – comedy has undermined the distinctions between acting and performance, and has therefore undermined the distinction between various social realms of behaviour, suggesting that neither is more legitimate.

Indeed, by making links between the two, and showing that everyday behaviour can be expressed through a mixture of performance and acting, contemporary sitcom critiques the generic distinctions commonly upheld between different kinds of programming and the appropriate representational strategies associated with them. Considering recent debates about generic blurring, especially those related to Reality TV and its supposed dismantling of the entertainment/information divide (Escoffery, 2006; Hill, 2007), it is perhaps unsurprising that comedy has similarly begun to question the representational limits placed on it for decades. In that sense, the movement in British sitcom from performance to acting may be seen as a significant statement about spheres of action inside and outside of broadcasting; the fact that audiences have, on the whole, been untroubled by this may be testament to the falsity of generic boundaries that have persistently attempted to uphold certain kinds of programming as more important, more worthy and more significant than others. The movement in sitcom from performance to acting is, then, a highly significant act.

References

Bakhtin, M. (1968 [1965]) *Rabelais and his World*, trans. H. Iswolsky, Cambridge and London: MIT Press.

BBC (2003) 'Gervais Tops List of the 50 Most Powerful People in TV Comedy', www.bbc.co.uk/pressoffice/bbcworldwide/worldwidestories/pressreleases/2003/01_january/rt_50_comedy.shtml (accessed June 2008).

BBC (2005) 'David Brent Dances to the Top of My BBC Poll', www.bbc.co.uk/pressoffice/bbcworldwide/worldwidestories/pressreleases/2005/02_february/mybbcpoll.shtml (accessed June 2008).

BBC (2008a) *BBC Statements of Programme Policy, 2008/9*, London: BBC.

BBC (2008b) 'The Office: Brentalikes', www.bbc.co.uk/pressoffice/bbcworldwide/worldwidestories/pressreleases/2005/02_february/mybbcpoll.shtml (accessed June 2008).

Bristol, M. D. (1989 [1985]) *Carnival and Theater: Plebeian Culture and the Structure of Authority in Renaissance England*, New York and London: Routledge.

Burns, E. (1972) *Theatricality: A Study of Convention in the Theatre and in Social Life*, London: Longman.

Butler, J. (2007) *Television: Critical Methods and Applications*, third edition, Mahwah and London: Lawrence Erlbaum.

Carlson, M. (1999) *Performance: A Critical Introduction*, London and New York: Routledge.

Cohen, W. A. (2005) 'Introduction: Locating Filth', in W. A. Cohen and R. Johnson, eds., *Filth: Dirt, Disgust, and Modern Life*, Minneapolis and London: University of Minnesota Press.

Davies, C. (2002) *The Mirth of Nations*, New Brunswick and London: Transaction.

Davis, M. S. (1993) *What's so Funny? The Comic Conception of Culture and Society*, Chicago and London: University of Chicago Press.

Davis, T. C. and T. Postlewait (eds.) (2003) *Theatricality*, Cambridge: Cambridge University Press.

Dyer, R. (1979) *Stars*, London: British Film Institute.

Dyer, R. (1986) *Heavenly Bodies: Film Stars and Society*, London: British Film Institute.

Escoffery, D. S. (ed.) (2006) *How Real is Reality TV? Essays on Representation and Truth*, Jefferson: McFarland and Company.

Féral, J. (1997) 'Performance and Theatricality: The Subject Demystified', in T. Murray, ed., *Mimesis, Masochism and Mime: The Politics of Theatricality in Contemporary French Thought*, Ann Arbor: University of Michigan Press.

Freud, S. (1960 [1905]) *Jokes and their Relation to the Unconscious*, trans. J. Strachey, London: Routledge.

Goddard, P. (1991) 'Hancock's Half-Hour: A Watershed in British Television Comedy', in J. Corner, ed., *Popular Television in Britain*, London: British Film Institute.

Goffman, E. (1971 [1959]) *The Presentation of Self in Everyday Life*, Harmondsworth: Penguin.

Grote, D. (1983) *The End of Comedy: The Sit-Com and the Comedic Tradition*, Hamden: Archon.

Hill, A. (2007) *Restyling Factual TV: The Reception of News, Documentary and Reality Genres*, London: Routledge.

Jenkins, R. (1994) *Subversive Laughter: The Liberating Power of Comedy*, New York and Toronto: The Free Press.

Kristeva, J. (1982) *Powers of Horror: An Essay on Abjection*, trans. L. S. Roudiez, New York: Columbia University Press.

Lockyer, S. and M. Pickering (eds.) (2005) *Beyond a Joke: The Limits of Humour*, Basingstoke: Palgrave Macmillan.

Lynch, O. H. (2002) 'Humorous Communication: Finding a Place for Humor in Communication Research', *Communication Theory*, 12, No. 4: 423–445.

Mayer, D. (1999) 'Acting in Silent Film: Which Legacy of the Theatre?', in A. Lovell and P. Krämer, eds., *Screen Acting*, London and New York: Routledge.

McGhee, P. E. (1979) *Humor: Its Origin and Development*, San Francisco: W. H. Freeman and Company.

Mellencamp, P. (1992) *High Anxiety: Catastrophe, Scandal, Age and Comedy*, Bloomington and Indianapolis: Indiana University Press.

Meyer-Dinkgräfe, D. (2001) *Approaches to Acting: Past and Present*, London and New York: Continuum.

Mills, B. (2004) 'Comedy Vérité: Contemporary Sitcom Form', *Screen* 45, No. 1: 63–78.

Mills, B. (2005) *Television Sitcom*, London: British Film Institute.

Mulkay, M. (1988) *On Humour: Its Nature and Its Place in Modern Society*, Cambridge: Polity Press.

Naremore, J. (1988) *Acting in the Cinema*, Berkeley: University of California Press.

Palmer, J. (1994) *Taking Humour Seriously*, London and New York: Routledge.

Pearson, R. E. (1992) *Eloquent Gestures: The Transformation of Performance Style in the Griffith Biograph Films*, Berkeley: University of California Press.

Purdie, S. (1993) *Comedy: The Mastery of Discourse*, Toronto: University of Toronto Press.

Radcliffe-Brown, A. R. (1952) *Structure and Function in Primitive Society*, London: Cohen & West.

Roscoe, J. and C. Hight (2001) *Faking It: Mock-Documentary and the Subversion of Factuality*, Manchester: Manchester University Press.

Schechner, R. (2002) *Performance Studies: An Introduction*, London and New York: Routledge.

Seidman, S. (1981) *Comedian Comedy: A Tradition in Hollywood Film*, Ann Arbor: UMI Research Press.

Seyler, A. (1990 [1939]) *The Craft of Comedy: An Exchange of Letters on Comedy Acting Techniques with Stephen Haggard*, London: Nick Hern Books.

Striff, E. (2003) *Performance Studies*, Basingstoke: Palgrave Macmillan.

Walters, B. (2005) *The Office*, London: British Film Institute.

Whitmore, J. (1994) *Directing Postmodern Theatre: Shaping Signification in Performance*, Ann Arbor: University of Michigan Press.

Wright, J. (2006) *Why is That so Funny? A Practical Exploration of Physical Comedy*, London: Nick Hern Books.

Yi-Fu (2001 [1990]) 'Space and Context', in C. Counsell and L. Wolf, eds., *Performance Analysis: An Introductory Coursebook*, London and New York: Routledge.

8

2-D performance and the re-animated actor in science fiction cinema

Christine Cornea

About 25 minutes into the science fiction film, *Hollow Man* (Paul Verhoeven, 2000), there is a striking scene that marks the literal disappearance of the central character, Dr. Sebastian Caine (Kevin Bacon), an ambitious young scientist working on an invisibility serum. Keen to try out his chemical creation, Sebastian persuades his team of fellow scientists to ignore normal protocols so that he can become the first human test subject. The film is basically an updated remake of *The Invisible Man* (1933), showcasing the wonders of cutting edge computer graphics technology, and the scene in question begins as Sebastian is strapped down to a gurney and injected with the serum. His gradual disappearance is displayed as layer upon layer of his body is stripped away, progressively revealing a network of veins, muscles, vital organs and skeletal structure, until all that is left is the indented outline of Bacon's body on the soft foam cover of the gurney.

The drama of this scene is accentuated as Bacon violently jerks and rolls his body to reveal the pain and agony of Sebastian's transformation and the surrounding team react with shock and amazement. In a somewhat playful twist, as Sebastian disappears from the screen Bacon's performance in this role becomes crucially evident. From then on the focus of attention is assuredly on Bacon, with the audience's gaze directed via point of view shots from various characters keeping tabs on his whereabouts through heat-detecting goggles and television monitors that register his bodily outline. Later in the film, Bacon's movements and gestures are rendered through digital graphics, as the character's body becomes vaguely perceptible when he takes a shower, walks through steam or is splashed with blood. Wearing a green or blue costume, Bacon was digitally 'painted out' of scenes in which the character was meant to be invisible, and then replaced with a three-dimensional, animated digital

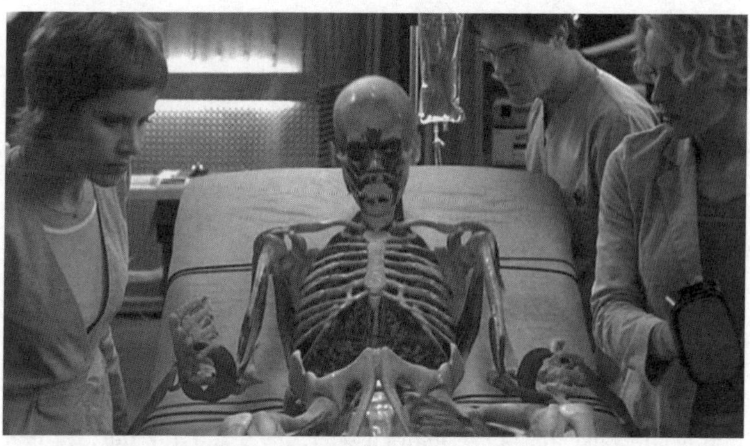

8.1 Sebastian Caine/Kevin Bacon makes the traumatic transition to invisible presence in *Hollow Man*

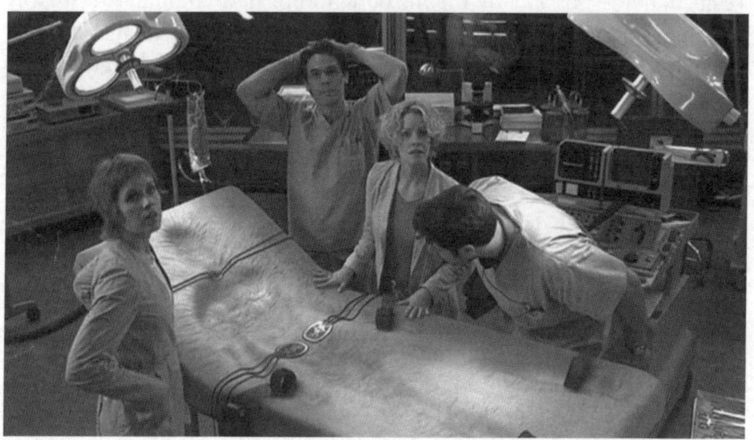

8.2 Indented outline on gurney marks the otherwise invisible presence of Caine/Bacon in *Hollow Man*

image in those moments when his bodily movements are discernible. As the film's director, Paul Verhoeven, described it:

> Kevin felt very uncomfortable at the end of shooting the movie because he realised that everything from then on would be replaced by another 'Kevin Bacon', a digital one. It was, I think, a hard thing to swallow, because he was giving us the tools for his performance - which was a physical,

> psychological and emotional one - then all these aspects were translated, as much as possible, into the digital world.[1]

If correct, perhaps Bacon need not have worried about his erasure from this film, as his presence is curiously intensified by his absence from the screen. While Sebastian's transformation into transparent psychotic killer justifies Bacon's amplified physicality, there is also a sense of hysteria in this performance. Aware that he was to be removed from the screen, it is as though the actor was adamantly imprinting his authority upon the film, the rendering of his excessive movement making his impact upon the film apparent.

By the time of *Hollow Man*'s release, CGI technologies had made a big impression in Hollywood, with hugely successful, comedy animation features like *Toy Story* (John Lasseter, 1995) and *Toy Story 2* (John Lasseter, 1999),[2] followed later by films like *Shrek* (Andrew Adamson, 2001).[3] Marketing of these films frequently laid claim to an unparalleled 'realism' made possible by the introduction of new computer technologies in animation. For instance, the treatment of animated characters as live players was signalled through their three-dimensional design, virtual camerawork, and fabricated cinematic lighting, alongside the familiar tones of recognisable star voices, which grounded the comic virtuosity of animated performances and supplied an additional aura.[4] Not only did all these films produce very healthy financial returns at the box office, but they received forthright critical acclaim in press reviews. Rita Kempley's review of *Toy Story* for the *Washington Post* praised the picture for its 'eye-popping parade of 3-D-seeming anthropomorphs' and its 'enormous humanity and heart', before moving on to state that 'all the digital gimmickry would count for nothing were it not for the zany and zealous vocal cast' (1995). Similarly, Todd McCarthy's review for *Variety* proclaimed, 'the writing is smart, the vocal performances are game, and the relatively lifelike look is stunningly realized' (2001). So, the combination of 3-D animated characters with energetic, star vocals in films aimed at a child and family market was judged as an acceptable and engrossing new form for feature filmmaking.

The trend towards CGI 'realism' was also seen at this time in attempts to produce greater degrees of visual veracity with science fiction animations like *Titan A. E.* (Don Bluth, 2000) and *Final Fantasy: The Spirits Within* (Hironobu Sakaguchi, 2001).[5] But as much as achievements in the rendering of dynamic movement in *Titan A. E.* and the photoreal human hair, skin texture and facial expression evident in *Final Fantasy* were celebrated in the marketing of these films, reviews and reports were less than enthusiastic. Discussions surrounding these films were frequently concerned with the disappearance of the human actor, replaced by the less than believable 'synthespian'. Stephen Holden, in his review for *The New York Times*, asked: 'why, given the movie's poignant notion of humans as intergalactic exiles, does so much of *Titan A .E.* feel emotionally flat and mechanically tossed off' (2000). In a review of *Final Fantasy* for *Sight and Sound*, film critic Dan Mayers complained, '*The Spirits Within* lacks emotional resonance: characterisation is excessively broad and its script routine' (2001: 43), while academic William Schaffer's account of *Final Fantasy* observed that 'the stunningly 3D virtual humans populating this film often display less depth than cardboard cutouts' (2004: 82). Unlike the children's cartoon-style comedies, these science fiction animations were aimed at a juvenile or adult audience and promised a convincing facsimile of human performance. However, it seemed it was the lack of believable human presence that brought about the less than positive reports of both *Titan A. E.* and *Final Fantasy* by critics and academics alike.

The difference in critical estimation of the cartoon-style comedies and science fiction animations, I would suggest, has much to do with the divergent modes of address and performance styles associated with the two genres. Certainly, *Titan A. E.* and *Final Fantasy* also featured star voices, although these tended to belong to actors new to animation voice-over and who had clearer previous attachments to 'straight' as opposed to comic performance. Although *Titan A. E.*'s wise-cracking action hero, Cale (Matt Damon), and street-wise heroine, Akima (Drew Barrymore), were voiced in a lively manner, these characters were not performed with the same degree of ostensiveness signalled in the overstated dynamism of the comedy vocals in *Toy Story* and *Shrek*. And, as if to place greater emphasis upon the visual construction of the film, *Final Fantasy*'s more serious dialogue was delivered in an especially flat manner: actors voicing the heroine, Dr. Aki Ross (Ming-Na), hero, Capt. Gray Edwards (Alec Baldwin) and father figure, Dr. Cid (Donald Sutherland), all employed an intimate but rather monotone style of delivery. My point is that the slapstick visual humour associated with children's animated cartoons and the string of verbal word plays and jokes as a feature of *Toy Story* and *Shrek* were aligned with a very different mode of vocal address from the more understated styles associated with the quasi-live-action science fiction dramas.

In his well-respected study of screen acting, James Naremore categorised styles of performance ranging from the presentational to the representational: the former involving a degree of awareness and direct address to an audience, the latter involving the pretence that the audience does not exist. Film genres like the musical and certain comedy forms are frequently associated with a more presentational style of performance, whereas most 'narrative movies depend chiefly on representational – in other words, the characters seem to be speaking to one another even though their performance is aimed at an audience beyond the "fourth wall"' (Naremore, 1988: 6). In a later study of acting and performance, Philip Auslander argued that a variety of acting styles common to live dramatic performance rely on the presence of the 'actor's self as the *logos* of performance'. It is this presence that grounds the performance and 'provides the audience with access to human truths' (Auslander, 1997: 30). I believe that this same understanding of presence also grounds cinematic performance, at least in the minds of critics and some academics. It is this same perception of presence that underpins critical estimations of film performance. I would also contend that the more presentational style of vocal delivery in *Toy Story* and *Shrek* actually worked to assure critics and audiences of the presence of the actor/star and therefore the actor's self behind the animated images on screen. Certainly, as Paul Wells has pointed out, there is a long history of association between American vaudeville and what can be taken as performance in the animated cartoon comedy (see Wells, 1998: 127-138). Even as these animated cartoon films moved towards the convincing construction of a fanciful but material world, it is not surprising to find residual elements of vaudeville's energetic presentational mode of address in *Toy Story* and *Shrek*.

Having set up the idea of the actor's self as a vital constituent of performance, Auslander goes on to contest this very notion of a grounding presence, stating that the 'actorly self is, in fact, produced by the performance it supposedly grounds' (1997: 30). Of course, in the context of screen performance, a literal form of presence is traditionally inferred through the photo-indexicality of the celluloid image. Also, the construction of the actorly self is not simply a product of the on-screen performance but takes place in the marketing, reception and interpretation of a film. While the more ostensive voice-over performances in the animated cartoon comedies allowed critics to assume an actorly self at the heart of the performance, what can be taken as the more naturalistic vocal mode in *Titan A. E.* and *Final Fantasy* did not apparently compensate for the known lack of a visual human presence in the science fiction animations; a presence that critics apparently yearned to engage with in these films. I would suggest that the hyper-real visuals evident in *Titan A. E.* and especially in *Final Fantasy*, along with the more representational vocal style adopted in these science fiction films, ironically worked to deconstruct the 'actorly self' in these performances. Consequently, critics felt that these films failed to deliver because the illusion of the actorly self as a grounding force was severely disrupted. Used to the presentational mode allied with cartoon animation and without the obvious, anchoring presence of an identifiable actorly self, critics were largely at a loss as to how to interpret the performances in the science fiction animations.

In some ways the construction of performance in *Final Fantasy* was not dissimilar to the reconstruction of Bacon's performance in *Hollow Man*: both *Hollow Man*'s substituted performance via digital mapping and the extensive use of 'motion capture'[6] in the creation of characters in *Final Fantasy* relied initially on the recording of human performance. The difference is that where audiences were treated to a 'digital Kevin Bacon' in *Hollow Man*, the recorded movement in *Final Fantasy* did not emanate from the actors who gave voice to the characters. While *Hollow Man* did not fare that well among critics, Bacon's performance was often praised. Writing for *Variety*, Robert Koehler called this performance an 'expressionistic triumph of actor and physical effects, putting voice and form to the drama's tragic irony of a brilliant mind undone by his own work' (2000). Likewise, Eric Harrison, writing for the *Houston Chronicle*, said 'Bacon is terrifically venal. He gives the kind of performance that people would praise as courageous if he were Tom Cruise or Harrison Ford' (2004), and according to Steve Biodrowski of *Cinefantastique*, 'Bacon does a good job (even limited mostly to his voice), first at establishing character and then at creating fear' (2000). The majority of critics found the special effects astonishing and impressive, but it was the script, plot and director's obsession with sex and violence that was generally thought to mark this out as an unappealing film. For instance, J. Hoberman of *The Village Voice* said that '*Hollow Man* doesn't have too many dull patches [but] neither is there much subtext' (2000). Certainly, Sebastian's characterisation was fairly one-dimensional but this is not uncommon in popular action or science fiction cinema. What is interesting is that at the same time as some critics took this to be a weakness in the film, Bacon's presence was very much in evidence in the reviews. Even as the performance of this character slips into digital reconstruction, it was understood as sutured to what critics took to be a convincing 'actorly self', in much the same way as the enthusiastic vocals of Tom Hanks or Eddie Murphy were respectively understood as the grounding forces behind 'Woody' in

Toy Story or 'Donkey' in *Shrek*. Of course, this may partly be explained by the way in which *Hollow Man* set up a live-action Bacon/Sebastian at the beginning, and by the way the viewer is theatrically presented with his disappearance and digital reappearance, as well as the presence of the ongoing live-action performance of the other characters. Instead of deconstructing the notion of the actorly self, the film actually placed emphasis upon Bacon as a star performer. Although many critics were eager for more depth of characterisation and were not persuaded by what they understood as the poor attempts at dramatic realism in the scripting of Sebastian, they did believe in Bacon.

As I have argued elsewhere, science fiction films frequently work to question traditional notions of what constitutes the human subject and, to these ends, have developed generic styles of performance that question, undercut and deconstruct accepted principles surrounding the physical and psychological nature of being human (see Cornea, 2007: 215-245). For instance, performance in this film genre often involves an overly mechanical and seemingly emotionless manner of acting or a blatantly ostensive approach, and styles are repeatedly clashed together to emphasise or question the difference between self and Other (e.g. human/machine, human/alien). However, in critical circles it appears that when the actor's visual presence is overtly compromised in science fiction, a more exaggerated and ostensive performance style is deemed necessary. Embedded within the traditions of science fiction, *Final Fantasy*'s re-animated, quasi-human characters can be understood alongside the genre's recent preoccupation with the melding of human and machine, most obviously seen in the figure of cyborg. In this generic context, the understated, somewhat emotionless, performance style of the film might seem appropriate - remember Arnold Schwarzenegger's machine-like Terminator and Peter Weller's mechanical Robocop. What was missing in *Final Fantasy* was a direct or discernible link for the audience with the 'actorly self' behind the performance.

Then again, a similarly understated acting style was also read as deficient in the second *Star Wars* series of films that emerged during this period, only this time it was the live-action performances that were criticised. *Star Wars Episode 1: The Phantom Menace* (George Lucas, 1999), *Star Wars Episode II: Attack of the Clones* (George Lucas, 2002) and *Star Wars Episode III: The Revenge of the Sith* (George Lucas, 2005) all made extensive use of CGI in the creation of alien settings and 3-D digital characters which appeared beside the live-action performance of human characters. The series was generally applauded for its spectacular use of digitally constructed vistas and characters, but the live-action performances of well-known actors like Liam Neeson and Ewan McGregor were understood as lacking in affective substance. Critics of the first film found it necessary to forgive the stilted acting style of its stars, most taking a view similar to that expressed by Roger Ebert, who said of *The Phantom Menace*: 'If some of the characters are less than compelling perhaps that's inevitable . . . I do not attend with the hope of gaining insights into human behaviour' (1999). Nevertheless, several critics were irritated by what they saw as an incompatible allegiance between the performances of animated and live-action characters. On this topic, Bob Graham of *The San Francisco Chronicle* noted: 'Ironically in *The Phantom Menace*, the animated characters have more human juice to them than the live ones. The humans, low-key and one-dimensional, are the stick figures' (1999). As the series continued, complaints about live-action performance in the films grew. Taking up the point about disparity between performances, Roger Ebert's review of *Attack of the Clones* suggested that the only characters 'who have inimitable personal style are the beloved Yoda and the hated Jar-Jar Binks . . . The other characters – Obi-Wan Kenobi, Padme Amidala, Anakin Skywalker – seem so strangely stiff and formal in their speech that an unwary viewer might be excused for thinking they were the clones' (2002). Likewise, in his later review of *Revenge of the Sith*, Ebert complained that the human characters 'talk in what sounds like Basic English, without colour, wit or verbal delight' (2005). While A. O. Scott, writing for *The New York Times*, protested: 'Mr Lucas's indifference to two fairly important aspects of moviemaking – acting and writing – is remarkable' before declaring that 'nobody ever went to a *Star Wars* picture for the acting' (2005). On the contrary, it seems that acting is incredibly important in these films. In my view, what critics were really objecting to was the clash of styles that came with the mix of animated and live-action characters. While the animated characters remained sutured to an actorly self through the vitality of vocal delivery, the somewhat monotonous and declamatory delivery of the live-action performances worked against the visual presence of stars like Neeson and McGregor. A star performance relies on the recognition of a star identity, detectable across a number of roles and performances and produced by the discourses that construct the star persona. Also, star performances are often framed by the busier or more ostensive performances of lesser-known actors, which work to make the star actor appear more realistic by comparison. However, in these *Star Wars* films, the ostensive performance style associated with animated characters did not function in the same way, as it provided a remarkably reassuring sign of their presence. In comparative contrast, the live-action performances produced by the stars of these films were so obviously de-naturalised that belief in their star identity was undermined and a sense of presence was lost. So, the fact that Neeson and McGregor were visually recognisable as stars in this film was not enough for critics to accept their performances as grounded by their presence.

Darko Suvin reads science fiction as a literature of 'cognitive estrangement' (1979: 63) and science fiction film frequently works in similar ways by defamiliarising representational codes and naturalism in performance. Also, as a film genre, science fiction is unusually located in a generic liminal zone, sandwiched between fantasy film and the codes and conventions associated with filmic realism. Therefore, its aesthetic composition frequently oscillates between familiar realism and fantasy construction, which often operates to foreground the constituent features in the performance of the human subject. The exploration of the boundaries between digital animation and live-action in performance is therefore relevant to the genre, and it is notable that even given the critical failure of the science fiction animation films I have discussed, the genre has certainly not deserted this terrain. Indeed, the recent release of *A Scanner Darkly* (Richard Linklater, 2006)[7] reminds us that an identifiable mix of photo-indexical and animated performance is certainly not new to cinema. Revealing a nostalgia for earlier cinematic technology, *A Scanner Darkly* is constructed entirely through a computerised version of rotoscoping, a system that traditionally worked with recorded and projected live-action performance that was then traced and overlaid by animation artists. The patent for the rotoscope was taken up back in 1917 when Max and Dave Fleischer developed this method in order to produce relatively life-like cartoon characters. By tracing over the recorded movement, frame by frame, as it was projected onto a translucent screen, the animator avoided the painstaking work involved in creating the smooth transitions necessary to convey fluidity in character movement. Rotoscoping may well have been developed as an expedient tool in animation, but unlike today's motion capture, its construction as based upon live-action footage was overtly present in many films. As Mark Langer puts it in his introduction to a special issue of *Animation Journal*, rotoscoping is detectable in the '*simultaneous presence* of the drawn and the photo-indexical' image produced by the technique (2004: 6). Even when early animators attempted to hide the use of the rotoscope, live-action footage was usually visible as an underlying element of the animation.

A well-known example of the rotoscope can be found in the Fleischer

Studio's *Betty Boop's Snow White* (Dave Fleischer, 1933), in which Cab Calloway's famous dance-walk was captured and re-animated as a ghostly character from the underworld. Calloway was a renowned musician and performer, easily recognisable as a presence in this re-animated creation. In fact, this darkly comic characterisation relies upon the particularly eerie affect created in the overlaid animation of a highly recognisable presence. In a similar fashion *A Scanner Darkly* relies upon recognisable presence, but it also foregrounds and plays with the construction of the actorly self in its use of film stars. Based upon a Philip K. Dick novel published in 1977, the film closely follows its narrative, which is unsurprisingly concerned with conspiracy, surveillance and a growing sense of paranoia fuelled by drugs and counter-cultural clashes with government. For the most part the film concentrates on the antics of a group of friends, all apparently addicted to a powerful hallucinogenic drug called Substance D: Arctor/Fred (Keanu Reeves), Barris (Robert Downey Jr.), Luckman (Woody Harrelson), Freck (Rory Cochrane) and Arctor's girlfriend, Donna (Winona Ryder). The audience learns that Arctor is an undercover narcotics agent, called 'Officer Fred', assigned by the Sheriff's Department to trace the suppliers of Substance D. To this end, the house in which Arctor is living is wired up with surveillance equipment to gather evidence and record the behaviour of the motley crew he has befriended as part of his mission. Arctor's friends do not know he is an agent and many of the officials at the Sheriff's Department are not aware that Fred is in fact Arctor. At the Sheriff's Department his anonymity is made possible by the use of a 'scramble suit', a futuristic coverall that alters the sound of his voice and masks his identity behind a jumble of ever changing, alternative identities. Wearing this as Fred whenever he reports to the Department, the plot thickens when he is asked to pay particular attention to Arctor in the recorded surveillance tapes. In effect, he is asked to watch himself and to assess his own behaviour. This, along with the heady and destabilising effects of the drug, oblige Arctor to question his own identity, which eventually leads him to become disconnected from any certain sense of himself.

From the opening of the film the issue of Arctor's/Fred's identity and true character is brought to the fore when, clad in his 'scramble suit', he is presented to an audience of suited men at the 'Brown Bear Lodge'. A formal introduction establishes his role as undercover officer and clarifies the purpose of the 'scramble suit'. Described by the host as 'the ultimate everyman' in his 'scramble suit', Arctor/Fred begins his speech using the flat and disguised vocal tones supplied with the suit. Declaiming the

8.3 Wearing his 'scramble suit', Fred is asked to observe Arctor on the monitors at the Sheriff's Department in *A Scanner Darkly*

dangers of Substance D he goes on to define his hidden identity as law officer and father of two children. However, the film audience is privy to conversation inside the suit and learns that Arctor/Fred, as his undercover name implies, is simply following an officially prepared script. From the outset there are indications of an inner conflict, played out in his reluctance to follow the pre-assigned speech. Any sense of who Arctor/Fred really is or the role he is really playing for the purposes of the film's narrative is left in doubt. At this point, all that is really left for the viewer to identify is the re-created image of Keanu Reeves.

A Scanner Darkly is set in a near future ('7 years from now' the opening title announces), but the rotoscoped images also seem appropriate to the period during which Dick wrote his novel. After all, use of the rotoscope alongside risqué narrative subject matter was prominent in Ralph Bakshi's decidedly adult and experimental animations: for example, his fantasy animations, *Fritz the Cat* (1972) and *The Lord of the Rings* (1978), and his science fiction animation, *Heavy Metal* (1981). Through animation, Bakshi explored counter-cultural sensibilities of the period, emphasising a dark underside and loss of certainty as linked to the hallucinogenic haze of drug culture. In comparison with Disney's output, Bakshi's animations could only be described as radical. As an independent filmmaker, the rotoscoping process used in both *The Lord of the Rings* and *Heavy Metal* allowed him to produce these films at a fraction of the budget assigned to Disney productions. But, as much as the use of the rotoscope might have made the animation feature film accessible and more affordable for Bakshi, on an artistic level I would say that it also expressed the uncertain nature and experience of life during this turbulent and confusing period. In a 1978 interview about his use of the rotoscope in *The Lord of the Rings*, Bakshi explained: 'This is live action with the *design* of animation . . . The thing about the movie – why the technique will be different – is that it's *not* a cartoon but rather the first realistic painting in motion' (Zito, 1978: 61). However, with the possible exception of *Heavy Metal* (which used the voices of well-known comedians and comic actors[8]), his films did not rely on the presence of well-known performers. In fact, reviews and features around these films primarily focused upon Bakshi as the creator and authorial voice behind the images on screen. Similarly, reviews of *A Scanner Darkly* focused upon the film's director, Richard Linklater (with reference usually made to his earlier use of computerised rotoscoping in *Waking Life* [2001]), but the performances in the film also provoked a great deal of comment. *Variety*'s Justin Chang complained that the animation had a 'flattening effect on the actor's faces', but he had no trouble interpreting the character of Barris as 'a flippant opportunist played to the hilt by Downey Jr.' (2006). Conversely, Andrew Sarris, writing for *The New York Observer*, found the performances 'subtly engaging' and particularly liked 'the interplay between the impregnable passivity of Mr. Reeves' Fred/Bob and the antic energy of Mr. Downey's bee-like James Barris' (2006). One of the most interesting comments came from Carina Chocano of *The Los Angeles Times*, who said that the rotoscoping technique 'turns Reeves et al. into still-familiar yet somehow more authentic versions of their characters. Less mediated by the hyper-reality of the actors' movie stardom, the characters become more engrossing' (2006). For Chocano, characterisation is foregrounded over star identity in this film. At the same time Chocano seems reassured by the 'still-familiar' images of the actors on screen.

Flanking populist reviews of the film, the discussion given over to performance in the promotional documentaries available with the *A Scanner Darkly* DVD is also striking. During an interview with Linklater in the documentary 'special feature', *One Summer in Austin: The Story of Filming 'A Scanner Darkly'*, he describes the actor Woody Harrelson as 'kind of like a silent movie star – say a Buster Keaton type – physical, kind of physical humour, almost slapstick'. Here Linklater implies Harrelson's suitability for the role of Luckman as inherent in his known acting style, a style associated with the ostensive physicality of Keaton and the presentational mode of slapstick. Even more fascinating is the second DVD

8.4 The digitally rotoscoped Keanu Reeves (Arctor/Fred) and Winona Ryder (Donna) in *A Scanner Darkly*

documentary, *The Weight of the Line: Animation Tales,* which is largely given over to the animators and the actors. With the notable exception of Ryder, the main cast (Cochrane, Harrelson, Reeves and Downey Jr.) provide comment alongside the animators responsible for overlaying their performances. Here the star cast talked about how they responded to this rotoscoping project in their performances. Cochrane said: 'Well, I kept in mind that they were going to animate it, so I tried to do more kind of weird facial gestures and stuff. I don't know if that is going to work or not, but I took some liberties I guess that I normally wouldn't, because I thought, you know, it's an animated film.' Similarly, Harrelson spoke about how he exaggerated his performance for the animators: 'In some ways I probably went a little more over the top than I would, because I knew it was going to be animated. I don't know, it just seemed to give licence to go a little more nutty.' Downey Jr. indicated that any exaggeration in his performance was due to directorial prompting: 'In fact, sometimes Ricky would come and say, we're going to animate this after the fact, so you can kind of do stuff – chewing up the scenery as much as you like on this next take.' And when asked about the particular requirements of acting for the famous 'scramble suit' featured in the film, Reeves stated: 'No information is being passed from the face. So for me then it was just about architecture . . . I might make a move a little bigger.'

The animators interviewed in *The Weight of the Line* also stressed the importance of the star performances. One said, 'it is actually their performance', and repeatedly drew attention to his reliance upon the live-action video footage. Along similar lines, another animator said, 'the good thing about the rotoscope is that it really gives you a realistic sense of the people who are doing the acting' and the animator responsible for artwork on Downey Jr. enthused, 'he's got such an animated way of acting, especially in this. He's just all over the place. He's rubbery and his face is just going crazy.' Also, a link was blatantly forged between animator and actor in discussions of the artwork for the character of Donna. At this juncture, much was made of the fact that a female illustrator (referred to as 'Blue') was considered best placed to undertake this work and discussions were largely confined to Winona Ryder's good looks and physical attractiveness.[9] So, in one way or another, the documentary went to some lengths to stress the grounding presence of these star actors and the importance placed upon their presence and performance. In addition, what becomes obvious in the interviews with the male stars is their adoption of a more gregarious or exaggerated performance style. These actors appear to pick up on the energetic styles associated with either early film or animated cartoon comedy, but there is also a sense that they were simply adding a more ostensive dimension to the kinds of performance styles they more usually adopt. Although Cochrane and Harrelson appeared to find the experience liberating, all these performances are familiar: the exaggerated acting along with rotoscoping worked to accentuate signature styles associated with each star identity. Also, it has not been missed that the casting of the film seemed designed to bring star persona close to character, allowing for given personas to resonate with the concerns of the film. As Nick Bradshaw pointed out:

> Harrelson, Downey Jr. and Ryder all come with their different drug controversies (Ryder is also the goddaughter of Tomothy Leary, name-checked in the book). And if Keanu Reeves, playing Arctor, does not intentionally reference *The Matrix* (1999) with its pastiche of Dickian communal hallucinations, then the opening credits certainly do. (Bradshaw, 2006: 43)

At the same time, as if to echo the experiences of the characters in this film, the rotoscoping technique seemed to weaken the viewer's hold on the veracity of the star identities presented on screen. On some level, watching this film is testing: I certainly noticed my own attempts to penetrate and probe the overlaid artwork, to get a glimpse of the photo-indexical image underneath. The actors' movement and expression seem both masked and heightened by the artwork, which draws attention to the construction of their performances. This forges a noticeable gap between actorly self and star identity, simultaneously interrupting and encouraging close identification with the characters on-screen. Star identity is both shored up and destabilised and the nature of the actorly self and a sense of 'true' presence are questioned.

Unlike Bakshi, Linklater has had repeated access to star performers. The kudos now associated with the 'serious' independent film makes up for the star fees associated with higher budget features. For the independent filmmaker, the use of stars can assure a wider audience and sometimes open the door to more mainstream projects. A desire to reach a larger audience may well explain the casting of the film, but the use and meaning of performance mark the film apart from popular mainstream product. Moreover, the questioning focus upon and interpretation of performance in press reviews reveal that critics were prepared to approach and understand this film in a different way from conventional science fiction or animated film. Primed by some of the earlier science fiction films and animated films I have discussed, movie goers are well aware of the ubiquitous existence of the digitally crafted film world of today. The convincing status once conferred upon the filmic image has been eroded by the photorealism that is now possible with CGI technologies. If the filmic image was ever a marker of certainty, then it no longer functions as such. A reassuring degree of certainty might be retained in the children's animated cartoon comedy, but this is located in the presence assumed by the star voice-over. Alternatively, as a genre that has long been concerned with displacing ontological certainty, any sense of presence that a star performer might confer is often diluted in science fiction cinema. *A Scanner Darkly* works with the codes and conventions of both the animated cartoon and science fiction film and playfully puts the power of performance back on the agenda.

Notes

1 This quotation is taken from an interview that I carried out with Paul Verhoeven in 2004.

2 *Hollow Man* (budgeted at approximately $95,000,000) had grossed $73,209,340 by November 2000 in the US and £5,968,350 by November 2000 in the UK. *Toy Story* (budgeted at approximately $30,000,000) had grossed $191,773,049 by September 1996 in the US and £21,700,230 by June 1996 in the UK. *Toy Story 2* (budgeted at approximately $90,000,000) had grossed $245,823,397 by July 2000 in the US and £43,294,228 by April 2000 in the UK. Figures taken from box office, www.imdb.com.

3 *Shrek* (budgeted at approximately $60,000,000) had grossed $267,652,016 by December 2001 in the US and £91,207 by October 2001 in the UK. www.imdb.com.

4 Main characters were usually voiced by well-known stars associated with comedy: in *Shrek,* 'Shrek' was voiced by Mike Myers, 'Donkey' by Eddie Murphy, and 'Princess Fiona' by Cameron Diaz, and in *Toy Story* the two main leads, 'Woody' and 'Buzz Lightyear' were voiced by Tom Hanks and Tim Allen respectively.

5 *Titan A. E.* (budgeted at approximately $75,000,000) had grossed $22,751,979 by September 2000 in the US and £761,323 by August 2000 in the UK. *Final Fantasy* (budgeted at approximately $137,000,000) had grossed $32,131,830 by August 2001 in the US and £2,371,630 by August 2001 in the UK. www.imdb.com.

6 'An animation technique in which the precise position and movement of an actor is recorded so it can be applied to the skeleton of a 3D character.' Definition borrowed from Goulekas (2001: 332.)

7 Made on a budget of $8,500,000, this film grossed $5,480,996 by October 2006 in the US and £561,707 by August 2006 in the UK. Figures taken from box office reports provided by www.imdb.com.

8 John Candy, John Vernon, Eugene Levy, and Joe Flaherty figure in the cast list.

9 Presumably Ryder's conscious performance was not considered important in this context and her presence seems defined simply by her physicality. At one point, the male voice-over accompanying shots of Blue working on Ryder stated, almost apologetically, 'there were a lot of shots where the lighting just wasn't there for us to really prettify her'. It is also significant that when the character of Donna dons the 'scramble suit', she is presented as a man with a distinctly male voice, indicating that female identity is not really an issue in the film.

References

Auslander, P. (1997) *From Acting to Performance: Essays in Modernism and Postmodernism*, London and New York: Routledge.

Biodrowski, S. (2000) 'Hollow Man', *Cinefantastique* (4 August), http://cinefantastique.com/2000/08104/hollow-man-review-interview/ (accessed 23 March 2008).

Bradshaw, N. (2006) 'Lost in the Loop', *Sight and Sound*, XVI, No. 8 (August): 41–43.

Chang, J. (2006) 'A Scanner Darkly', *Variety* (25 May), www.variety.com/award central_review/VE1117930642.html?nov=reviews07&categoryid=2352&cs=1&p=0 (accessed 26 March 2008).

Chocano, C. (2006) 'A Scanner Darkly', *Los Angeles Times* (7 July), www.

candendarlive.com/movies/reviews/cl-et.scannerdarkly7jul07,0,5662926.stay (accessed 26 March 2008).

Cornea, C. (2007), *Science Fiction Cinema: Between Fantasy and Reality*, Edinburgh: Edinburgh University Press/New Jersey: Rutgers University Press.

Ebert, R. (1999) 'Star Wars Episode 1: The Phantom Menace', *Chicago Sun Times* (17 May), http://rogerebert.suntimes.com/apps/pbcs.dll/article?AID=/19990517/REVIEWS/905170301/1023 (accessed 25 March 2008).

Ebert, R. (2002) 'Star Wars Episode II: Attack of the Clones', *Chicago Sun Times* (10 May), http://rogerebert.suntimes.com/apps/pbcs.dll/article?AID=/20020510/REVIEWS/205100305/1023 (accessed 20 March 2008).

Ebert, R. (2005) 'Star Wars Episode III: Revenge of the Sith', *Chicago Sun Times* (19 May), http://rogerebert.suntimes.com/apps/pbcs.dll/article?AID=/20050519/REVIEWS/50503002/1023 (accessed 20 March 2008).

Goulekas, K. E. (ed.) (2001) *Visual Effects in a Digital World*, San Francisco: Academic Press/Morgan Kaufmann.

Graham, B. (1999) '*Star Wars* Battles to a Draw: Breathtaking Animation, Flat Human Study', *San Francisco Chronicle* (16 May), www.sfgate.com/cgi-bin/article.cgi?f=/c/a/1999/05/16/PK1259.DTL (accessed 20 March 2008).

Harrison, E. (2004) *Houston Chronicle* (3 April), www.chron.com/disp/story.mpl/ae/movies/review/6244116.html (accessed 23 March 2008).

Hoberman, J. (2000) 'Men Will Be Boys', *The Village Voice* (8 August), www.villagevoice.com/film/0032,hoberman,17091,20.html (accessed 23 March 2008).

Holden, S. (2000) 'May a Slightly Different Force Be With You', *The New York Times – on the Web* (6 June), www.nytimes.com/library/film/061600titan-film-review.html (accessed 21 March 2008).

Kempley, R. (1995) '*Toy Story*: From Plastic to Fantastic' (22 November), www.washingtonpost.com/wp-srv/style/longterm/movies/videos/toystory.htm (accessed 20 March 2008).

Koehler, R. (2000) 'Hollow Man', *Variety* (1 August), www.variety.com/review/VE1117787726.html?categoryid=31&cs=18p=0 (accessed 23 March 2008).

Langer, M. (2004) 'From the Guest Editor', *Animation Journal*, 12: 3–6.

Mayers, D. (2001) 'Final Fantasy: The Spirits Within', *Sight and Sound*, No. 9 (September), 43.

McCarthy, T. (2001) 'Shrek', *Variety* (4 May), www.variety.com/review/VE111779795-/html?categoryid=31&cs=18p=0 (accessed 21 March 2008).

Naremore, J. (1988) *Acting in the Cinema*, Berkeley, Los Angles and London: University of California Press.

Sarris, A. (2006) 'Linklater's *A Scanner Darkly* Finds Slackers of the Future', *The New York Observer* (30 July), www.observer.com/node/39175 (accessed 26 March 2008).

Schaffer, W. (2004) 'The Importance of Being Plastic: The Feel of Pixar', *Animation Journal*, 12: 72–95.

Scott, A. O. (2005) 'Some Surprises in that Galaxy Far, Far Away', *The New*

York Times, (16 May), http://movies.nytimes.com/2005/05/16/movies/16star.html?_r-1&oref=slogin (accessed 20 March 2008).

Suvin, S. (1979) *Metamorphosis of Science Fiction: On the Poetics and History of a Literary Genre*, New Haven, Connecticut: Yale University Press.

Wells, P. (1998), *Understanding Animation*, London and New York: Routledge.

Zito, S. (1978) 'Bakshi Among the Hobbits', *American Film*, Part 10 (September): 58–63.

9

The multiple determinants of television acting

Roberta Pearson

Gene Roddenberry, legendary creator of the legendary *Star Trek* franchise, believed that viewers more readily recognise actors' work than that of other television workers: 'When Picard makes a wonderful, thrilling statement, the audience will say . . . "isn't he marvellous – isn't he intelligent?" And maybe "I would like to be like that" . . . They don't say "Wow – isn't that writer John Doe fabulous? . . . I would like to be like that" . . . It is the actors who carry the message' (Fern, 1995: 182). But the actors would have no message to carry without their colleagues' input – the producers' overview, the scriptwriters' words, the directors' shot selections. Actors' individual contributions to a programme's meaning are enabled or constrained by their colleagues as well as by the uniquely televisual conditions of production under which all the creative personnel labour. This chapter explores the multiple determinants of the televison actors' agency and creativity: time; the actor's status within the cast; the visual nature of the medium; input from other creative personnel and, last and most importantly in terms of this volume, the genre. The science fiction genre poses unique challenges for actors, as will become apparent. And what better science fiction show to choose than one of the most long running and beloved of all, *Star Trek*? Given their centrality both to the production process and to public perceptions of *Star Trek*, I focus on the two best-known captains, William Shatner – James Kirk in the original *Star Trek* (*TOS*) (Desilu/Paramount, 1966–69) – and Patrick Stewart – Jean-Luc Picard in *Star Trek: The Next Generation* (*TNG*) (Paramount, 1987–94) – supplementing the analysis with discussions of other *Trek* actors (much of what follows is taken from personal interviews conducted by myself and Maire Messenger Davies with *Star Trek* personnel).

Time

Time, not money, is the most precious resource in television production. It takes months to rehearse a play or shoot a feature film, weeks to shoot a television film or mini-series and approximately seven days to shoot a weekly episode of a television series. The need for speed most fundamentally determines the television actor's work. Speaking in 1968 while *TOS* was still on air, Leonard Nimoy (Mr. Spock) said, 'Time to cogitate, to digest or to live with an idea before committing it to film is strictly forbidden . . . On the *Star Trek* set we've actually had rewrites arrive seconds and even minutes after the scene had been shot' (Van Hise, 1997 [1968]: 49). Television changed a great deal between the 1960s and the beginning of the twenty-first century but time pressures remain a universal constant. Brannon Braga, executive producer on *Enterprise* (Paramount, 2001–05) said, '[the actors] get the script, they're shooting the script, and then on the last day of that episode, they get the script for the next episode and then they go right into that. When they rehearse it, they're rehearsing it right before the scene is shot. It's intensely high pressure. It's non-stop' (20 January 2002, Pearson and Messenger Davies).

Theatre actors have months or at least weeks to rehearse and build their characters. Film actors rehearse before shooting and can perfect their performance in retakes. Television actors have minimal rehearsal and need to get the shot right on the first take – retakes waste time. Time constraints exert tremendous pressure on television actors, making their jobs in some respects more difficult than that of their theatre and film counterparts. William Shatner characterised his three years of *TOS* as a 'workaday struggle, learning all those lines every day, learning the next day's lines every day. You have to be completely prepared, you have to know every one of your lines, you have to know exactly what you want to do with those lines, where your character's going, what you're doing, how you're going to do it'(19 January 2002, Pearson and Messenger Davies). If the actor doesn't know his lines or where his character is going, he won't get much help when he arrives on the set. Asked about rehearsals for *TNG*, Patrick Stewart responded, 'We would rehearse a scene in that we would walk onto the set and go through the lines and the moves but basically that would be it. This would be done very, very quickly' (12 March 1999, Pearson and Messenger Davies).

Shatner's and Stewart's pre-*Trek* careers predisposed them to respond differently to television's demands. Both actors began their careers in the classical theatre, but while Shatner soon concentrated on television

Stewart remained primarily a stage actor until getting the Picard role in his late 40s. Shatner found television's pace exhilarating: 'There is in television an excitement, an immediacy, a bravura if you will, because you know that if you miss a line, they'll give you the line right away, you go with it, you stay in the mood, in the tempo and it can be exciting'(19 January 2002, Pearson and Messenger Davies). Stewart, by contrast, discovered that the medium's hectic schedule denied him some of the pleasures of theatrical performance: 'I've often found, as many actors have, that the rehearsal process was as enjoyable as the performance. Rehearsal was a whole section of my life that ceased to exist and that investigative process, that building a character' (12 March 1999, Pearson and Messenger Davies). Television's fast-paced production means that character building takes place not in rehearsal but through an accumulation of episodes which establish a character's narrative arc and backstory. This is television's temporal paradox: actors spend far less time shooting each episode than they would mounting a play or shooting a film but over the course of a long-running series they spend far more time with a character than they would in the theatre or the cinema. Stewart described television's character-building process:

> I began to feel that I was not making individual episodes in themselves. That I was telling a story that had an unknown number of scenes or moments and that each episode represented a scene. The arc of Picard would not be complete until the camera rolled for the last time and the end of the story would have been told. Wherever you stop it, that would have been Picard's story. It was always moving forward, that's why I was always finding things. I made myself a promise early on that I would try to introduce something original into every single episode, a gesture or an attitude or some aspect of his life that hadn't been seen before just to keep something fresh always occurring. (12 March 1999, Pearson and Messenger Davies)

Over the course of 178 episodes Stewart found revealing new aspects of the character increasingly difficult and finally 'there came a point when there really was nothing more to be said about him or new to be done'. Stewart became frustrated at the absence of 'the process of investigation and analysis' that he had been accustomed to in the theatre and felt relief at Paramount's decision to end the series after seven years and transfer the cast to the big screen (12 March 1999, Pearson and Messenger Davies). It is not only the fear of typecasting or the chance of a film career that causes actors to leave long-running series; it is sheer boredom. Contributing to a character's narrative arc helps to alleviate boredom, although it requires access to writers and producers not granted to all cast members. In the *Star Trek* universe, captains come first.

Status

Production designer Herman Zimmerman said that the very design of the Enterprise's bridge emphasised the captain's centrality. Originally, the bridge was oval with 'a big oval conference table' but that lacked dynamism. Worse, 'it didn't give the captain precedence. And one of the things that Gene was really regretting, but then he realised that he had no other choice, was the star of the series had to be the captain. He wanted every one of the crew members to be the star . . . but always the captain has to have the last word, and the captain has to have the bulk of the action or the audience is confused' (20 January 2002, Pearson and Messenger Davies). William Shatner told *TV Guide* during the first season of *TOS*, 'I've gotten great insight into the omnipotence of the series' lead . . . It's an almost unique position few in the entertainment world achieve . . . it's like absolute power'(Van Hise, 1997 [1966]: 22). Stewart put it more succinctly: 'There are aspects of being the captain which benefit me' (21 January 2002, Pearson and Messenger Davies). If time primarily determines a television actor's performance, the actor's status within the cast is an important secondary determinant, with those playing the central roles perforce having greater agency and creative input than the supporting cast.

Accustomed from the theatre to the investigative process of building a character, Stewart took full advantage of the star's/captain's status to lobby for his version of Picard. As early as the second season of *TNG*'s seven-year run, Stewart was complaining about Picard's development and the writers' disregard of previously established traits. A letter to Gene Roddenberry outlined Stewart's conception of the character: 'Picard is leader, negotiator, peacemaker, ombudsman. He thinks, he talks, he assesses, he bluffs.' Stewart felt that Picard should display more humour and get involved in action sequences (Shrager, 1998: 30–32). Asked whether he encouraged the writers to explore different aspects of the Picard character, Stewart replied: 'in that I used to yell and shout when things weren't very good, yes, if you can call that encouragement. But I never worked directly with the writers on the scripts, the producers would not have allowed that.' In television, it is the producer, rather than the writer or the director, who most directly regulates the degree of actor input into a character. 'I did talk every day to Rick Berman [executive producer] about the scripts. I don't think a day passed that he and I didn't have some conversation about the current script. And he was always tremendously supportive of what I was trying to do, encouraging.'

But Stewart couldn't change dialogue without Berman's permission. 'You always had to get approval. No director was allowed to roll the camera if there'd been a script change without its being given the Rick Berman seal of approval.' With Berman's permission, Stewart regularly changed dialogue to make it truer to his conception of the character or of *Star Trek*: 'Any scene of any substance that I played throughout the seven years would somewhere in it have some tweakings or fine tunings from me.' Asked for examples, Stewart mentioned the second season episode 'Measure of a Man', in which Starfleet wants to dismantle Data (Brent Spiner) to see what makes him tick. Picard defends the android, arguing that he is a sentient life form entitled to self-determination:

> There is a speech in there that I have about slavery and Whoopi [Goldberg, who played Guinan] and I pretty much put that together between us. Let me be absolutely clear that the subject matter of the scene was the writers' but the intensifying theme and the specific words that I said very much belonged to me and some of it came from Whoopi as well, as I remember. (12 March 1999, Pearson and Messenger Davies)

When asked whether others in the cast had the same opportunities to contribute to their characters, Stewart confirmed that status is a powerful determinant: 'I think leading actors in series have done that [change dialogue] a lot. They can do it because they have the power to do it. It was not always as easy for my colleagues to do that. More often they were told shut up and say what's in the script. It was easier for me' (12 March 1999, Pearson and Messenger Davies). Lesser ranks have also sought to protect their visions of their characters but lack of clearly defined star status sometimes militates against their success. During *TOS*'s third season, Leonard Nimoy had frequent conflicts with Fred Freiberger, who had taken over from Roddenberry as executive producer. For example, in the episode 'All Our Yesterdays', in which Kirk and Spock are transplanted to an ice-age planet, Spock acts in a most un-Vulcan-like manner, falling in love with a woman stranded there and eating meat. Nimoy felt that Spock 'would never permit himself to behave in such a manner'. Freiberger agreed and the writers inserted a few lines explaining that Spock's transportation to the past had caused him to revert to primitive behaviour (Nimoy, 1995a: 119). But relations between actor and producer deteriorated and the frustrated Nimoy went over Freiberger's head, writing to Roddenberry and studio head Doug Cramer to complain about efforts to change Spock's image. A scene in 'Whom Gods Destroy' in which Spock has to decide which Kirk is real and which an impostor particularly incensed Nimoy.

In the past, said Nimoy in his memo (October 1968), Spock could have quickly resolved the situation through a Vulcan mind meld but now 'he is unable to cleverly, dramatically, or fascinatingly arrive at a solution' (Nimoy, 1995b: 125–126).

In *Star Trek Memories*, William Shatner reproduces Nimoy's memo but also recounts an interview with Freiberger. Freiberger acknowledged that Nimoy's concerns with regard to 'All Our Yesterdays' had been valid, but felt that the actor's expectations for his character were incommensurate with his position in the cast. At one meeting, Freiberger reminded Nimoy that Shatner was the star but the actor 'insisted that he was a co-star of equal stature'. Nimoy's belief in his equal stature, thought Freiberger, was the basis of their misunderstandings: 'Although the Spock character was heavily involved in almost all of our episodes, the "star" of a show *would* have gotten more emphasis.' After this meeting, Freiberger phoned Roddenberry for clarification: 'It was my understanding that Bones and Spock were very important but that Kirk was the star . . . Roddenberry assured me that my original understanding was accurate' (Shatner, 1993: 271–272). Freiberger believed that the desire for more screen time motivated Nimoy. The actor himself asserted that he was simply striving for character consistency:

> I thought it was *my* responsibility to look after the character. You see, after a television series has been on the air for a period of time, the staff will undergo a good deal of turnover. Writers, directors and producers all come and go; only the actors, usually, remain. So the actor is ultimately the 'keeper of the flame' for his or her character. It often falls to the actor to point out to incoming producers and directors any inconsistencies in the character . . . If the actor doesn't take on the responsibility, a character 'drift' is likely to take place, and not necessarily for the better. (Nimoy, 1995a: 121)

Nimoy's successor as first officer, Jonathan Frakes also had producer problems, since Gene Roddenberry's conception of the Will Riker character did not necessarily play to his acting strengths: 'One of the things he wanted was for me not to smile, and for Jonathan Frakes not to smile is really a tough chore. He used to insist that Riker has a military bearing, and a derring-do, and he wanted a Gary Cooper, Midwestern stare. And I used to have that physicalisation of looking like I had a stick up my ass.' In the second season, perhaps aware that fans disliked the character and had nicknamed him 'Will the Stick', Roddenberry, together with Berman and first season producer Morris Hurley, 'allowed a little more Frakes to slide into Riker. So, I was able to smile. I started to play the trombone in the show. And they wrote to that a little bit. I sort of incorporated a kind of a John Wayne mien and walk into it, so I had a little more laconic kind of a cowboy thing going on' (22 January 2002, Pearson and Messenger Davies). Frakes, like many actors in long-running shows, drew on aspects of his own personality to round out his character. In retrospect, judging from my own and fan reactions, Roddenberry's valuing of his own agency over that of Frakes seems a bad choice and Berman and Hurley's recognition of Frake's agency a good one. Making his character more like himself, Frakes emphasised Riker's humour and playfulness. These character traits become more pronounced in the two Frakes-directed features, *First Contact* and *Insurrection*, during the production of which Frakes, as director as well as co-star, had greater agency than in the television series.

Status is determined not only by televisual but by cultural expectations, with gender being a key factor. Female characters, even captains, have to exhibit greater conformance to gender norms than do male characters, particularly with regard to appearance, as Canadian actor, Genevieve Bujold, found during her brief association with the franchise. Originally cast as the captain of *Star Trek: Voyager* (Paramount, 1995–2001), Bujold quit a short while into the shooting of the pilot, 'Caretaker'. During her brief time in command she had to endure constant changes of hairstyle as the producers sought to solve the culturally imposed conundrum of a female character's being simultaneously authoritative and attractive. Winrich Kolbe, director of 'Caretaker', talked about the 'hair problem':

> For some odd reason, the gods had not quite figured out what kind of hairdo Captain Janeway would be wearing. I remember one scene where she comes on the bridge with one hairdo, then we shot a closeup with another hairdo, then she leaves and there's a third hairdo. And then we cut to the following scene where she comes down the hallway, and the fourth hairdo. They were futzing around with her hair, and then finally we got it. To a degree. I think they switched it later on. I think there must have been just, you know, an assault on femininity. Because nobody would have dared do it with a man. But with a woman, always have to futz around with her hair. You know, is it up, is it down, the lifts, why is it dark, is it black, is it brown? So, that was, I think we spent five days to just reshoot for hair. (23 January 2002, Pearson and Messenger Davies)

Kate Mulgrew, Bujold's successor, also suffered from the hair problem, her coiffure frequently altering during *Voyager*'s seven-year run.

Marina Sirtis, ship's counsellor Deanna Troi on *TNG*, had her agency constrained not only by being lower down the fictional chain of command than Mulgrew but also by her designation as the show's 'babe', the female character intended to appeal to the key male adolescent (or males with adolescent inclinations) audience. Having felt unattractive as a teenager, Sirtis generally relished being the babe although she did find one aspect of the role objectionable: 'I was happy to be the babe, less happy to be the object in Rick's office being poked and prodded. I was literally put in the costume, and then, go and show Rick. I stood there like a non-person almost, while they decided how I was gonna look.' Acutely aware of her position in the cast hierarchy, Sirtis rarely fought for input:

> Pretty early on I realised that there was a pecking order on *Star Trek*. And I realised that I really didn't have an awful lot of power. I never was comfortable asking for changes, questioning the authority figures if you like. I kind of left that to Patrick and Brent. I felt they had more clout. The only time that I ever really made a phone call to Rick was if it was so obvious that they'd been going through the script, and they thought, 'Oh, look, Troi hasn't said anything in ten pages, let's give her one of Data's lines.' And I would call and say either fix it to make it a Troi line or just give it back to Data or Geordi or whoever it is. (23 January 2002, Pearson and Messenger Davies)

The visual

Producers and writers exert great control over actors' dialogue; only the most privileged or aggressive can make changes. But the speed of television production, with no time for retakes, ensures that no one exercises much control over the non-verbal aspects of actors' performances. Since the days of pre-Hollywood cinema, actors have used facial expressions, looks and glances to convey implicit meanings not necessarily overtly present in the script. For example, Jonathan Frakes and Marina Sirtis, annoyed by the writers' dropping the romantic relationship between Riker and Troi established in the first season, kept it going through non-verbal means. Said Frakes:

> They had made such a big deal of it in the pilot and then essentially brushed it under the table. Marina and I refused to let it go. We always believed that our two characters were still in love with each other, and that would inform our behaviour in scenes, and we'd often have meaningful looks, or we'd be together in social functions on the ship. We decided, without the writers' help, that we would maintain this thing. (22 January 2002, Pearson and Messenger Davies)

Viewers picked up on the visual cues and the Riker/Troi relationship, according to research that Frakes had seen, became 'a very popular element of *Star Trek: The Next Generation*' (22 January 2002, Pearson and Messenger Davies). Like Frakes, Patrick Stewart wondered why the writers seemed to have abandoned his character's romantic relationship, in Picard's case with ship's doctor Beverly Crusher (Gates McFadden): 'I know there is a school of thought that a Picard/Crusher relationship never existed but I am a little puzzled by this as I spent hours in front of the camera last season assuming – and acting – that it did' (Shrager, 1998: 30–32). And like Frakes, Stewart constructed the relationship 'without the writers' help', through non-verbal performance; posture, gestures, facial expression. For example, in the first season episode 'Angel One', a virus incapacitates most of the crew, including the captain. Crusher comes to care for Picard in his quarters, where he has collapsed into his bed. As she raises his head to the cup to administer the liquid antidote, he gives her what can only be described as a yearning look. No words are exchanged; the look alone makes clear Picard's unspoken feelings; this presumably was Stewart's doing, not the writer's or director's.

Facial expression is perhaps the most important component of a screen actor's non-verbal repertoire. The smaller screen size makes facial expression even more important in television than in the cinema; much of television consists of close-ups of the actors' faces. As has been the case since the establishment of the classical editing system in the silent cinema, narratively central characters are accorded the greatest number of close-ups. *Star Trek*, not surprisingly, privileges the captains over all other characters; many scenes, particularly those before commercial breaks, end with a reaction shot of the star. Whatever the actor is thinking or not thinking, the viewer probably infers that the captain is planning a course of action, since that is the character's narrative role. Other characters' narrative roles warrant reaction shots as well. Marina Sirtis didn't ask for more dialogue partly because she knew that her character would get a fair number of reaction shots; these dialogue-less shots show captains planning and empathic counsellors feeling: 'I did a lot of what we call, jokingly, face acting. Reacting acting. I got a lot of screen time making faces, so it didn't matter to me so much that I wasn't actually saying anything' (23 January 2002, Pearson and Messenger Davies).

Experienced and accomplished actors like Patrick Stewart use non-verbal performance to augment the script and round out their characters. In scenes set in the captain's ready room, for example, Picard would often pick up and play with a stylus-shaped crystal. Stewart used this and the other small props on the captain's desk to convey the captain's state of mind. Said Stewart, 'I used to make those choices if I was trying to show some sort of state of mind because for the most part Picard tended to be rather passive – or focused really rather than passive.' Stewart said that he used such techniques to

> make [Picard] seem more complex than perhaps he really was. I think that's quite a commonplace technique that if there is a tendency in a character it's more interesting to conceal the tendency and disguise it as something else which may not be as authentic as the tendency itself and so something immediately becomes multi-layered . . . When I go to watch actors act, the kind of people I like to watch are those who are all suggesting that there's more than one thing going on which there always is in all our lives. I tended to be very secretive with Picard. Often not show what he was thinking or feeling but to submerge behind duty and responsibility and so forth. (12 March 1999, Pearson and Messenger Davies)

Collaborators' influences

Stewart had not, of course, bought that stylus-shaped crystal or placed it on the captain's desk; that's the job of the set dresser. Roddenberry may have been right in thinking that viewers ascribe the message to the character, but that character emerges from the combined efforts of numerous people. As we have seen, producers, particularly the 'show runner', and writers have a great deal of influence. But television directors don't, for the most part, contribute a great deal to characterisation, lacking the time or incentive to work with the actors on their performances. William Shatner believes that a television director's reputation is based on sticking to a shooting schedule not on quality of output: 'Most television directors are traffic directors. If they can bring their show in on or under budget, on or under time, they'll be rehired . . . He doesn't have time for vision. What he has time for is to set the camera up, you sit there, I'll shoot you, now you don't move, I'll turn the camera over there, same lighting, I'll shoot you' (19 January 2002, Pearson and Messenger Davies). Television's temporal paradox – fast-paced production of each episode, long run of tens or hundreds of episodes – also militates against directorial input. Directors come and go while, as Leonard Nimoy said, actors come to own their characters and resist inconsistent input. Patrick Stewart confirmed this: 'So far as the seven of us that were with the series through to the end were concerned there was nothing to rehearse because it would take a brave director to tell us what we should do because very quickly we knew better than anybody else' (12 March 1999, Pearson and Messenger Davies). Winrich Kolbe, director of 'Caretaker' as well as several episodes of each of the spin-off *Trek* series, did not entirely go along with this: 'In every long run, whether it's Broadway or the West End, or television, people get into a rut. "We've always been doing it this way." "I always come in this way." "I never would do something like that."' Kolbe is critical of this attitude; he 'liked to shake people up a little' (23 January 2002, Pearson and Messenger Davies).

But the weekly grind of turning out the next episode often causes television actors to cling to what they've 'always been doing'. Directors, even those like Kolbe who return for several episodes, simply aren't around long enough to have much effect on actors' conceptions of their characters. Just as the actors benefit from television's temporal paradox of rapid production schedules and very long runs, so do the craft workers – set and costume designers, set decorators, and so on – who have the time to establish great mastery of their individual tasks and to build good working relationships with the rest of the production team, including the actors. Costume designer Robert Blackman said that working with the actors on a regular basis made him very aware of their concerns about costumes.

> I'm very good at getting past things that actors are nervous about, that they're afraid of, and getting them to see that you think that's an issue, but it's really not an issue. It may make you too uncomfortable to wear it but we ought to try once. And if it does, we'll never do it again. But since we're doing seven years of 26 episodes a year, why not have all of us experiment? (24 January 2002, Pearson and Messenger Davies)

Blackman regularly persuaded the actors to experiment, particularly with new looks for their characters. The actors' ability to persuade Blackman depended, as it does with the executive producer and the writers, upon status and the time spent playing the character. 'With the actors, it's kind of a collaborative thing,' but the nature of the collaboration changes as the actors 'get more confident and more power in their position.' With costumes as with everything else, captains/stars come first. When Blackman joined the *TNG* production crew in the third season, he redesigned the officers' uniforms. Said Blackman, 'I added the collar because I thought [the old ones] just looked like pyjamas. They just needed more formality. They needed to be heroes.' A captain played by Patrick Stewart needed a particularly heroic costume: 'I thought because of his language, the way he spoke, and who the captain was. He was this very dignified man in pyjamas.' Unlike the other six members of the ensemble cast, Stewart had the power to ask for specific and distinct costumes for his character. Blackman responded to these requests. 'Later we went into civilian clothes, we started doing the heroic stuff on him, and cutting it down, so that he could feel more heroic and less tight (24 January 2002, Pearson and Messenger Davies). Stewart confirmed that costume influences his performance:

> It makes you feel a certain way. I know [a costume] affects the way I move, the way I sit, my attitudes and so forth and the uniform for Picard was especially persuasive. You just have to stand in a certain way. And no pockets means you always have to find something for your hands to do or do nothing with them at all, which is usually the best thing to do. The costumes required a certain physical attitude all the time and that helps to produce these appropriate feelings about being the character. (12 March 1999, Pearson and Messenger Davies)

Stewart's comment on pockets shows how small details, perhaps unnoticed by the viewer, can affect performance. Props and sets also affect performance and produce appropriate feelings about being a character. As set dresser Jim Mees told us, 'It was the personal items that developed the character that were much more important to the actors than more impersonal items such as furniture.' Mees always consulted with the actors about the personal items in their quarters:

> I always think of myself as somebody who is there to make you look good, as the actor. And I went to theatre school and I really do understand these issues, so whenever I've got to do a set, even if I'm given quite specific instructions from the producers or from Rick or whoever it is, I do go to the actor. So I remember many times having conversations with Marina or Jonathan or Levar [Burton who played engineer Geordi Laforge], who was supposed to be blind, but, you know, still had to have some sensibility of the space he was in. (24 January 2002, Pearson and Messenger Davies)

Mees worked closely with one of the key actors in *TNG*, Brent Spiner, on the Data character's development over the show's seven-year run. 'Brent's character has progressed so much from what it was in the beginning, and so, yeah, we always work that through.' Data's quarters originally contained only a desk and a computer but 'as he had a quest to become more human, we had to keep bringing in more things' (24 January 2002, Pearson and Messenger Davies).

Graphics designer Michael Okuda sometimes had to explain twenty-fourth-century technology to actors wanting to make their performances more convincing:

> Patrick Stewart has on a couple of occasions said, 'I need to do this, I want to make sure that I'm doing this in a believable way.' I remember one specific time I said, 'Well, just punch a few buttons there and there.' And Patrick said, 'No, no, I want to know what does this do?' And fortunately, on that particular occasion, it was something where I had actually thought about how you would do this. So I said OK, you tap this and then you do this to activate the system and then you enter the coordinates in this.

Okuda had a similar conversation with Marina Sirtis, who, as the counsellor, didn't often interface with the technology:

> Marina Sirtis had a particularly complex thing that she needed to do and she was afraid that it might not come across credibly. And I explained to her that the control panels were software defined, which means that the panel reconfigures itself to whatever the task at hand is. And she thought about it and said, 'Oh, OK, that makes sense.' My giving the help to her I think it made her feel more at ease with what she was doing. (24 January 2002, Pearson and Messenger Davies)

Genre

Stewart and Sirtis adapted to acting science fiction by believing in the universe and making it believable for their viewers but other actors never feel at ease in the science fiction genre. Robert Beltrane, who played first officer Chakotay in *Voyager* didn't feel comfortable with the science fiction genre:

> The writers are very open to ideas, but my problem is that because I don't think in terms of Science Fiction, I'm hindered in being able to come up with inventive ideas . . . Science Fiction is not one of my favourite genres . . . I prefer to let the writers do the writing, because they seem to be more in the frame of mind than I am . . . As far as the general arc of my character is concerned, I guess that I should get more involved, but I honestly have very few ideas of my own. In another genre, I'd probably be more creative. (Joy, 1998: 58)

The complexity of the *Star Trek* universe may have partly accounted for Beltrane's reluctance to get involved and certainly accounts for the executive producer's close monitoring of dialogue changes. Patrick Stewart told us, 'I know of shows where there's a terrific amount of almost improvisation. With science fiction it's hard. You've got to get the techno babble right' (12 March 1999, Pearson and Messenger Davies). Jonathan Frakes said that working in the science fiction genre increased the need for the executive producer's oversight: 'Part of it has to do with maintaining control of the ship, no pun intended. It's easier to make changes on other shows. If you're directing a contemporary show, and you're changing a line, you're changing it because it feels more colloquial, or it feels more appropriate, and it doesn't generally become a megillah that has to get called up to the Bochcos' (22 January 2002, Pearson and Messenger Davies).

The demands upon *Star Trek* actors to operate the technology in a credible fashion or get the techno babble right aren't necessarily specific to the science fiction genre; *ER* actors, for example, must convincingly deliver reams of high-speed medical babble and manipulate life-saving equipment. But *Star Trek* actors face a further set of challenges posed by the non-realist universes of the science fiction and fantasy genres. As director Winrich Kolbe put it, 'There's a lot of make believe. If Picard welcomes a non-existent alien, it's kind of tough. How do you act to that person? Is he wider than he is tall?' (23 January 2002, Pearson and Messenger Davies). The non-existent alien will only be realised in post-production but the cast has to imagine his presence and interact with or react to him. To stray from *Trek* for a moment, *The X-Files* actors had the same problem. David Duchovny (Fox Mulder) spoke to *The New York Times* about the challenge of acting with the show's monsters and aliens:

> The hardest thing about the show was modulating his reactions to the various creatures. Early on he and Ms. [Gillian] Anderson had to watch a blank night sky and react to some UFOs that the special effects people would insert later. 'We're acting all amazed at the technology, shaking with excitement,' he recalls. 'And then we saw the show and it looked like a Pong game, these little things in the sky. We got burned on that.' So in an attempt to underplay his surprise, he offered a dead-pan expression when the director told him to react to the Fluke Man, a six foot intestinal worm that would also be photographed later. 'And then I see the show and the Fluke Man is the most amazing thing that anyone could have seen and there's no way that this' – he makes a deadpan face – 'was an appropriate reaction. In any universe.' The safest policy, the actors have found, is to change facial expressions rarely. Mr. Duchovny always has a sad, obsessed, bemused look, and Ms. Anderson always has a serious, open-mouthed, disbelieving look. (Dowd, 1995: H37)

Actors get better at these interactions over the run of a series. Kolbe said:

> When I came into *Star Trek* [*TNG*] all the guys knew already what they had to do with the blue screen [the ship's view screen] ahead of them. But when

> you have a new cast, like on *Voyager*, it's an interesting challenge to actors, because they now suddenly have to imagine things. It's my job to tell them what they imagine. (23 January 2002, Pearson and Messenger Davies)

Here at least, the director seemed to have a useful function for the actors, serving as the liaison between them and the visual effects staff who designed what eventually appeared on the view screen. The director also helped the actors to respond to the impact of photon torpedoes and other weapons. All the *Trek* casts, Kolbe pointed out, had to internalise a carefully calibrated set of 'ship-shake' staggers to convey their starship's instability: 'If the camera goes this way, the ship goes the other way, so they have to make those movements. The ship shakes. One two three' (23 January 2002, Pearson and Messenger Davies).

Conveying a character's thoughts and feelings while burdened with the elaborate and often cumbersome wigs, make-up and costumes of the science fiction/fantasy genres poses yet another challenge for actors. Michael Westmore, the supervising make-up designer responsible for some of the discomfort that *Trek* actors regularly had to go through in being made up as aliens, told us a story about one of his favourite make-up jobs on an actor who had a part as an android in *TNG*'s 'The Offspring':

> The actor couldn't see, he had thick contact lenses on . . . The rubber head that he had came right over his ears, because the character had no ears. He had no nose, so he couldn't smile. He had a mouth that was down here . . . He had a rubber chest on, and we built a rubber diaper for him, since he couldn't go to the bathroom all day once he got put into his appliance. And then once we glued all this on, we painted him all this coppery gold colour. And there he was. It took four hours to get him in, he'd work a 12 hour day, and it would take about an hour and a half to pull it off at night. During that entire time, he wouldn't eat or drink and he really couldn't lay down. But he was a dancer, and he was very strong. (24 January 2002, Pearson and Messenger Davies)

Some of the craft workers, like Blackman, seem quite sensitive to an actor's physical needs, while others like Westmore don't really mind the discomfort they impose upon the cast.

Imaginary aliens and cumbersome costumes made acting in *Star Trek* different from acting in *ER* or *The Sopranos*, but there is a more general distinction between acting in science fiction/fantasy and a realist drama. Performance in most television drama is suited to the intimate, close-up, domestic nature of the medium – cool, low key, realist. But the epic quality of some science fiction or fantasy programmes – *Star Trek*, *Buffy the Vampire Slayer*, *Battlestar Galactica* – requires the greater intensity of a theatrical performance mode.[1] In *Get a Life!*, William Shatner reveals the motivation for his oft-parodied, over-the-top performances:

> There's actually a pretty valid reason for all that scenery chewing . . .When you're an actor standing around in a cardboard-and-Christmas-light starship . . . you can never be too sure that your scripted lines won't just seem completely ridiculous. It often seemed to me that *without* all of Kirk's emotion, and intensity and high-octane hand-wringing, our villains of the week might have seemed more ridiculous than frightening; the ship's crisis of the week might have seemed a lot less threatening were Kirk not up in arms. (Shatner with Kreski, 1999: 166, 167)

Original series producer Robert Justman agreed that Shatner's acting style precisely matched the needs of the original series. In the first pilot, film actor Jeffrey Hunter (perhaps best known as Jesus in Nicholas Ray's 1961 *King of Kings*) had played Captain Christopher Pike. Justman thought that Hunter 'was too brooding, too turned inward. He didn't have any energy.' By contrast Shatner, who 'has incredible energy', was 'a brilliant job of recasting' (19 January 2002, Pearson and Messenger Davies). Shatner told us that his theatrical training contributed to his portrayal of the heroic Kirk: 'in order to sustain a scene, learn your lines, discipline, techniques, confidence, all of that is theatrical' (19 January 2002, Pearson and Messenger Davies). *Trek*'s most high-profile classical actor, Patrick Stewart, agreed with Shatner that his theatrical training was essential to his portrayal of Picard: 'In the early years of the series, it was perpetually suggested to me that I might be slumming or selling out by coming to Hollywood to do this television series – that in some way, I was betraying my Royal Shakespeare Company past . . . All the time I spent sitting around on the thrones of England as various Shakespearean kings was nothing but a preparation for sitting in the captain's chair on the Enterprise.'[2] Several of the other actors have told interviewers that playing Shakespeare was a particularly useful preparation for *Star Trek*'s epic tone. *Voyager*'s Robert Duncan McNeil (Tom Paris), who had a great deal of stage experience before entering the *Trek* universe, has said that he had 'always [been] particularly interested in classic stories: Shakespeare, Greek drama, classical theatre. So when I got on this show, I kind of felt a sense of *déjà vu*. The style of the show is very classical; the stories are big and mythic in proportion and really exciting to do' (Bassom, 1998: 47). A Shakespearean background is apparently especially helpful for actors playing Klingons. Robert O'Reilly, Klingon chancellor Gowron in *TNG* and *DS9*, said, 'it helps to have done a lot of Shakespeare. Shakespeare lends itself to being a Klingon' (Fisher, 1999: 27). Richard Herd, L'Kor in *TNG* agreed: 'I'd done a bunch of Shakespeare when I was younger . . . So, I found L'Kor very Shakespearean. I wouldn't say that we were playing the Klingons as Shakespearean characters, but L'Kor reminded me of a Shakespearean character, just in the way he was a warrior, the way he carried himself, and the clothing' (Spelling, 2000: 69).

Genre seems a particularly strong determinant of television performance style, science fiction (and fantasy as well) requiring actors to suit their interpretations to the oft-times larger-than-life nature of the text. But genre must be considered in conjunction with those other determinants of television acting discussed above: time, the actor's status within the cast, the visual nature of the medium and input from other creative personnel. This interpretive schema can reveal a great deal not only about *Star Trek* and similar shows but about any television show.

Notes

1 There is simply not space in this chapter to fully consider the meanings of such vexed words as 'realist' and 'theatrical'. I use them fairly imprecisely in their generally understood meanings.

2 This quotation was originally read on the website: www.efr.hw.ac.uk/EDC/StarTrek/picard.html (website no longer active).

References

Bassom, David (1998) 'Tom Foolery: Robert Duncan McNeil', *Star Trek: The Official Monthly Magazine* (March): 47.

Dowd, Maureen (1995) 'Looking for Space Aliens (and Denying Yale)', *The New York Times*, 26 March, H37.

Fern, Y. (1995) *Inside the Mind of Gene Roddenberry, the Creator of Star Trek*, London: HarperCollins Publishers.

Fisher, Deborah (1999) 'Gowron: A Warrior's Portfolio', *Star Trek Communictor*, No. 122 (April/May): 27.

Joy, Nick (1998) 'Chakotay Chats', *Starburst*, No. 371998: 58.

Nimoy, Leonard (1995a) *I Am Spock*, New York: Hyperion.

Nimoy, Leonard (1995b) Memo to Gene Roddenberry and Doug Cramer, 15 October 1968, in *I Am Spock*, New York: Hyperion.

Shatner, William (1993) *Star Trek Memories: The Inside Story of the Classic TV Series*, London: HarperCollins Publishers.

Shatner, William with Chris Kreski (1999) *Get A Life!*, New York: Pocket Books, 166, 167.

Shrager, A. (1998) *The Finest Crew in the Fleet: The Next Generation Cast on Screen and Off*, Chichester: Summersdale Publishers Ltd.

Spelling, Ian (2000) 'Following the Herd,' *Star Trek: The Official Monthly Magazine*, 67 (July): 69.

Van Hise, J. (1997 [1966]) 'No One Ever Upsets the Star,' *TV Guide*, 15 October, quoted in *The Unauthorized History of Trek*, London: Voyager.

Van Hise, J. (1997 [1968]) Leonard Nimoy writing in *Variety*, quoted in *The Unauthorized History of Trek*, London: Voyager.

10

Bollywood blends: genre and performance in Shahrukh Khan's post-millennial films

Rayna Denison

Film genres are always already mixed; as the process of making films requires ever new combinations of generic elements (Altman, 1999: 54-68). Despite this, there are very few discussions of the effects of genre mixing and hybridisation, even in relation to Hollywood cinema. A blind spot in genre criticism has therefore emerged and the effects of genre mixing on the whole of the circuit of culture related to filmmaking (from production through to reception, see Hesmondhalgh, 2002) consequently remains under-scrutinised. In particular, the challenges for actors represented by genre mixing have also gone largely unremarked. Where film studies has dealt with genre hybridisation and mixing, it has tended to do so as a means to show the progression in genres over time (Altman, 1999; Neale, 1993, 2000) or as a means to discuss the primacy of one generic element over another (Neale and Krutnik, 1990). As Henry Jenkins argues, 'genre criticism takes for granted that most works fall within one and only one genre, with genre mixing the exception rather than the norm' (2008: 230; see also Neale, 2000: 25). Demonstrating the wide-reaching nature of genre mixing, Jason Mittell's work on television genre mixing offers intriguing parallels with popular cinema's uses of genre. Mittell views genre mixing as normal within television and argues that 'genre mixing brings generic practices to the surface, making the conventions and assumptions clustered within individual categories explicit' (2004: 157). However, as well as foregrounding existing conventions, genre mixing is also concerned with various kinds of balancing acts: it functions to meet the needs of competing generic codes, works to produce generic hierarchies and highlights dominant generic elements at given points within a film text.

In practice, Mittell's approach appears similar to the blending spoken of in the title of this chapter, a term borrowed from Rosie Thomas's article on popular Indian cinema, in which she writes:

> Film-makers talk about 'blending the *masalas* in proper proportions' as one might discuss cookery; and . . . they have a clear perception that these elements, including the inexcusably maligned songs and dances, are an important part of the work of the film, which is to achieve an overall balance of 'flavours'. (1985: 124; see also Mittell, 2001: 3)

Thomas's account provides examples of how popular Indian, or at least Hindi language, cinema is understood by its makers as overtly mixed. Popular Indian Hindi language cinema, with its typically multi-generational audiences, long running times and complex integration of domestic and foreign filmmaking styles, provides an extreme case for the examination of genre mixing. However, the extremity of the case of popular Hindi language cinema does not make it exceptional per se. Rather, genre blending offers an alternative way to think about how genre is used in the media, from Hollywood to Bollywood and beyond; a way which sees *how* generic components are utilised in film as important, particularly as they are discussed and mobilised by those who create and watch the films in question.

As Thomas's article implies, the masala film has, all too often, been used as an imprecise way of describing popular Hindi language cinema's complex relationship to genre:

> Indian popular films are sometimes referred to contemptuously as 'masalas' (spices). Just as different spices are used in cooking, so the filmmaker, it is contended, uses the standard elements associated with the given formula for success, namely: song, dance, melodrama, stunts, fights, cabaret sequences, exaggerated humour. (Gokulsing and Dissanayake, [1998] 2004: 31)

Comparing this statement with Thomas's we can see how imprecision, if not reductive denigration, lurks at the edges of masala as an explanation of popular Hindi genre cinema. Furthermore, the way such accounts generalise about the roles played by these masala elements (glossing over the ways in which they help to form or integrate with narratives and the impact they have on the content and look of popular Hindi cinema) results in a loss of understanding about how important *any* given generic element might be to the finished film. Adding to the complexity of the matter, in addition to these masala elements several Indian cinema genres are regularly outlined by academics before being rapidly recuperated into the notion of a masala formula film (Dudrah, 2006; Pendakur, 2003).

To borrow a second time from K. Moti Gokulsing and Wimal Dissanayake's discussion of genre in popular Hindi cinema, they list the following as the central genres under which masala blending might take place: mythologicals and devotionals (based directly or in part on India's classical theatrical and literary Hindu texts, especially the *Ramayana* and *Mahabharata*); social dramas (often dealing with India's caste system); the erotic/romantic genre (into which Rajinder Kumar Dudrah places the majority of Shahrukh Khan's contemporary films (2006: 179–180)); stunt films (notably also cited as a masala 'element') and, in an off-shooting cycle, angry young man films (Gokulsing and Dissanayake, 2004 [1998]: 25–28). The overlaps between the masala elements and more substantified genres in popular Hindi cinema are only part of Hindi cinema's generic picture, however. In addition to domestic generic categories, popular Hindi film has a long relationship with foreign cinema, which is regularly borrowed from and adapted for the domestic marketplace (Gokulsing and Dissanayake, 2004 [1998]; Pendakur, 2003). While concurring with Thomas's claims that the application of Hollywood's genres to Indian cinema in many cases would miss the point (1985: 120), it still seems necessary to carefully analyse these 'Bollywood' genres in order to examine the extent to which traditional terms remain applicable to an increasingly internationalising national cinema.

Within popular Hindi cinema criticism, what seems to emerge is a genre hierarchy starting with basic elements (like songs or stunts) which then appear under the auspices of a number of wider organising generic frameworks (for instance, devotionals or angry young man films), which themselves could be thought of as operating within or against an internationalised notion of the masala or 'Bollywood' cinema (similar to Vasudevan, 1995 and Gopalan, 2002: 19). Up to this point the terms 'masala', 'Bollywood' and 'popular Hindi cinema' have been purposefully separated. The latter accurately describes the large number of films being produced in Mumbai each year (for statistics see Dudrah, 2006 and Kaur and Sinha, 2005), whereas the internationally coined label 'Bollywood' more accurately describes the films from within that larger corpus that travel beyond India, and that are received and reviewed under the auspices of diasporically and foreign applied notions of transnational or global Indian cinema (Kaur and Sinha, 2005: 11–29). The internationally successful films of Shahrukh Khan that will be discussed here are, by this categorisation, Bollywood films and it is their generic relationship with the masala 'spices' and genres of popular Hindi cinema (and beyond) that form the focus of the investigations into genre and acting that follow.

Among those who create films, perhaps the group most affected by the demands of genre mixing are those put in front of the cameras. As Pamela Robertson Wojcik argues, 'modes of performance differ sufficiently among melodrama, the Western, comedy, film noir, and the musical to enable genre theorists to characterize acting styles as a defining feature of genre', and yet, she goes on, 'for the most part, genre theorists have attended more to visual style, narrative structure, thematic opposition, and historical context than on performance' (2004: 6). However, academic critics like James Naremore and Henry Jenkins have argued that actors' performances require more rounded and generically and culturally organised analyses (Jenkins, 2004 [1992]: 111–112; Naremore, 1988: 3–4; Robertson Wojcik, 2004: 8). Following these lines of thought, it stands to reason that the work of the actor, in creating expressively coherent performances, frequently requires them to perform across the modes of generic acting cited by Robertson Wojcik, as they alter their modes of performance to fit a film's shifting genre needs. Indeed, in moving beyond genre studies' predilection for viewing genre as a product largely of Hollywood cinema, it is also reasonable to assert that Indian actors have a doubly difficult job, performing to meet the needs of both domestic genres and foreign ones. It would stand to reason too that the actors most affected by this process would be those with the most screen time: namely, stars.

Stars, or at least those performing protagonist and antagonist roles within films, have a complex set of genre-related issues to deal with. Meeting the demands of directors, post-production crews and their fellow cast members, the actors at the centre of film productions tend also, by virtue of screen time, to have the most generically complex parts to play. Consequently, the central actor is typically required to produce a more generically nuanced performance than those around him or her, while at the same time producing a performance that often becomes the benchmark for expressive coherence across the film (Jenkins, 2004 [1992]: 112). The choices that the central actor makes, therefore, have wide-reaching impact on film production, and all the more so when the actor is a star who plays multiple production roles behind the scenes in addition to acting.

Many stars now have their own production companies, both within and outside Hollywood. For example, there has been a trend over the past decade or so for female stars in Hollywood to begin their own production companies, including high-profile figures such as Sandra Bullock and Drew Barrymore (Kramer, 2004). These stars are accordingly able to exert much more control over the productions in which they appear, and over their performances within those productions. Likewise, this trend has been taken up outside Hollywood in recent years, with director–stars like Takeshi Kitano in Japan and actor–producers such as Shahrukh Khan in India starting up production companies to afford them more control over the films they make. Khan is a particularly interesting example in this case as he seems to have built up a roster of personnel that he continually works with through his production companies, first Dreamz Unlimited and then Red Chillies Entertainment. Fostering close working relationships with directors like choreographer-director Farah Khan and producer-costume designer-director Karan Johar, as well as a multitude of post-production and production personnel, helps to create a degree of quality and consistency in the Red Chillies productions that goes beyond that found in Khan's previous films. In fact, Khan has been instrumental in driving Indian popular cinema into the realm of computer visual effects technologies, with his Red Chillies Entertainment and Red Chillies VFX companies, founded in 2004. Through his investments in Indian cinema and his collaborations with the filmmaking teams around him, Khan offers a pertinent example of how film stars engage with the processes of filmmaking beyond their ostensible production roles, parlaying their popularity and high salaries into greater industrial control. It is for this reason that this chapter will focus on the films that Khan has made since he first set up Red Chillies Entertainment: *Main Hoon Na* (2004), *Paheli* (2005) and *Om Shanti Om* (2007).

Shahrukh Khan is also a useful figure to focus on here because critical opinion about his performances is decidedly mixed. He is frequently compared with two other Khans currently working in popular Hindi cinema: Salman Khan and Aamir Khan, and it is the latter who is consistently described as being the 'best actor' within contemporary Bollywood cinema (e.g. Deshpande, 2005: 197). The negative responses to Khan within the English language Indian news press seem to focus on two areas: his 'average' qualities and his highly charged emotional acting style. Parul Gupta, reviewing *Main Hoon Na*, for example, writes that 'With SRK [a commonly used abbreviation of Shahrukh Khan] around, mawkishness couldn't be far behind. He shifts in with his father's other family to find their love' (2004). Here then, the implication is that it is *Main Hoon Na*'s melodramatic elements, and Khan's presentation of them, that the reviewer finds unsatisfactory.

Likewise, there is a consistent presentation of Khan as average. Sandipan Deb, writing in *The Indian Express*, comments that Khan's star persona and acting style utilise a variety of notions of the 'average' from being 'happy to dance like any other fan in a cricket stadium', to performing as a 'playmate' on television when acting as a game-show host, to 'not taking himself seriously' in interviews or when acting and, finally, in being 'non-threatening': 'it's very likely that you wouldn't mind too much if your wife stuck a poster of Shahrukh on the cupboard door. And if your sister brought him home, you would instantly make him your drinking buddy' (2008). However, the notion of the average or everyday aspects of Khan's star persona is not being mobilised here in quite the same way as Richard Dyer (1998 [1979]) has discussed stars' ordinary extraordinariness in Hollywood cinema. Instead it becomes a signifier of Khan's unexceptional performances, where Khan 'is not as handsome as Hrithik Roshan, is hardly a great actor. He is not as good at fights and stunts as Akshay Kumar is, and does not have the comic timing or dancing skills of a Govinda' (Deb, 2008). Ordinariness is not just juxtaposed against Khan's megawatt star persona here (to make him a special everyman); it is used specifically to question how he has achieved that persona and status, and his acting skills are made a key part of the question.

On the flip side of this review culture, positive responses to Khan use almost uniform language, citing his energy on-screen as a major source of audience pleasure. To quote Deb again, 'in every film he has appeared in, Shahrukh, you can make out, is doing his best to entertain you' (2008). Others concur, writing, for example, 'he jumps out like a Jack in the box and sets the screen on fire with his rumbustious energy' (writing of Khan's performance in *Don* [2006]: Kazmi, 2006). Another popular respondent on Bollywood cinema writes that 'if Aamir is focused and Salman, laidback, Shahrukh is an energy field. He is intense, single-minded and irradiates sheer force' (Sippy and Ramachandran, 2006: 96). However, none of these reviewers is entirely clear about what they mean by energy. Therefore, it would seem that a good place to begin an analysis of Khan's acting in Bollywood cinema would be to attempt to unpack this idea; to attempt to make sense of how Khan's 'energetic' performances work across the many genres in which he appears, and perhaps why these have led to him being dubbed 'King Khan', the 'King of Bollywood cinema' (Goodridge, 2005; 'Living Life Khan-Size!', 2007).

Narrative, generic hybridity and performance in Bollywood

The three films selected for analysis in this chapter are purposefully diverse ones that relate to Khan's changing star status since the millennium. Khan has played a variety of characters within popular Hindi cinema over the last decade or so, beginning with villains before moving on to play diasporically oriented romantic protagonists, to which he has recently added a growing number of action-oriented (anti)heroes in films like *Main Hoon Na* and *Don*. In fact, since 2000 Khan's acting choices have shown a high degree of variation, often playing with the Non-Resident Indian (NRI) 'type' that made him famous (Dyer, 1998 [1979]: 47–48, 1993: 11–18), developing it in new directions. For example, in *Swades* (2004), Khan's character Mohan Bhargav rejects his high-profile NASA career and NRI status to return to rural India as an aid worker; or, in *Devdas* (2002), Khan's upper caste, British-educated lawyer slowly drinks himself to death after the loss of his childhood love. Additionally, Khan has begun to take on an increasing number of roles that parody his star persona, as can be seen most clearly in the highly self-reflective *Om Shanti Om*, where in the second half of the film Khan plays a Bollywood superstar named Om Kapoor, who in one scene wins a high profile-award for playing an NRI hero (excerpts from two films-within-the-film are played for comedy by Khan, gleefully overacting). Since taking on the role of producer, however, Khan has also begun to move away from the NRI hero type, as in *Asoka* (2001) and *Paheli*, both of which present historical versions of Indian life that are uninflected by western modernity (in content, if not in film style), and whose characters therefore work to re-inflect Khan's star image as domestically and traditionally Indian.

Going hand in hand with the variety evident in Khan's choice of roles is a concomitant experimentation with different generic modes of acting. The genre mixing seemingly inherent to these films relates to the manner in which their narratives unfold. Gokulsing and Dissanayake, for example, argue that popular Hindi cinema 'does not progress in a linear fashion but meanders, with detours and stories within stories' (2004 [1998]: 31). This meandering and detouring presents problems for even Mittell's elastic version of genre mixing, in which he most frequently compares how just two sets of generic codes might be operating in relation to one another, rather than considering the impact that the combination of many across a single text might produce (2004: 148-157). As becomes obvious from the complexity of Bollywood's uses of genre, it is beyond the scope of this chapter to attempt detailed micro-analyses of performance within the entirety of even three of Khan's films. Instead, key generic and performance techniques from across the films will be selected and offered as examples of Khan's acting choices in relation to coherency and the nuance of his performance style. To begin, a mutated version of John O. Thompson's commutation test will be used to compare Khan's performances in two very different films: *Main Hoon Na* and *Paheli*, in order to analyse how he has been experimenting with performances that fall into ostensibly opposed generic categories (Thompson, 1978; MacDonald, 2004: 26–32).

Main Hoon Na and *Paheli* make disparate uses of genre: the former bombastically mixing genres episodically with little hybridisation, while the latter disperses its masala elements in a more integrated fashion, diffusing songs and dances, melodrama and stunts within a narrative that presents a romantic, period ghost story. *Main Hoon Na* also overtly borrows from non-domestic genre traditions, most notably from the musical *Grease* (1978) and John Woo's *Mission: Impossible 2* (2000), itself a fusion of Hong Kong and American action genres; whereas *Paheli* is more subtle about its influences, integrating western special effects computer technologies into a narrative based in traditional Indian folk tales (and the 1973 film *Duvidha* [Jha, 2006]). Due to the different handling of generic materials in evidence in these films, Thompson's commutation test can be applied in relation not to the different choices made by two actors as would be normal, but to the choices made by one actor under different circumstances (Thompson, 1978): in particular, Khan's acting in stunt sequences from the two films and his performances in sequences that require him to mix modes. It is hoped that attention to these details of performance will begin to elucidate Khan's approach to genre and acting, and how he maintains coherence across his performances.

In *Main Hoon Na*, it is easy to see how Khan's performance might be considered 'energetic': his character dangles from wires while killing hostage-takers, shoots henchmen in slow motion while seemingly flying through the air, and literally bursts onto the set by dropping through a ceiling in a shower of sparks and glass, and all this in the opening sequence alone. What is remarkable about this sequence, however, is not the use it makes of John Woo's slow motion shooting style for action, but the way in which that shooting style emphasises Khan's confidence in performing the action hero role. The use of slow motion highlights every potential performance flaw (such as many of the actors, including Khan, closing their eyes while shooting guns or performing stunts), while at the same time highlighting moments of virtuosity. The overall successful creation of Khan as an action hero, after the style of Woo's film heroes, is reliant on the stunts performed in these shots being done convincingly. The fact that so many of the shots are provided in slow motion indicates the filmmakers' conviction that this was, indeed, the case. Khan's confidence in the role can similarly be read by the fact that he performs his own stunts throughout the sequence, thereby physically embodying the role of military hero Major Ram Prasad Sharma.

This sequence can therefore be read as an example of popular Hindi cinema 'stunt films where the focus is on the action and physicality'

(Gokulsing and Dissanayake, 1999: 26), but also, because it follows Woo's action style, should reasonably be expected to replicate the kinds of truncated performance techniques noted in Woo's films by Cynthia Baron (2004: 303). Indeed, this would seem to be the case, as Khan's Major Ram Prasad Sharma, on a protection detail to an Indian General, is shown in glimpses as he begins to thwart antagonist Raghavan Datta's (Sunil Shetty's) attempt to blackmail the General into stopping a prisoner exchange between India and Pakistan while on live television. However, while Khan's performance is truncated in this opening, it is inter-cut with a passionate debate about the relationship between the two nations, adding associative emotional depth to Khan's performance. Moreover, Sharma's father (Naseeruddin Shah) is grievously injured in the sequence, and slow motion shots are included to capture the character's response to his father's shooting. It is here that the Indianisation of Woo's techniques becomes clear: Sharma/Khan's initial stunned reaction shot is held for almost ten seconds, inter-cut with a shot of his father falling to the ground, both in slow motion. As with the rest of the slow motion action in this sequence, the shot displays every nuance of Khan's performance, from his running stance to the 'momentary' concern that registers across his face, before he exits the shot. This emotional response is echoed at the end of the sequence when Sharma hears his father's call and returns to his side. In a racking focus shot that shifts perspectives between his father's bloody, outstretched hand and Sharma/Khan in a medium shot, eyes tearing up as he stands under the still sparking roof he had earlier dropped through, we see melodrama intruding on the space of truncated action performance in *Main Hoon Na*. In mixing the codes of melodrama and action here, Khan's performance goes beyond merely puncturing the 'smooth surface' of the film's mise-en-scène, as Baron argues happens in Woo's *The Killer* (1989) (2004: 323). Instead we get competing generic codes of performance presaging the shift from scenes of action to ones of melodrama.

Paheli's presentation of stunts is dissimilar in many ways, and significantly it places Khan to one side of their performance. For example, the major stunt element of *Paheli* revolves around the Ghost (Khan) using his supernatural powers to ensure that his father-in-law's (Anupam Kher's) camels win a local race, in order to restore the family's honour. The action sequence of the race is inter-cut with images of the Ghost/Khan casting spells on the camels and their riders. During this sequence Khan is framed in medium close-up, with light playing across his eyes to indicate his magical nature, against a backdrop of chaotically gesturing crowds. He moves with deliberate slowness, emphasising the importance of each of his character's gestures and, by holding his hands roughly parallel with his face, he draws attention to the link between the Ghost's actions and the reactions of the camels and riders in the surrounding shots. Khan's facial expressions are important here, ranging between the serious (eyes closed to indicate the gathering of power) to the comedic (smiling as the rival camels stop racing, and biting his bottom lip in profile to indicate the character's mischievous nature). Additionally, the editing of the sequence also emphasises Khan's gestures, at times focusing shots on his hands alone before shifting to frame his face along with them.

Interestingly, this is another largely silent performance, but the manner in which it is performed by Khan means that it is comedic rather than straight-faced, and shown almost as a shot–reverse shot conversation that works to place Khan's character within the action of the sequence, rather than alongside it. In this stunt or action sequence then, Khan's performance shifts between registers, demonstrating a command over the mise-en-scène that affords his character authority, while also displaying comedic elements that stop the Ghost from becoming threatening, despite his ability to manipulate the world around him. By meeting the needs of the generic elements of the sequence simultaneously, Khan's performance in *Paheli* provides a contrast with that examined in *Main Hoon Na*, but in both cases Khan's delivery of physical acting plays a central role in defining the generic tones of the scenes in which he appears.

This is especially true of sequences in both films that show Khan's characters falling in love. In a reverse of the action sequences, it is *Main Hoon Na* that emphasises genre hybridisation in Khan's romantic scenes, while in *Paheli* these scenes are largely played for melodramatic or emotional affect. When Major Ram Prasad Sharma meets chemistry teacher Chandni Chopra (Sushmita Sen) in *Main Hoon Na* for the first time (while undercover to protect General Amarjeet Bakshi's [Kabir Bedi's] daughter), for example, it is as he undertakes a forfeit for a lost bet, wherein he will have to sing for the first woman he meets. Parodying his star persona, which is integrally linked with the many song and dance numbers Khan has performed, the character is shown first as a bad singer (as Khan sings), but, on the arrival of Chopra, a playback singer's voice is used (with the backing of the full musical score) to show the depth of Sharma's feelings for his teacher (for more on playback singers see Pendakur, 2003: 119-169). The staging of this scene deconstructs Bollywood song and dance numbers, as Sharma/Khan is shown looking on in mild horror at his outstretched arms, a pose that Khan usually strikes emphatically while performing declarative love songs. Essentially this works to divide

Khan's performance from the more manufactured elements of his star persona, demonstrating his capacity for self-deprecation while at the same time playing with generic conventions, foregrounding the artificiality of Bollywood formula films. At the same time, however, this meeting actually reinforces Khan's musical star persona by showing his character's capacity to perform musical numbers successfully.

By contrast, the first meeting between Lachchi (Rani Mukherjee) and Khan's Ghost in *Paheli* takes place well into the film narrative, when the Ghost inveigles his way into Lachchi's home by impersonating her husband. Repeating an earlier scene in which Kushinlal, the husband, ignores his wife on their wedding night, the Ghost declares his love for Lachchi emphatically, trying to convince her to love him. Khan delivers the Ghost's dialogue in hushed and sincere tones initially, holding Lachchi/Mukherjee by the tops of her arms and gazing intently at her face as she averts her eyes, and then following her as she moves, bending at the waist in order to put his face on the same level as hers as he tries to impress her with his sincerity. As the Ghost tries to confess his true nature, however, Khan's performance shifts, becoming less intimate and more frontal, moving away from Lachchi/Mukherjee as he faces the camera, his voice shaking and tears appearing in his eyes as the character asks, 'How could I live a dream? I am a ghost after all.' This sequence provides an example of another kind of potential energy from Khan, a commitment to the role and genre that results in seemingly whole-hearted embodiment of character, or what Barry King among others has discussed as 'personation' (1991; Naremore, 1988: 23). Khan's commitment can be read in these examples as emanating from a variety of sources: from the desire to play with his star persona, to a desire to meet the needs of competing generic requirements, to attempts to embody character while drawing attention to his status as an actor. Frontal display acting like that seen in *Paheli* provides an example of this latter, and it is also a particularly common technique used in relation to Khan's performances in song and dance numbers.

Dual roles and performance virtuosity: *Paheli*, special effects and acting

One other prominent repetition visible in Khan's post-millennial films is his adoption of double roles. In at least three of his post-millennial films, Khan has explored different types of dual roles: in *Paheli* he plays both Kishanlal (the husband) and the Ghost, in *Don* he plays the eponymous lead villain as well as that of Don's double, Vijay, and in *Om Shanti Om*,

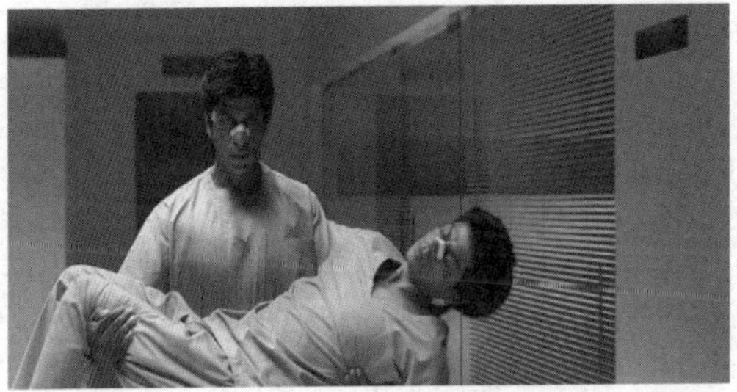

10.1 Don/Khan carries the unconscious Vijay/Khan in *Don*

he plays Om Prakash Makhija and his reincarnation, Om Kapoor. Even where he plays only a single role, Khan's character identities are often played with, as in *Veer-Zaara* (2004), which sees him age 22 years during the film, and in *Asoka*, where his aristocratic character is banished from court and forced to cut his hair and change his name to Pawan for a time. Effectively, these roles require Khan not just to act within different generic modes in a single film, but to respond to those genre requirements in multiple ways. In *Don*, for instance, Khan's performances as Vijay and Don are commingled, with audiences often kept guessing as to which of the characters is being performed at a given moment. In one short scene near the film's conclusion there are even three Khans: Don in the present, Don in a flashback and Vijay. In a seamless CGI composite shot, Don and Vijay are pictured together, 'simultaneously' performed by Khan, with Don glowering unblinkingly, chin lowered to show his ruthless determination, carrying Vijay, unconscious, in his arms. Both are identically dressed, but the character differentiation is clearly expressed through Khan's acting which, throughout the longer sequence of the flashback, shows Don's sociopathic tendencies. For instance, Khan performs Don by moving decisively and smoothly, and with a focused, yet unblinking, stare compared with Vijay's deferential behaviour, broader gestures and tense facial expressions. In doing so, Khan responds to the needs of the genre (predominantly narrated here in the thriller or espionage modes), but from two opposing positions.

Without special effects such seamless simultaneity of acting would be nearly impossible, and the many dual roles performed by Khan in his post-millennial films make extensive use of both new and old special effects technologies. *Paheli*, like *Don*, largely uses computer technologies to achieve the doubling necessary to the narrative. While the two versions of Khan's Kishanlal are kept apart for most of the film, towards the end a shepherd (Amitabh Bachchan) is asked to reveal the real Kishanlal.

For an extended period, two Khans occupy the screen, and Khan's performance as both shows the demarcations between the 'true' and false husband. Again stillness and movement are used as markers, with the 'true' husband being the least flinching and gestural of the two. More than this, too, the sincerity of the two characters' emotions is performed by Khan in different ways, with Kishanlal shown to be quicker to take up tasks but more fearful of them (he refuses to hold hot coals for example, while the Ghost simply stands off to one side, looking pained). In a final test of faithfulness to Lachchi, the shepherd asks the real husband to get into a water carrier, a test which the Ghost cannot refuse. Here special effects are used to end the doubling of Khans on screen, as he stands relatively still, closes his eyes and then begins to dissolve into a sand-like substance. Significantly, it is the use of special effects here which decisively indicates the 'true' husband, and significantly this chimes with Khan's extra-diegetic statements about the importance of special effects technologies to Indian cinema (Goodridge, 2005).

Perhaps just as significantly, these dual roles increase Khan's screen time and force him to engage with genre in original ways. The differences between Khan's double performances in *Paheli* (and, to a lesser extent, in *Don*) showcase his varied skills as an actor. For, while stardom could be used to explain the extra screen time afforded to Khan, the notion that audiences understand him as a singular, pre-existing 'persona' is undercut by the multiplicity of his types of presence within these films (contrary to Dyer, 1998 [1979]: 126). In these dual roles, Khan not only responds to the needs of multiple genres, he also responds to generic codes with a perhaps surprising degree of elasticity for a star actor who is rarely described as a skilled performer. The range of character types performed by Khan in his post-millennial films provides evidence of an actor who has mastered not only a wide range of different character types, but who can also perform these types in relation to the needs of a broad set of historical, contemporary, action and romantic film genres. In doing so, Khan's dual role performances showcase his skills as an actor, and work to highlight his virtuosity.

Genre as/in process: performing the present and the past in *Om Shanti Om*

Virtuosity in acting, when discussed in relation to western actors, tends to be identified in association with the Method, as opposed to emerging from a performer's adherence to generic codes. Alignment with the

Method is also frequently used to relate actors' fluctuating weight and bodies to notions of 'quality' in their performances: Marlon Brando's weight gain for *Raging Bull* (1980) being one popular example. However, recent changes in Hollywood action adventure cinema have been affecting the types of male body seen on screens. Moving away from the body-builder physiques of the 1980s, it would seem a newer, sculpted male physique is emerging, but to relatively little academic comment thus far (see, for exceptions, Tasker, 2004). Sudhanva Deshpande (2005) sees a correlation between the new Hollywood action star and the trend towards well-muscled Bollywood actors, a good example of which would be *Dhoom 2* (2006) in which Hrithik Roshan's defined muscular torso is repeatedly and prominently displayed, especially during song and dance numbers. Trends like these suggest that there are competing understandings of the male body and its role in acting. Genres that include displays of the sculpted or 'built' body for the sake of spectacle (action) are typically presented in these accounts as ranking below transformations that take place 'on-screen' as part of the narrative logic of a film (as in Method acting, often male-oriented dramas; Tasker, 1993). Khan's recent performance in *Om Shanti Om* challenges this divide, in that it offers bodily transformation on-screen but not in a Method film; rather, his transformation takes place to meet the needs of genre acting and Bollywood acting norms.

Khan's dual role as Om Prakash Makhija and Om Kapoor fulfils two distinct sets of historical generic expectations and he changes his body to meet those demands. In his role as 1970s junior artiste Om Prakash Makhija, Khan alters his acting style to parody that of the original period but retains his 'normal' physique. For example, in song and dance number 'Dhoom Taana' (see Figure 10.2, also the main poster image for *Om Shanti Om*), Khan's character is shown shirt-less, with a trim but relatively undefined torso. In this sequence, Makhija imagines himself transported into the film being shown at a premiere he is attending. This allows the special effects team and choreographer–director Farah Khan to intersperse shots of Khan between those of real 1970s performers, composited into shots using CGI technologies. The effervescence of Khan's performance, exaggerating dance movements beyond the performance of backing dancers and purposefully over-using facial expressions, draws attention to Khan's performance-within-a-performance, and especially to his adherence to the acting styles of a previous historical period. This can also be seen in a scene he shares with Makhija's mother (Kirron Kher), which stands out from those surrounding it as a parody of 1970s acting styles. Pulling

10.2 Publicity still taken from 'Dhoom Taana', *Om Shanti Om*

out from an initial close-up of Kher, the two are framed in a two-shot using wild gesticulations while melodramatically discussing the over-elaborate nature of Om Prakash Makhija's name. Calling attention to the parody, at the end of the scene, Khan's character remonstrates, 'Quit overacting Mom!' In both examples, however, the parodic uses made of previous Hindi popular cinema provide more than just surface dressing for *Om Shanti Om*, and are, rather, central markers of its period nature and comedy-oriented generic mode. Conversely, in song number 'Dard-e-Disco', a parody of contemporary Bollywood cinema is performed. In a remarkable bodily transformation, Khan plays Bollywood star Om Kapoor as a parody of the contemporary sculpted, muscular Indian actor. While the number is largely performed with a serious tone, the set-ups are once again exaggerated to draw attention to the performance of Bollywood acting taking place. For example, in two sequences with very rapid shot turn-overs, Khan is shown in slow motion rising shirtless out of a pool of water, with lighting and low camera angles emphasising his newly sculpted upper body. In a second set-up from the end of the number, Khan performs complex choreography covered in oil wearing a miner's costume. Several interesting things emerge out of this parody: first, an awareness of the importation of Hollywood-inflected action genre expectations within contemporary Bollywood cinema; second, an awareness of the importance of the muscular body to successful contemporary actors, performed by Khan despite the fact that Deshpande (2005) cites him specifically as an exception to this rule; and third, an awareness that bodily transformation can be used to create hype for a film. This was certainly the case for *Om Shanti Om*, with pictures comparing Khan's newly muscled body to his 'normal' physique being used in promotional materials (see Figures 10.2 and 10.3), and being widely discussed in interviews and reviews for the film. For instance, Nikhat Kazmi, in *The Times of India*, writes:

> The film is essentially Shahrukh's who manages to add life to the tardy second half . . . He is the cool dude with the low waist jeans threatening to slip down and the six pack abs giving muscle to a story that goes dreadfully off-track. (2007)

Here it is Khan's physical transformation that is viewed, not only as a main attraction for audiences, but as the saving grace of the second half of the film. In a somewhat contrasting example, Khalid Mohamed writes in the *Hindustan Times*:

> Above all, the enterprise belongs to Shahrukh Khan, who tackles comedy, high drama and action with his signature style – spontaneous and intuitively intelligent. Six-pack or no-packs, he's the entertainer of the year in this valentine to movies. (2007)

This hyperbole indicates the level of fervour with which fans greeted Khan's transformation, which even he has called 'hyped' (Jain, Shaw and Nanda 2007). More than this though, the review returns to the aspects of Khan's acting that have been under examination here: commitment, energy (and intelligence), used in the service of genre performance.

Conclusions

Khan's performances could be viewed, in light of these discussions, as largely generic in nature. His use of a variety of modes of acting, and his ability to tie them together into coherent performances even in disparate

10.3 Publicity still from Khan's performance in 'Dard-e-Disco', *On Shanti Om*

types of film, is at least partly responsible for his success. It is not, therefore, that Khan is an 'exceptional' actor, but rather that Khan's ability to act to meet the needs of genre has become a central part of the notion of 'ordinariness' that lurks in his star persona. Moreover, his ability to make shifting across generic boundaries seem effortless feeds understandings of him as 'average', while also ensuring that his star persona has not devolved into his typecasting as the 'NRI hero' of popular Indian cinema.

The concept of energy that circulates around him seems, therefore, to stem from Khan's commitment to performance styles that range across genres, but which typically make use of contrasting generic codes (the melodramatic and action or stunt genres being commonly repeated motifs). Moreover, Khan's body is important here from his 'unthreatening' or 'average' good looks to his ability to perform complex choreography while displaying his body. It would seem also, from the examples studied here, that Khan uses his body extensively to show characterisation and variation: from a fake moustache and period costuming in *Paheli* to actual physical transformation in *Om Shanti Om*, changes to the surface of the body are a frequent marker of Khan's acting choices. These changes show a balancing act at work in Khan's acting: he would seem to meet the competing demands of the various genre extremes in his films not by ignoring their shifting registers but by personifying them.

More than this, however, Khan is important because his generically aware acting has implications for acting more generally. The brief discussion here indicates how cinemas outside Hollywood are adapting to challenge globalising notions of genre in film, taking Hollywood's ideas and localising them (as with the sculpted male body). Moreover, the range of mixing seen here is extreme, but perhaps not unusual even beyond Bollywood. For example, complex generic blending is being undertaken extensively in Hollywood, where Hollywood's masalas (a central couple, romance, special effects, comic relief, and so on) belie the simplicity of reading their movies under single-genre auspices. More to the point, the production of films as franchises with multiple sequels also points to a need to read Hollywood films as increasingly similar to television's approaches to genre and narrative. By viewing genres as inherently blended and as operating within hierarchies, it becomes possible to show the complexities of contemporary filmmaking with greater clarity: acting need not surpass the needs of genre to be remarkable, because the actor's ability to tie together competing generic threads of a film into a unified performance is a considerable skill in itself. What Khan's career and acting choices demonstrate is that actors frequently have nuanced understandings of the importance of genre blending, and the global rise of the actor–producer is indicative of actors taking greater control of their generic filmmaking environments.

References

Altman, R. (1999) *Film/Genre*, London: BFI Publishing.

Banaji, S. (2006) *Reading 'Bollywood': The Young Audience and Hindi Films*, Basingstoke: Palgrave Macmillan.

Baron, C. (2004) 'Suiting up for Postmodern Performance in John Woo's The

Killer', in C. Baron, D. Carson and F. P. Tomasulo, eds., *More than a Method: Trends and Traditions in Contemporary Film Performance*, Detroit: Wayne State University Press, 297–329.

Baron, C., D. Carson and F. P. Tomasulo (eds.) (2004) *More than a Method: Trends and Traditions in Contemporary Film Performance*, Detroit: Wayne State University Press.

Deb, S. (2008) 'Superstar and Everyman. Why this Khan is King', *The Indian Express* (4 May), www.indianexpress.com/printerFriendly/305007.html (accessed 12 August 2008).

Deshpande, S. (2005) 'The Consumable Hero of Globalised India', in R. Kaur and A. J. Sinha, eds., *Bollyworld: Popular Indian Cinema through a Transnational Lens*, New Delhi: Sage, 186–203.

Dudrah, R. K. (2006) *Bollywood: Sociology goes to the Movies*, New Delhi: Sage.

Dyer, R. (1993) 'The Role of Stereotypes', in *The Matter of Images: Essays on Representations*, London: Routledge, 11-18.

Dyer, R. (1998 [1979]) *Stars*, London: BFI Publishing.

Gokulsing, K. and W. Dissanayake (2004 [1998]) *Indian Popular Cinema: A Narrative of Cultural Change*, Stoke on Trent: Trentham Books.

Goodridge, M. (2005) 'King Khan takes on Hollywood', *Screen International* (2 December): 10.

Gopalan, L. (2002) *Cinema of Interruptions: Action Genres in Contemporary Indian Cinema*, London: BFI Publishing.

Gupta, P. (2004) 'Main Hoon Na – So What?', *The Times of India* (30 April), http://timesofindia.inditimes.com/articleshow/msid-651114,prtpage-1.cms (accessed 3 March 2008).

Hesmondhalgh, D. (2002) *The Cultural Industries*, London: Sage Publications.

Hunt, L. (2004) 'The Hong Kong/Hollywood Connection: Stardom and Spectacle in Transnational Action Cinema', in Y. Tasker, ed., *Action Adventure Cinema*, London: Routledge, 269-283.

Jain, P., S. Shaw and M. Nanda (2007) 'Six-pack abs is hyped: Shah Rukh Khan' *Hindustan Times* (14 October), www.hindustantimes.com/Story Page/StoryPage.aspx?sectionName = NLetter&id = de9bcaf0-e852-4f39-948f-dbb42508724&Headline=Six-pack+abs+is+huped%2c+says+Shah+Rukh+Kh an (accessed 12 June 2008).

Jenkins, H. (2004 [1992]) '"A High-Class Job of Carpentry": Toward a Typography of Early Sound Comedy', in P. Robertson Wojcik, ed., *Movie Acting:The Film Reader*, New York: Routledge, 111-125.

Jenkins, Henry (2008) '"Just Men in Tights": Rewriting Silver Age Comics', in L. Geraghty and M. Jancovich, eds., *The Shifting Definitions of Genre: Essays on Labeling Films, Television Shows and Media*, Jefferson: McFarland, 229–243.

Jha, S. K. (2006) '"Paheli" is a Whim of Mine, says Shahrukh', *Hindustan Times* (4 November), www.hindustantimes.com/StoryPage/Print.aspx?Id=7d6854bd-e88a-4d78-96c0-8330b2341c3d (accessed 13 June 2008).

Kaur, R. and A. J. Sinha (eds.) (2005) *Bollyworld: Popular Indian Cinema through a Transnational Lens*, New Delhi: Sage.

Kazmi, N. (2006) '*Don*', *The Times of India* (21 October), http://timesofindia.indiatimes.com/articleshow/msid-2220076,partpage-1.cms (accessed 3 March 2008).

Kazmi, N. (2007) 'Review: Om Shanti Om', *The Times of India* (10 November), http://timesofindia.indiatimes.com/articleshow/msid-2531081,partpage-1.cms (accessed 3 March 2008).

King, B. (1991) 'Articulating Stardom', in J. Butler, ed., *Star Texts: Image and Performance in Film and Television*, Detroit: Wayne State University Press, 125–154.

Kramer, P. (2004) 'The Rise and Fall of Sandra Bullock: Notes on Starmaking and Female Stardom in Contemporary Hollywood', in A. Willis, ed., *Film Stars: Hollywood and Beyond*, Manchester: Manchester University Press, 89-112.

'Living Life Khan-Size!' (2007) *The Times of India* (2 November), http://timesofindia.inditimes.com/articleshow/msid-2509211,prtpage-1.cms (accessed 3 March 2008).

Lovell, A. and P. Kramer (eds.) (1999) *Screen Acting*, London: Routledge.

MacDonald, P. (2004) 'Why Study Film Acting?', in C. Baron, D. Carson and F. P. Tomasulo, eds., *More than a Method: Trends and Traditions in Contemporary Film Performance*, Detroit: Wayne State University Press, 23-41.

Mishra, V. (2002) *Bollywood Cinema: Temples of Desire*, New York and London: Routledge.

Mittell, J. (2001) 'A Cultural Approach to Television Genre Theory', *Cinema Journal*, 40, No. 3 (Spring): 3–24.

Mittell, J. (2004) *Genre and Television: From Cop Shows to Cartoons in American Culture*, London: Routledge.

Mohamed, K. (2007) 'Quite a Mughal-e-masala', *Hindustan Times* (10 November), www.hindustantimes.com/StoryPage/Print.aspx?Id=4c53bac6-5c3d-4821-baa2-230c15d5569b (accessed 12 June 2008).

Naremore, J. (1988) *Acting in the Cinema*, Berkeley: University of California Press.

Neale, S. (1993) 'Melo-Talk: On the Meaning and Use of the Term "Melodrama" in the American Trade Press', *Velvet Light Trap*, 32 (Fall): 66–89.

Neale, S. (2000) *Genre and Hollywood*, London: Routledge.

Neale, S. and F. Krutnik (1990) *Popular Film and Television Comedy*, London: Routledge.

Pendakur, M. (2003) *Indian Popular Cinema: Industry, Ideology and Consciousness*, Cresskill, NJ: Hampton Press, Inc.

Robertson Wojcik, P. (2003) 'Typcasting', *Criticism*, 45, No. 2 (Spring): 223–249.

Robertson Wojcik, P. (ed.) (2004) *Movie Acting: The Film Reader*, New York: Routledge.

Sippy, S. and N. Ramachandran (2006) *Lights, Camera, Masala*, Mumbai: India Book House.

Tasker, Y. (1993) *Spectacular Bodies: Gender, Genre and the Action Cinema*, London: Routledge.

Tasker, Y. (ed.) (2004) *Action Adventure Cinema*, London: Routledge.

Thomas, R. (1985) 'Indian Cinema: Pleasures and Popularity', *Screen*, 26, Nos. 3–4: 116–131.

Thompson, J. O. (1978) 'Screen Acting and the Commutation Test', *Screen*, 19: 55–69.

Vasudevan, R. S. (1995) 'Addressing the Spectator of a "Third-World" National Cinema: The Bombay Social Film of the 1940s and 1950s', *Screen*, 36, No. 4: 305–324.

Willis, A. (2003) Locating Bollywood: Notes on the Hindi Blockbuster, 1975 to the Present', in J. Stringer, ed., *Movie Blockbusters*, London: Routledge, 255–268.

Index

Note: page numbers in italics denote illustrations

acting style
  backstage/frontstage 137–8, 144
  on film 3, 151–2, 167, 187
  film noir 21, 27, 28
  Khan, Sh. 15, 188, 191, 194, 197–8, 199–201
  Naremore 3, 151–2, 187
  overplaying 19, 28, 29, 31–2
  and performance 1, 14, 143–4, 145
  Shatner 181
  on television 38–9, 166, 167, 168, 174, 181–2
action films 191, 192
actuality 13, 64, 67, 76–7, 81, 82
Adamson, Andrew 150
  see also Shrek
Alexander, Scott 76
Altman, Rick 8, 9, 184
Amazing Grace 84
American Splendor 80, 82–6, 93–4
Amy Fisher: My Story 69
And Now the Screaming Starts! (Baker) 52
And Soon the Darkness (Fuest) 53
animation 150–1, 158–9, 160–1
  see also rotoscoping technique
Animation Journal 156
archive footage 63
Armbruster, Ben 114
Artaud, Antonin 55
Asher, Jane 42, *43*
Asoka 190, 195
Astor, Mary 19
audience
  biopic 77, 78, 81, 82
  Colbert 115, 122, 125, 128–9
  comedy 132–3, 135, 136
  cultural reality 24
  docudrama 59–62, 64, 67, 69–70, 73
  film noir 12, 18, 19, 23–7
  genre 7, 8, 9, 12, 13, 145
  horror 48, 51, 52, 55
  identification 4, 62, 65, 66
  Khan, Sh. 189, 195, 196, 199
  as market 73
  news 114, 115, 116–19, 122
  performance 12, 65–8
  postmodernism 123
  science fiction 148, 153
  sitcom 130–1, 132, 139, 140, 143
  Star Trek 166
  tough guy portrayals 23, 26–7, 29–30
Auslander, Philip 2, 5, 16n.1, 152
auteur 6, 7, 79
Avengers, The 50, 51
Aviator, The (Scorsese) 73, 88–90

backstage behaviour 137–8, 144
Bacon, Kevin 148, *149*, 150, 153–4

Baker, Roy Ward 52
Bakhtin, Mikhail 133
Bakshi, Ralph 158–9
Bale, Christian 88, 91, 92
Band of Brothers 73
Banks, Elizabeth 80
Bannen, Ian 52
Baron, Cynthia 5, 12, 21, 67, 192
Barrymore, Drew 151, 187
Barrymore, John 54
Barthes, Roland 77
Bates, Ralph 53
Baudrillard, Jean 117–18
Beasts 38, 40, 51, 55
Beatty, Warren 79, 80, 82
Beckett, Samuel 53
Beckinsale, Kate 88
Beltrane, Robert 178
Benny, Jack 132
Berardinelli, James 22
Berman, Rick 169–70
Berman, S. S. 87
Bernhardt, Sarah 77
Betty Boop's Snow White 157
Big Brother 64
Big Sleep, The (Hawks) 18, 19, 26, 28, 30
Bignell, Jonathan 13, 52, 68, 70
Bingham, Dennis 13
Biodrowski, Steve 153
biopics 11, 12–13
  audience 77, 78, 81, 82
  awards 78
  body too much concept 81–2, 86, 90, 93
  neo-classical 90
  performance 76–82
  postmodernism 84
Blackman, Robert 176–7, 180
Blanchett, Cate *94*
  Aviator, The 88–90
  I'm Not There 88–9, 91, 92–3
Blick, Hugo 140
Bluth, Don 150
  see also Titan A. E.
body 131–2, 133, 138
  see also male body
body too much concept 81–2, 86, 90, 93
Bogart, Humphrey 19, 21–2, 23, 26, 28, 30
Bollywood 15, 185, 186, 190, 197, 198–9
Borde, Raymond 20
Bould, Mark 20
Bradshaw, Nick 161
Braga, Brannon 167
Brando, Marlon 196–7
Brick (Johnson) 18, 26, 27, 30, 31
Brokeback Mountain (Lee) 108
Brooks, P. 70
Bryant, Michael 42, *43*, 52, *53*
Brydon, Rob 140, 141
Bugsy 79
Bujold, Genevieve 172
Burrows, James 135
Bush, George W. 115, 116, 122–3
Butler, Jeremy G. 4, 67, 135
Butler, Judith 4

Calloway, Cab 157
camerawork 39, 71, 135, 136, 193, 199
Capote 73, 79
carnivalesque 133
Carpenter, Karen 90–1, 92–3
Carson, Diane 5, 67
Carson, John 54–5
cartoons 151, 152
  see also animation
Casualties of Love 69
Caughie, John 38–9
Cavell, Stanley 109
censorship 102–3
CGI realism 150–1, 154–5, 162
Chang, Justin 159
Chaplin 80

character actors 53, 78, 81
character types 10, 23, 96, 108
Chaumeton, Étienne 20
Chelsea Girls, The (Warhol) 118
Cheung, Maggie 86–7
chiaroscuro 20
Chinatown (Polanski) 18, 21–2, 26, 29, 30–1, 99
Chocano, Carina 159
Citizen Kane 76, 82, 88
Clark, Lawrence Gordon 39, 47
Clemens, Brian 38, 50, 55
  see also Thriller
Clockwork Orange, A (Kubrick) 51, 52
Cochrane, Rory 157, 160, 161
Coen Brothers 108
Cohen, Mitchell 21
Colbert, Stephen
  audience 115, 122, 125, 128–9
  and Bush 122–3
  in drag 118, 119, 120, 122
  irony 14, 122, 123
  parody 116, 124
Colbert Report, The 14, 114, 115, 117, 118–21
comedian comedy 134, 135, 141, 142, 143
comedy
  audience 132–3, 135, 136
  body 131–2, 135, 136, 138
  camera style 136
  cartoon 151, 152
  editing process 135
  laugh tracks 134
  performance 130–1, 132–3
  run lengths 142–3
  see also sitcoms
comedy vérité 14, 136, 138, 139
comics, underground 82, 83–5, 87–8
Comolli, Jean-Louis 77, 81–2
Cornea, Christine 154
Cosby, Bill 134
costume design 176–7
Cotillard, Marion 78
Cox, Michael Graham 41–2
Crumb, R. 83–4
Custen, George F. 79
Cuthbertson, Iain 48, 52, *53*

Daily Show, The 14, 114, 116, 117, 122, 123
Dale, Alan 116
Damon, Matt 151
Davis, Hope 80, 84–5, *86*
Davis, Julia 140
Day Britain Stopped, The 66
Day-Lewis, Daniel 79
De Cordova, Richard 6, 12, 18, 19, 34, 35
De Niro, Robert 77, 79
Dead of Night series 51
Deadwood
  boundaries 99, 100–1, 104–5, 108, 112n.2
  gender/space 106–7
  language 99–100, 102–3
  Merrick *104*
  money as structure 101, 103–4
  negotiation of roles 107–8
  Swearengen 13, 102–3, *105*
  Westerns 13, 96–7, 108–10, 111
Deb, Sandipan 188–9
Denison, Rayna 15
Depp, Johnny 80
Deshpande, Sudhanva 197, 199
Devdas 190
Devil in a Blue Dress (Franklin) 18, 22, 26, 28, 29, 31, 32–3
Diana: Her True Story 68, 69–71, 72
Diana, Princess of Wales 68–71
Dillahunt, Garret 107–8
Dimendberg, E. 20
Dirty War 66
Dissanayake, Wimal 185–6, 190, 192
dissimulation 12, 18
Doane, Mary Ann 91

Dobbs, Lou 121, 127–8
docudrama
  and actuality 66–7, 71
  audience 59–62, 64, 67, 69–70, 73
  British/US compared 60
  celebrity 11–13
  and melodrama 68–72
  performance 59–65, 73–4
documentary 11, 59–65, 72–3, 136–7, 139–40
Don 190, 194, *195*, 196
Don't Look Back (Pennebaker) 92
double roles 194–6, 197
Dowd, Maureen 123, 179
Downey, Robert Jr. 80, 157, 159, 160, 161
Dr Jekyll and Mr Hyde (Robertson) 54–5
Dr Strangelove 90
Dudrah, Rajinder Kumar 185, 186
Durgnat, Raymond 21
Duvidha 191
DVD industry 38, 159–60
Dyer, Richard 2–3, 4, 119, 134, 189
Dylan, Bob 77, 88, 90, 91–3
Dynasty 71, 72

Earp, Wyatt 97
Eastwood, Clint 97
Ebert, Roger 22, 80, 155
Elsaesser, Thomas 21
emotion 23, 62, 69–72, 100–1, 144
ER 179, 180
Erin Brockovich 81
expression
  appliquéd 19, 28, *29*
  facial 27, 174, 193
  under wraps 22, 23
Exton, Clive 47

fantasy 124–5, 158–9
Farber, Manny 110
femmes fatales 19
film noir 21, 35n.2
  audience 12, 18, 19, 23–7
  heroes 27–8, 29–30, 32–3
  Naremore 20, 21–2, 27, 31
  performance 18, 21, 22–6, 29–30, 34
  tough guys 18–19, 23, 26–30, 33–5
Final Fantasy (Sakaguchi) 14, 150–1, 152–3
Fires Were Started (Jennings) 60–1
Flaming Creatures (Smith) 119
flashbacks 27, 34
Fleischer, Max and David 156–7
Fonda, Henry 97–8, 111
Forbes, Bryan 53
Ford, John 97
  see also My Darling Clementine
Foster, Gwendolyn Audrey 13–14
Foucault, Michel 4
Fox News 113, 123
Foxx, Jamie 79
Frakes, Jonathan 171–2, 173, 178–9
Francis, Jan 47, 48
Franklin, Carl 18
  see also Devil in a Blue Dress
Freiberger, Fred 170, 171
Frenzy (Hitchcock) 51
Freud, Sigmund 133
Freund, Karl 135
Fritz the Cat 158
Fuest, Robert 53

Gangster genre 99
Garbo, Greta 77
Gas Attack 66
gaze theory 4
gender 4, 71–2, 106–7
genre
  audience 7, 8, 9, 12, 13, 145
  blurring of 145
  gender 71–2
  hybridity 9–10, 59, 74
  and performance 6, 7, 10, 18

rules 18, 34
Star Trek 178–82
genre mixing 184, 185–6, 190, 201
Geraghty, Christine 72
Gervais, Ricky 137–9, 140–1
gesture 18, 19, 22, 26–7
Ghost Story for Christmas, A 38, 39, 40, 52
Giamatti, Paul 80, 84, *85*, 87, 88
Goffman, Erving 137–8, 143, 144
Gokulsing, K. Moti 185–6, 190, 192
Goldman, Emma 79
Good, Christopher 48
Goodman, Tim 108, 111n.1
Goodridge, M. 189, 196
Gordon-Levitt, Joseph 22–3, 26, 27, 30, 31
Gould, Elliott 19
Graham, Bob 155
Grand-Guignol horror theatre 48–9, 55
Grant, Barry 19, 20
Griffith, D. W. 3
Grotowski, Jerzy 25
Guerro, Ed 22
Gunsmoke 96–7
Gupta, Parul 188

Hammer horror 42, 53, 54, 55
Hancock, Tony 132, 140
Hand, Richard J. 12, 49, 55
Hanks, Tom 153–4
Harrelson, Woody 157, 159, 160, 161
Harrison, Eric 153
Haunted Airman, The 56
Hawks, Howard 18
see also Big Sleep, The
Haynes, Todd 77, 88, 90–1, 93
see also I'm Not There
Hayward, Susan 81, 89, 93
Heath, Stephen 19, 23–4
Heavy Metal 14, 158, 159
Henry Irving and The Bells (Meyer) 55
Hepburn, Katharine 88, 89
Herd, Richard 182
Herrmann, Bernard 50
Hideo, Nakata 47
Hindi language cinema 184–6, 190, 191–2, 196
Hiroshima 63
history programmes 73
Hitchcock, Alfred 50, 51
Hoberman, J. 153
Hockenberry, John 125
Hoffman, Phillip Seymour 79
Holbrooke, Richard 126
Holden, Stephen 151
Hollinger, Karen 4
Hollow Man (Verhoeven) 14, 148–50, 153–4, 162n.2
Hollywood 5, 197, 201
Hopkins, Anthony 80, 91
Hopkins, Stephen 90
Hordern, Michael 42, 43, *44*, 45, *46*
horror genre
audience 48, 51, 52, 55
real 48–56
supernatural 42–8
television 12, 38, 39, 52
Hughes, Howard 88, 89
Human Remains 136, 140, 141
humour 115, 130–1, 133, 140
see also comedy
Hunter, Jeffrey 181
Hurt, John 63
Huston, John 18

I Want to Live! 81
identification 4, 62, 65, 66
If . . . series 66, 67
I'm Not There (Haynes) 77, 88, 90, 91–2, 93–4
Indian cinema, popular: *see* Bollywood; Hindi language cinema
intensities 19, 24

Invisible Man, The 148
irony 14, 122, 123
Irving, Henry 55

James, M. R. 38
  'Casting the Runes' 47–8
  'Mr Humphreys and his Inheritance' 45, 47
  'Number 13' 56
  'Treasure of Abbot Thomas' 52
  'View from a Hill' 55–6
  'Warning to the Curious' 39, 40
  'Whistle and I'll Come to You' 42–5
James, Sid 140
Jenkins, Henry 184, 187
Jennings, Humphrey 60–1
JFK 79, 82
Johar, Karan 188
Johnson, Jeffrey 101, 109
Johnson, Laurie 50
Johnson, Rian 18
  see also Brick
Jones, Freddie 53
Jones, Toby 79
Jones, Tommy Lee 79
Joy, Nick 178
Justman, Robert 181

Karaszewski, Larry 76
Kempley, Rita 150
Kennedy, John F. 79
Khan, Aamir 188, 189
Khan, Farah 188, 197
Khan, Salman 188, 189
Khan, Shahrukh 185–9
  acting/genre 15, 188, 191, 194, 197–8, 199–201
  audience 189, 195, 196, 199
  double roles 194–6
  facial expressions 193–4
  in *Om Shanti Om 200*
  physique 198, 199, 201
  production companies 187–8
  self-parody 190
King, Barry 194
Kitano, Takeshi 187
Kneale, Nigel 38, 40–2: *see also Stone Tape, The*
Koehler, Robert 153
Kolbe, Winrich 172, 176, 179–80
Kouvaros, George 5
Kristeva, Julia 133
Kristofferson, Kris 92
Kubrick, Stanley 51

Laban Movement Analysis 12, 19, 24–6
Lacey, Stephen 52
Langer, Mark 156
Langham, Chris 141–2
Lasseter, John 150
  see also Toy Story
Law, Jude 88
Le Fanu, J. Sheridan 39
Le Mesurier, John 52
Ledger, Heath 88, 92
Lee, Ang 108
Lee, Spike 82
Leigh, Mike 81
Letheren, Mark 56
Levinson, Barry 80
Limbaugh, Rush 115
Linklater, Richard 159, 162
  see also Scanner Darkly, A
Lipman, Maureen 52
Littlewood, Joan 24
Long Goodbye, The 19
Lord of the Rings, The 158, 159
Lucas, George 124, 154–5
Lury, Karen 50

McCarthy, Todd 150
McColl, Ewan 24
McGregor, Ewan 90, 155, 156
McKenna, T. P. 52

McNeil, Robert Duncan 181
McShane, Ian 13, 100, 101, *105*, 109, 110–11
Magee, Patrick 52–3
Main Hoon Na 188, 190, 191–2, 193–4
Malcolm X 79, 80, 82
male body 197, 199, 201
Maltese Falcon (Huston) 18, 19
Man Who Shot Liberty Valance, The 110
Mansfield, Richard 55
Marion and Geoff 14, 133, 136, 140, 141
Marx Brothers 115, 116, 120
masala formula films 185–6, 201
Mass Observation 63–4
Mayers, Dan 151
Mees, Jim 177
Meldrew, Victor 143
melodrama 57n.1, 68–72, 192
Messenger Davies, Maire 166, 167–81
meta-performance 123
Method acting 24–5, 79, 196–7
Meyer, David 55
Mighty Quinn, The 91
Miller, Jonathan 42–5
Miller, Toby 51
Mills, Brett 14
Mills, Hayley 53
mise-en-scène 4, 39, 59, 135, 193
misogyny 51–2
Mission Impossible 2 (Woo) 191
Mitchum, Robert 21, 26, 27, 28, *29*, 31–2
Mittell, Jason 184–5, 190
Mnookin, Seth 126, 127
mock-documentary 73, 136–7
Mohamed, Khalid 199
Môme, La (La Vie en Rose) 78
Morton, Andrew 68
Mukherjee, Rani 194
Mulder, Fox 179
Mulgrew, Kate 172–3
Mulvey, Laura 4
Murder, My Sweet 19
Murphet, Julian 35n.4
Murphy, Eddie 153–4, 163n.4
music 50, 69–70
My Darling Clementine (Ford) 97–8, 105
My Left Foot 79

Napolitano, Andrew 125–6
Naremore, James
  facial expression 27
  film acting 3, 151–2, 187
  noir films 20, 21–2, 27, 31
  overplaying 28
  performance styles 4, 19, 143, 151–2, 187
naturalism 3, 14–15, 65, 67, 140–1
Neale, Steve 8, 27, 34, 184
Neeson, Liam 155, 156
Newman, Kim 41, 42, 55, 56–7, 57n.1
news agencies 113, 118
Nicholson, Jack 21–2, 23, 26, 29, 30–1
Nimoy, Leonard 167, 170–1, 175
Nixon, Richard 80, 91
No Country for Old Men (Coen Brothers) 108
noir film: *see* film noir

Office, The 14, 73, 133, 136, 137–41, 144
Okuda, Michael 177–8
Olyphant, Timothy 100, 105–6, 111
Om Shanti Om 188, 190, 194–5
  'Dard-e-Disco' *200*
  'Dhoom Thana' *198*
  genre as process 196–201
Omnibus 39, 42
One Foot in the Grave 143
O'Reilly, Bill 114, 115, 126
O'Reilly, Robert 182
O'Reilly Factor, The 121, 126
O'Rourke, Meghan 22–3, 27

Out of the Past (Tourneur) 18, 26, 27, 30, 31
overplaying 19, 28, 29, 31–2

Paget, Derek 59–60, 65, 69
Paheli 188, 190–1
  double roles 194, 195–6
  mise-en-scène 193
  physicality 201
  special effects 195–6
  stunt elements 192–3
Parker-Bowles, Camilla 68, 69
parody 76, 120, 124, 198–9
  self-parody 28, 190
pastiche 119
Patriot Act 126
patriotism 120, 126
Patton 89
Peacock, Steven 13
Pearson, Roberta 3, 4, 15, 167–81
Peckinpah, Sam 51
Pekar, Harvey 83–5, 88
Pennebaker, D. A. 92
People Like Us 136, 141–2, 144
performance 2, 5
  acting 1, 14, 143–4, 145
  audience 12, 65–8
  biopics 76–82
  comedy 130–1, 132–3
  docudrama 59–65, 73–4
  documentary 11
  and genre 6, 7, 10, 18
  Goffman 144
  horror television 52
  live-action 155–6
  Naremore 4, 19, 143, 151–2, 187
  narrative 27, 30, 34
  noir 18, 21, 22–6, 29–30, 34
  non-verbal 173–5
  postmodernism 93–4, 123
performance-within-performance 197–8
personation 194
Pew Report 113, 114
Piaf, Edith 78
Pitney, Nico 113
Pitt, Ingrid 53
Polanski, Roman 18
  see also Chinatown
postmodernism 10
  audience 123
  biopics 84
  humour 115, 117
  performance 2, 93–4, 123
  simulacrum 78–9
Powell, Dick 19, 21
presentational modes 3, 14, 152, 153
production companies 187–8
Psycho (Hitchcock) 50
Pulcini, Robert 87

Quatermass series 40, 41

Rabin, Nathan 120–2, 123–4
Rabinowitz, Paula 35n.4
Raging Bull 77, 79, 196–7
Raimi, Sam 108
Rawhide 96–7
Reality TV 64, 73, 145
Red Chillies Entertainment 188
Reds 79, 82
Reeves, Keanu 157, *158*, 159, 160, *160*, 161
rehearsal time 167, 168
Remnick, David 125
representational modes 3, 70–1, 152, 153
Rhys-Meyers, Jonathan 90
Ringu (Hideo) 47
Roberts, Julia 81
Robertson, John S. 54–5
Robertson Wojcik, Pamela 6–7, 186–7
Roddenberry, Gene 166, 169, 170, 171, 172, 175
Rodway, Norman 51
Rosenstone, Robert 77

Roshan, Hrithik 197
rotoscoping technique 156–62, 163n.6
Ruan Ling-Yu 86–7
Rush, Geoffrey 90
Russell, Geoffrey 45, 47
Ryder, Winona 157, *160*, 161, 163n.9

Safer, Morley 118
Sakaguchi, Hironobu 150
  see also Final Fantasy
Sands, Julian 56
Sarris, Andrew 159
Sasdy, Peter 40–2, 54
Saturday Night Live 135
Saunders, John 112n.3, 112n.4
Scanner Darkly, A (Linklater) 14, 156, 157, *158*, 159–62, 163n.7
Schaffer, William 151
Schechner, Richard 1, 143
Schickel, Richard 22
science fiction 11
  animation 150–1, 152–3, 158
  audience 148, 153
  film/television 14–15, 166
  as genre 178–82
  realism/fantasy 156
  subjectivity 154
Scorsese, Martin 73, 88, 89–90
Scott, A. O. 155
Scott, George C. 89
Sculls, Tony 45, 47
Seidman, Steve 134
Sellers, Peter 90
set design 120–1
Shaffer, Lawrence 19
Shah, Naseeruddin 192
Shakespeare, William 41, 53
Shatner, William 166, 167–8, 169, 171, 175, 181
Shaviro, Steven 118
Shaw, Ian 63
Shot in the Dark, A 90
shot-reverse shot 193
Shrek (Adamson) 150, 151, 152, 153–4, 163n.3, 163n.4
Siegel, Ben 'Bugsy' 79, 80
Silver, Alain 20
simulacrum 78–9, 124
Sirtis, Marina 173, 174, 178
sitcoms
  audience 130–1, 132, 139, 140, 143
  mise-en-scène 135
  performance/acting 143–4, 145
  US/Britain compared 136
Smallpox: Silent Weapon 66
Smith, Jack 119
Soderbergh, Steven 81
Sopranos, The 11, 180
special effects 195–6
  see also visual effects
Spicer, Andrew 21, 23
Spiner, Brent 177
Stanfield, Peter 98–9, 100, 103
Stanislavskian techniques 24–5
Stapleton, Maureen 79
Star Trek series 15
  audience 166
  costume design 176–7
  female hair styles 172–3
  genre 178–82
  graphics design 177–8
  make-up design 180
  props/set dressing 177
  speed of production 167
  status 169–73
  theatrical performance 181–2
  visual effects 173–5, 179–80
Star Wars films 154–6
stars 2–5, 23–4, 134, 155–6, 159, 162, 189
Stern, Lesley 5
Stewart, Jon 14, 115–16, 121, 126–7
Stewart, Patrick 166, 167, 169–70, 174–8, 181

Stone, Oliver 80, 82, 91
Stone Tape, The (Kneale) 38, 40–2, 55, 56–7
Straw Dogs (Peckinpah) 51, 52
Streep, Meryl 79
Streisand, Barbara 81
stunt films 191–3
subjectivity 65, 67, 154
supernatural 38, 42–8, 57n.3
Superstar (Haynes) 93
Suvin, Darko 156
Swank, Hilary 80
Syms, Sylvia 70

Takakura, Akiko 63
Tasker, Y. 197
Tati, Jacques 45
television 9–10
  horror 12, 38, 39, 52
  immediacy 62
  intimacy 62, 180–1
  location shooting 39–40
  naturalism 65, 67
  as window/mirror 61–2
television production 167–8, 173
terrorism films 73
testimony 62, 63
Thatcher, Margaret 68–9, 71
Thatcher: The Final Days 68, 70–1, 72
Theatre Workshop 24
Theron, Charlize 79
Thirty-Minute Theatre 53
Thomas, Deborah 98
Thomas, Rosie 184–5
Thomas, Serena Scott 69
Thompson, J. Lee 53
Thompson, John O. 190
Thomson, David 97–8
Thriller (Clemens)
  DVD 38
  formula for 57n.2
  location shooting 40
  misogyny 51–2
  music 50
  'Possession' 54–5
  supernatural 57n.3
  themes 48–9, 50–1
Tibbetts, Paul 63
Tiger Bay (Thompson) 53
Titan A. E. (Bluth) 14, 150, 151, 152–3, 163n.5
Toback, James 80
Tomasulo, Frank P. 5, 67
Tourneur, Jacques 18
  see also Out of the Past
Toy Story (Lasseter) 150, 151, 152, 153–4, 163n.4
truthiness 14, 121–2
Turner, Graeme 8, 10

Veer-Zaara 195
Velvet Goldmine 90, 93
Verhoeven, Paul 15, 148, 149–50
  see also Hollow Man
Video Diaries 64
Video Nation 64
visual effects 39, 173–5, 179–80, 195–6
voice-over 27, 34, 63, 66, 85–6, 150, 151

war films 73
Warhol, Andy 118, 119
Washington, Denzel
  Devil in a Blue Dress 22, 28, 30, *33*
  Malcolm X 79, 80, 82
  Mighty Quinn, The 91
Wayne, John 110
Weight of the Line, The 160–1
Wells, Paul 152
Westerns 13, 96–8, 108–10, 111
Westmore, Michael 180
Westmoreland, Lynn 127
Wexman, Virginia Wright 4
Wheatley, Dennis 56

Wheatley, Helen 51
Whistle Down the Wind (Forbes) 53
Williams, Kenneth 140
Wilson, M. 49, 55
Wilson, Neil 41
Wise, Greg 56
witnessing 62, 63–4
Woo, John 5, 191, 192
World Trade Centre 73
Wymark, Jane 55

X-Files, The 11, 179

Young Mr. Lincoln 84

Zimmerman, Herman 169
Zukor, Adolph 77